WILEY SERIES 65 EXAM REVIEW 2015

WILEY FINRA SERIES

This series includes the following titles:

Wiley Series 3 Exam Review 2015 + Test Bank: National Commodities Futures Examination

Wiley Series 4 Exam Review 2015 + Test Bank: The Registered Options Principal Qualification Examination

Wiley Series 6 Exam Review 2015 + Test Bank: The Investment Company Products/Variable Contracts Limited Representative Examination

Wiley Series 7 Exam Review 2015 + Test Bank: The General Securities Representative Examination

Wiley Series 9 Exam Review 2015 + Test Bank: The General Securities Sales Supervisor Qualification Examination—Option Module

Wiley Series 10 Exam Review 2015 + Test Bank: The General Securities Sales Supervisor Qualification Examination—General Module

Wiley Series 24 Exam Review 2015 + Test Bank: The General Securities Principal Qualification Examination

Wiley Series 26 Exam Review 2015 + Test Bank: The Investment Company Products/Variable Contracts Limited Principal Qualification Examination

Wiley Series 55 Exam Review 2015 + Test Bank: The Equity Trader Qualification Examination

Wiley Series 62 Exam Review 2015 + Test Bank: The Corporate Securities Limited Representative Examination

Wiley Series 63 Exam Review 2015 + Test Bank: The Uniform Securities Examination

Wiley Series 65 Exam Review 2015 + Test Bank: The Uniform Investment Adviser Law Examination

Wiley Series 66 Exam Review 2015 + Test Bank: The Uniform Combined State Law Examination

Wiley Series 99 Exam Review 2015 + Test Bank: The Operations Professional Qualification Examination

For more on this series, visit the website at www.wileysecuritieslicensing.com.

WILEY SERIES 65 EXAM REVIEW 2015

The Uniform Investment Adviser Law Examination

The Securities Institute of America, Inc.

WILEY

Cover Design: Wiley
Cover Image: © iStockphoto.com / LuisB

Published by John Wiley & Sons, Inc., Hoboken, New Jersey.
Previous editions published by The Securities Institute of America, Inc.
Published simultaneously in Canada.

For general information on our other products and services or for technical support, please contact our Customer Care Department within the United States at (800) 762-2974, outside the United States at (317) 572-3993 or fax (317) 572-4002.

Wiley publishes in a variety of print and electronic formats and by print-on-demand. Some material included with standard print versions of this book may not be included in e-books or in print-on-demand. If this book refers to media such as a CD or DVD that is not included in the version you purchased, you may download this material at http://booksupport.wiley.com. For more information about Wiley products, visit www.wiley.com.

ISBN 9781118857069 (Paperback)
ISBN 9781118844465 (ePDF)
ISBN 9781118857182 (ePub)

Printed in the United States of America

10 9 8 7 6 5 4 3 2 1

Contents

CHAPTER 2 CORPORATE AND MUNICIPAL DEBT SECURITIES 35

About the Series 65 Exam

Congratulations! You are on your way to becoming licensed to represent an Investment Adviser in all states that require the Series 65 license. The Series 65 exam will be presented in a 130-question multiple-choice format. Each candidate will have three hours to complete the exam. A score of 72% or higher is required to pass.

The Series 65 is as much a knowledge test as it is a reading test. The writers and instructors at The Securities Institute have developed the Series 65 textbook, exam prep software and videos to ensure that you have the knowledge required to pass the test, and to make sure that you are confident in the application of the knowledge during the exam. The writers and instructors at The Securities Institute are subject matter experts as well as a Series 65 test experts. We understand how the test is written and our proven test-taking techniques can dramatically improve your results.

TAKING THE SERIES 65 EXAM

The Series 65 exam is presented in multiple-choice format on a touch-screen computer known as the PROCTOR system. No computer skills are required and candidates will find that the test screen works in the same way as an ordinary ATM machine. Each test is made up of 130 questions that are randomly chosen from a test bank of several thousand questions. The test has a time limit of three hours and is designed to provide enough time for all candidates to complete the exam. Each Series 65 exam will have 10 additional questions that do not count toward the final score. The Series 65 exam comprises questions that focus on the following areas:

Ethics and legal guidelines	40 questions	31%
Investment strategies	40 questions	31%
Investment vehicles	31 questions	24%
Economics and analysis	19 questions	14%
TOTAL	**130 Questions**	**100%**

HOW TO PREPARE FOR THE SERIES 65 EXAM?

For most candidates the combination of reading the textbook, watching the videos and using the exam prep software is enough to successfully complete the exam. It is recommended that the individual spend at least 40 hours preparing for the exam by reading the textbook, underlining key points watching the video class and by taking as many practice questions as possible. We recommend that a student schedule their exam no more than one week after completing your Series 65 exam prep.

Test-Taking Tips

- ☐ Read the full question before answering
- ☐ Identify what the question is asking
- ☐ Identify key words and phrases
- ☐ Watch out for hedge clauses, for example except and not
- ☐ Eliminate wrong roman numeral answers
- ☐ Identify synonymous terms
- ☐ Be wary of changing answers

WHY DO I NEED TO TAKE THE SERIES 65 EXAM?

In order to conduct fee-based securities business, most states require that an agent successfully complete the Series 65 exam, Passing the Series 65 exam will allow an agent to receive asset based management and other advisory fees. The Series 65 is often taken in addition to obtaining a Series 6, 7, or 62 registration, which allow an agent to receive transaction based compensation.

WHAT SCORE IS NEEDED TO PASS THE EXAM?

A score of 72% or higher is needed to pass the Series 65 exam.

ARE THERE ANY PREREQUISITES FOR THE SERIES 65 EXAM?

A candidate is not required to have any other professional qualifications prior to taking the Series 65 exam.

HOW DO I SCHEDULE AN EXAM?

Ask your firm's principal to schedule the exam for you, or for a list of test centers in your area. You may be self-sponsored to take the exam. You must fill out and submit form U10 prior to making an appointment. The Series 65 exam may be taken any day that the exam center is open.

WHAT MUST I TAKE TO THE EXAM CENTER?

A picture ID is required. All other materials will be provided, including a calculator and scratch paper.

HOW SOON WILL I RECEIVE THE RESULTS OF THE EXAM?

The exam will be graded as soon as you answer your final question and hit the Submit for Grading button. It will take only a few minutes to get your results. Your grade will appear on the computer screen and you will be given a paper copy from the exam center.

If you do not pass the test, you will need to wait 30 days before taking it again. If you do not pass on the second try, you'll need to wait another 30 days. After that, you are required to wait 6 months to take the test again.

About This Book

The writers and instructors at The Securities Institute have developed the Series 65 textbook, exam prep software, and videos to ensure that you have the knowledge required to pass the test, and to make sure that you are confident in the application of the knowledge during the exam. The writers and instructors at The Securities Institute are subject matter experts as well as Series 65 test experts. We understand how the test is written and our proven test-taking techniques can dramatically improve your results.

Each chapter includes notes, tips, examples, and case studies with key information, hints for taking the exam, and additional insight into the topics. Each chapter ends with a practice test, to ensure you have mastered the concepts before moving on to the next topic.

About the Test Bank

This book is accompanied by a test bank of more than 350 questions to further reinforce the concepts and information presented here. The access card in the back of this book includes the URL and PIN code you can use to access the test bank. This test bank provides a small sample of the questions and features that are contained in the full version of the Series 65 exam prep software.

If you have not purchased the full version of the exam prep software with this book, we highly recommend it to ensure that you have mastered the knowledge required for your Series 65 exam. To purchase the exam prep software for this exam, visit The Securities Institute of America online at www.SecuritiesCE.com or call 877-218-1776.

About The Securities Institute of America

The Securities Institute of America, Inc. helps thousands of securities and insurance professionals build successful careers in the financial services industry every year.

Our securities training options include:

- On-site training classes
- Private tutoring
- Classroom training
- Interactive online video training classes
- State-of-the-art exam-preparation software
- Printed textbooks
- Real time tracking and reporting for managers and training directors

As a result, you can choose a securities training solution that matches your skill level, learning style, and schedule. Regardless of the format you choose, you can be sure that our securities training courses are relevant, tested, and designed to help you succeed. It is the experience of our instructors and the quality of our materials that make our courses requested by name at some of the largest financial services firms in the world.

To contact The Securities Institute of America, visit us on the Web at www.SecuritiesCE.com or call 877-218-1776.

CHAPTER 1

Equity Securities

INTRODUCTION

This first chapter will build the foundation upon which the rest of this text is built. A thorough understanding of equity securities will be necessary in order to successfully complete the Series 65 exam. Equity securities are divided into two types: common and preferred stock. We will examine the features of common stock and preferred stock, as well as the benefits and risks associated with their ownership, but first we must define exactly what meets the definition of a security.

WHAT IS A SECURITY?

A security is any investment product that can be exchanged for value and involves risk. In order for an investment to be considered a security, it must be readily transferable between two parties and the owner must be subject to the loss of some, or all, of the invested principal. If the product is not transferable or does not contain risk, it is not a security.

Types of Securities	Types of Nonsecurities
Common stock	Whole life insurance
Preferred stock	Term life insurance
Bonds	IRAs
Mutual funds	Retirement plans

(Continued)

Types of Securities	Types of Nonsecurities
Variable annuities	Fixed annuities
Variable life insurance	Prospectus
Options	Confirmations
Rights	
Warrants	
ETFs/ETNs	
Real Estate Investment Trusts	
CMOs	

EQUITY = STOCK

The term equity is synonymous with the term stock. Throughout your preparation for this exam and on the exam itself, you will find many terms that are used interchangeably. Equity or stock creates an ownership relationship with the issuing company. Once an investor has purchased stock in a corporation, they become an owner of that corporation. The corporation sells off pieces of itself to investors in the form of shares in an effort to raise working capital. Equity is perpetual, meaning there is no maturity date for the shares and the investor may own the shares until they decide to sell them. Most corporations use the sale of equity as their main source of business capital.

COMMON STOCK

There are thousands of companies whose stock trades publicly and who have used the sale of equity as a source of raising business capital. All publicly traded companies must issue common stock before they may issue any other type of equity security. There are two types of equity securities: common stock and preferred stock. While all publicly traded companies must have sold or issued common stock, not all companies may want to issue or sell preferred stock. Let's take a look at the creation of a company and how common stock is created.

CORPORATE TIME LINE

The following is a representation of the steps that corporations must take in order to sell their common stock to the public, as well as what may happen to that stock once it has been sold to the public.

AUTHORIZED STOCK

Authorized stock is the maximum number of shares that a company may sell to the investing public in an effort to raise cash to meet the organization's goals. The number of authorized shares is arbitrarily determined and is set at the time of incorporation. A corporation may sell all or part of its authorized stock. If the corporation wants to sell more shares than it's authorized to sell, the shareholders must approve an increase in the number of authorized shares.

ISSUED STOCK

Issued stock is stock that has been authorized for sale and that has actually been sold to the investing public. The total number of authorized shares typically exceeds the total number of issued shares so that the corporation may sell additional shares in the future to meet its needs. Once shares have been sold to the investing public, they will always be counted as issued shares, regardless of their ownership or subsequent repurchase by the corporation. It's important to note that the total number of issued shares may never exceed the total number of authorized shares.

Additional authorized shares may be issued in the future for any of the following reasons:

- Pay a stock dividend
- Expand current operations
- Exchange common shares for convertible preferred or convertible bonds
- To satisfy obligations under employee stock options or purchase plans

OUTSTANDING STOCK

Outstanding stock is stock that has been sold or issued to the investing public and that actually remains in the hands of the investing public.

EXAMPLE: XYZ corporation has 10,000,000 shares authorized and has sold 5,000,000 shares to the public during its initial public offering. In this case, there would be 5,000,000 shares of stock issued and 5,000,000 shares outstanding.

TREASURY STOCK

Treasury stock is stock that has been sold to the investing public, which has subsequently been repurchased by the corporation. The corporation may elect to reissue the shares or it may retire the shares that it holds in treasury stock. Treasury stock does not receive dividends, nor does it vote.

A corporation may elect to repurchase its own shares for any of the following reasons:

- To maintain control of the company
- To increase earnings per share
- To fund employee stock purchase plans
- To use shares to pay for a merger or acquisition

To determine the amount of treasury stock, use the following formula:

Issued stock – outstanding stock = treasury stock

EXAMPLE If, in the case of XYZ, the company decides to repurchase 3,000,000 of its own shares then XYZ would have 5,000,000 shares issued, 2,000,000 shares, and 3,000,000 shares of treasury stock.

It's important to note that once the shares have been issued, they will always be counted as issued shares. The only thing that changes is the number of outstanding shares and the number of treasury shares.

VALUES OF COMMON STOCK

A common stock's market value is determined by supply and demand and may or may not have any real relationship to what the shares are actually worth. The market value of common stock is affected by the current and future expectations for the company.

BOOK VALUE

A corporation's book value is the theoretical liquidation value of the company. The book value is found by taking all of the company's tangible assets and subtracting all of its liabilities. This will give you the total book value. To determine the book values per share, divide the total book value by the total number of outstanding common shares.

PAR VALUE

Par value, in a discussion regarding common stock, is only important if you are an accountant looking at the balance sheet. An accountant uses the par value as a way to credit the money received by the corporation from the initial sale of the stock to the balance sheet. For investors, it has no relationship to any measure of value, which may otherwise be employed.

RIGHTS OF COMMON STOCKHOLDERS

As an owner of common stock, investors are owners of the corporation. As such, investors have certain rights that are granted to all common stock holders.

PREEMPTIVE RIGHTS

As a stockholder, an investor has the right to maintain their percentage interest in the company. This is known as a preemptive right. Should the company wish to sell additional shares to raise new capital, they must first offer the new shares to existing shareholders. If the existing shareholders decide not to purchase the new shares, then the shares may be offered to the general public. When a corporation decides to conduct a rights offering, the board of directors must approve the issuance of the additional shares. If the number of shares that are to be issued under the rights offering would cause the total number of outstanding shares to exceed the total number of authorized shares, then shareholder approval will be required. Existing shareholders will have to approve an increase in the number of authorized shares before the rights offering can proceed.

TESTFOCUS!

Number of Existing Shares	Number of New Shares	Total Shares After Offering
100,000	100,000	200,000
10,000	10,000	20,000
10% ownership	10% of offering	10% ownership

In this example, the company has 100,000 shares of stock outstanding and an investor has purchased 10,000 of those original shares. As a result, they own 10% of the corporation. The company wishing to sell 100,000 new shares to raise new capital must first offer 10% of the new shares to the current investor (10,000 shares) before the shares may be offered to the general public. So if the investor decides to purchase the additional shares, as is the case in the example, the investor will have maintained their 10% interest in the company.

A shareholder's preemptive right is ensured through a rights offering. The existing shareholders will have the right to purchase the new shares at a discount to the current market value for up to 45 days. This is known as the subscription price. Once the subscription price is set, it remains constant for the 45 days, while the price of the stock is moving up and down in the market place.

There are three possible outcomes for a right. They are:

1. **Exercised:** The investor decides to purchase the additional shares and sends in the money, along with the rights to receive the additional shares.
2. **Sold:** The rights have value and if the investor does not want to purchase the additional shares, they may be sold to another investor who would like to purchase the shares.
3. **Expire:** The rights will expire when no one wants to purchase the stock. This will only occur when the market price of the share has fallen below the subscription price of the right and the 45 days has elapsed.

CHARACTERISTICS OF A RIGHTS OFFERING

Once a rights offering has been declared, the company's common stock will trade with the rights attached. The stock in this situation is said to be trading cum rights. The company's stock, which is the subject of the rights offering, will trade cum rights between the declaration date and the ex date. After the ex date, the stock will trade without the rights attached or will trade ex rights. The value of the common stock will be adjusted down by the value of the right on the ex-rights date. During a rights offering, each share will be issued one right. The subscription price and the number of rights required to purchase one additional share will be detailed in the terms of the offering on the rights certificate. During a rights offering, the issuer will retain an investment bank to act as a standby underwriter and the investment bank will stand by, ready to purchase any shares that are not purchased by the rights holders.

DETERMINING THE VALUE OF A RIGHT CUM RIGHTS

In order to determine the value of one right before the ex-rights date, you must use the cum-rights formula. Subtract the subscription price of the right from the market price of the stock. Once the discount (if any) has been determined, divide the discount by the number of rights required to purchase one share plus one. This will determine the value of one right.

EXAMPLE

XYZ has 10,000,000 shares of common stock outstanding and is issuing 5,000,000 additional common shares through a rights offering. XYZ is trading in the marketplace at $51 per share and the rights have a subscription price of $48 per share. Keep in mind that the stock price reflects the value of the right that is still attached to the stock.

The value of a right is determined as follows:

Stock price
– Subscription price

The number of rights required to purchase one share + 1

$51
– $48
$ 3

$3/3 rights = $1

Because each one of the 10,000,000 shares is entitled to receive one right and the company is offering 5,000,000 additional shares, it will require $48, plus two rights, to subscribe to one additional share. The rights agent will handle the name changes when the rights are purchased and sold in the market place.

DETERMINING THE VALUE OF A RIGHT EX RIGHTS

In order to determine the value of one right after the ex-rights date, subtract the subscription price of the right from the market price of the stock. Once the discount (if any) has been determined, divide the discount by the number of rights required to purchase one share. This will determine the value of one right. The price of the stock on the ex-rights date is adjusted down by the value of the right to reflect the fact that purchasers of the stock will no longer receive the rights.

EXAMPLE

XYZ has 10,000,000 shares of common stock outstanding and is issuing 5,000,000 additional common shares through a rights offering. XYZ is trading in the marketplace at $50 per share and the rights have a subscription price of $48 per share. The value of a right is determined as follows:

Stock price
– Subscription price

The number of rights required to purchase one share

$50
–$48
$2

$2/2 rights = $1

Because each one of the 10,000,000 shares is entitled to receive one right and the company is ffering 5,000,000 additional shares, it will require $48, plus two rights, to subscribe to one additional share.

VOTING

As a common stockholder, you have the right to vote on the major issues facing the corporation. You are a part owner of the company and, as a result, you have a right to say how the company is run. The biggest emphasis is placed on the election of the board of directors.

Common stockholders may also vote on:

- Issuance of bonds or additional common shares
- Stock splits
- Mergers and acquisitions
- Major changes in corporate policy

METHODS OF VOTING

There are two methods by which the voting process may be conducted: statutory and cumulative. A stockholder may cast one vote for each share of stock owned and the statutory or cumulative methods will determine how those votes are cast. The test focuses on the election of the board of directors, so we will use that in our example.

TESTFOCUS!

An investor own 200 shares of XYZ. There are two board members to be elected and there are four people running in the election. Under both the statutory and cumulative methods of voting, take the number of shares owned and multiply them by the number of people to be elected to determine how many votes the shareholder has; in this case, 200 shares × 2 = 400 votes. The cumulative or statutory methods dictate how those votes may be cast.

Candidate	Statutory	Cumulative
1	200 votes	400 votes
2		
3		
4	200 votes	

The statutory method requires that the votes be distributed evenly among the candidates for whom the investor wishes to vote.

The cumulative method allows the shareholder to cast all of their votes in favor of one candidate, if they so choose. The cumulative method is said to favor smaller investors for this reason.

LIMITED LIABILITY

A stockholder's liability is limited to the amount of money invested in the stock. They cannot be held liable for any amount past their invested capital.

FREELY TRANSFERABLE

Common stock and most other securities are freely transferable. That is to say that one investor may sell their shares to another investor without limitation and without requiring the approval of the issuer. The transfer of a security's ownership, in most cases, is facilitated through a broker dealer. The transfer of ownership is executed in the secondary market on either an exchange or in the over-the-counter market. Ownership of common stock is evidenced by a stock certificate which identifies the:

- Name of the issuing company
- Number of shares owned
- Name of the owner of record
- CUSIP number

In order to transfer or sell the shares, the owner must endorse the stock certificate or sign a power of substitution known as a stock or bond power. Signing the certificate or a stock or bond power makes the securities transferable into the new buyer's name.

THE TRANSFER AGENT

The transfer agent is the company that is in charge of transferring the record of ownership from one party to another. The transfer agent:

- Cancels old certificates registered to the seller
- Issues new certificates to the buyer
- Maintains and records a list of stockholders
- Ensures that shares are issued to the correct owner
- Locates lost or stolen certificates
- Issues new certificates in the event of destruction
- May authenticate a mutilated certificate

THE REGISTRAR

The registrar is the company responsible for auditing the transfer agent to ensure that the transfer agent does not erroneously issue more shares than are authorized by the company. In the case of a bond issue, the registrar will certify that the bond is a legally binding debt of the company. The function of the transfer agent and the registrar may not be performed by a single department of any one company. A bank or a trust company usually performs the functions of the transfer agent and the registrar.

CUSIP NUMBERS

The Committee on Uniform Securities Identification Procedures issues CUSIP numbers that are printed on the stock or bond certificates to help identify the security. CUSIP numbers must also appear on trade confirmations.

INSPECTION OF BOOKS AND RECORDS

All stockholders have the right to inspect the company's books and records. For most shareholders, this right is ensured through the company's filing of quarterly and annual reports. Stockholders also have the right to obtain a list of shareholders, but they do not have the right to review other corporate financial data that the corporation may deem confidential.

RESIDUAL CLAIM TO ASSETS

In the event of a company's bankruptcy or liquidation, common stockholders have the right to receive their proportional interest in residual assets. After all the other security holders have been paid (along with all creditors of the corporation), common stockholders may claim the residual assets. For this reason, common stock is the most junior security.

WHY DO PEOPLE BUY COMMON STOCK?

The main reason people invest in common stock is for capital appreciation. They want their money to grow in value over time. An investor in common stock hopes to buy the stock at a low price and sell it at a higher price at some point in the future.

EXAMPLE An investor purchases 100 shares of XYZ at $20 per share on March 15, 2012. On April 30 of 2013, the investor sells 100 shares of XYZ for $30 per share, realizing a profit of $10 per share or $1,000 on the 100 shares.

INCOME

Many corporations distribute a portion of their earnings to their investors in the form of dividends. This distribution of earnings creates income for the investor, and investors in common stock generally receive dividends quarterly.

The amount of income that an investor receives each year is measured relative to what the investor has paid—or will pay—for the stock and is known as the dividend yield or the current yield.

EXAMPLE

ABC pays a $.50 quarterly dividend to its shareholders. The stock is currently trading at $20 per share. What is its current yield (also known as dividend yield)?

Current yield = annual income/current market price

$.50 × 4 = $2.00 $2/$20 = 10%

The investor in this example is receiving 10% of the purchase price of the stock each year in the form of dividends, which, by itself, would be a nice return for the investor.

WHAT ARE THE RISKS OF OWNING COMMON STOCK?

The major risk in owning common stock is that the stock may fall in value. There are no sure things in the stock market and, even if you own stock in a great company, you may end up losing money.

DIVIDENDS MAY BE STOPPED OR REDUCED

Common stockholders are not entitled to receive dividends just because they own part of the company. It is up to the company to elect to pay a dividend. The corporation is in no way obligated to pay a dividend to common shareholders.

JUNIOR CLAIM ON CORPORATE ASSETS

A common stockholder is the last person to get paid if the company is liquidated. It is very possible that after all creditors and other investors are paid, there will be little or nothing left for the common stockholder.

HOW DOES SOMEONE BECOME A STOCKHOLDER?

We have reviewed some of the reasons why an investor would want to become a stockholder. Now we need to review how someone becomes a stockholder. Although some people purchase the shares directly from the corporation when the stock is offered to the public directly, most investors purchase the shares from other investors. These investor-to-investor transactions take place in the secondary market on the exchange or in the over-the-counter market. Although the transaction in many cases only take seconds to execute, trades actually take several days to fully complete. Let's review the important dates regarding transactions, which are done for a "regular-way" settlement.

TRADE DATE

The trade date is the day when your order is actually executed. Although an order has been placed with a broker, it may not be executed on the same day. There are certain types of orders that may take several days or even longer to execute, depending on the type of order. A market order will be executed immediately (as soon as it is presented to the market), making the trade date the same day the order was entered.

SETTLEMENT DATE

The buyer of a security actually becomes the owner of record on the settlement date. When an investor buys a security from another investor, the selling investor's name is removed from the security and the buyer's name is recorded as the new owner. Settlement date is three business days after the trade date. This is known as T+3 for all regular-way transactions in common stock, preferred stock, corporate bonds, and municipal bonds. Government bonds and options all settle the next business day following the trade date.

PAYMENT DATE

The payment date is the day when the buyer of the security has to have the money in to the brokerage firm to pay for the purchase. Under industry rules, the payment date for common and preferred stock and corporate and municipal bonds is five business days after the trade date or T+5. Payment dates are regulated by the Federal Reserve Board under Regulation T of the Securities Exchange Act of 1934. Although many brokerage firms require their customers to have their money in to pay for their purchases sooner than the rules state, the customer has up to five business days to pay for the trade.

VIOLATION

If the customer fails to pay for the purchase within the five business days allowed, the customer is in violation of Regulation T. As a result, the brokerage firm will "sell out" and freeze the customer's account. On the sixth business day following the trade date, the brokerage firm will sell out the securities for which the customer failed to pay. The customer is responsible for any loss that may occur as a result of the sell out and the brokerage firm may sell out shares of another security in the investor's account in order to cover the loss. The brokerage firm then will freeze the customer's account, which means that the customer must deposit money up front for any purchases they want to make in the next 90 days. After the 90 days have expired, the customer is considered to have reestablished good credit and then may conduct business in the regular way and take up to five business days to pay for their trades.

PREFERRED STOCK

Preferred stock is an equity security with a fixed income component. Like a common stockholder, the preferred stockholder is an owner of the company. However the preferred stockholder is investing in the stock for the fixed income that the preferred shares generate through their semiannual dividends. Preferred stock has a stated dividend rate or a fixed rate that the corporation must pay to its preferred shareholders. Growth is generally not achieved through investing in preferred shares.

TAKENOTE!

While not the norm, some companies issue adjustable rate preferred shares. The dividend rate on these shares will be adjusted based on a benchmark such as Treasury bill rates. Because the dividend rate adjusts with market interest rates the price of the shares tends to be stable.

FEATURES OF ALL PREFERRED STOCK

There are a number of different types of preferred stock but all preferred stock have the same basic features.

PAR VALUE

Par value on preferred stock is very important because that's what the dividend is based on. Par value for all preferred shares is $100 unless otherwise stated. Companies generally express the dividend as a percentage of par value for preferred stock.

EXAMPLE

How much would the following investor receive in annual income from the investment in the following preferred stock?

An investor buys 100 shares of TWT 9% preferred.

$100 × 9% = $9 per share × 100 = $900

PAYMENT OF DIVIDENDS

The dividend on preferred shares must be paid before any dividends are paid to common shareholders. This gives the preferred shareholder a priority claim on the corporation's distribution of earnings.

DISTRIBUTION OF ASSETS

If a corporation liquidates or declares bankruptcy, the preferred shareholders are paid prior to any common shareholder, giving the preferred shareholder a higher claim on the corporation's assets.

PERPETUAL

Preferred stock, unlike bonds, is perpetual with no maturity date. Investors may hold shares for as long as they wish or until the shares are called in by the company under a call feature.

NONVOTING

Most preferred stock is nonvoting. Occasionally the holder of a cumulative preferred stock may receive voting rights in the event the corporation misses several dividend payments.

INTEREST RATE SENSITIVE

Because of the fixed income generated by preferred shares, their price will be more sensitive to changes in interest rates than the price of their common stock counterparts. As interest rates decline, the value of preferred shares tends to increase and when interest rates rise, the value of the preferred shares tends to fall. This is known as an inverse relationship.

TYPES OF PREFERRED STOCK

Preferred stock, unlike common stock, may have different features associated with it. Most of the features are designed to make the issue more attractive to investors and, therefore, benefit the owners of preferred stock.

STRAIGHT/NONCUMULATIVE

The straight preferred stock has no additional features. The holder is entitled to the stated dividend rate and nothing else. If the corporation is unable to pay the dividend, it is not owed to the investor.

CUMULATIVE PREFERRED

A cumulative feature protects the investor in cases when a corporation is having financial difficulties and cannot pay the dividend. Dividends on cumulative preferred stock accumulate in arrears until the corporation is able to pay them. If the dividend on a cumulative preferred stock is missed, it is still owed to the holder. Dividends in arrears on cumulative issues are always the first dividends to be paid. If the company wants to pay a dividend to common shareholders, they must first pay the dividends in arrears, as well as the stated preferred dividend, before common holders receive anything.

> **TESTFOCUS!**
>
> GNR has an 8% cumulative preferred stock outstanding. It has not paid the dividend this year or for the prior three years. How much must the holders of GNR cumulative preferred be paid per share before the common stockholders are paid a dividend?
>
> The dividend has not been paid this year nor for the previous three years, so the holders are owed four years' worth of dividends or:
>
> $$4 \times \$8 = \$32 \text{ per share}$$

PARTICIPATING PREFERRED

Holders of participating preferred stock are entitled to receive the stated preferred rate as well as additional common dividends. The holder of participating preferred receives the dividend payable to the common stockholders over and above the stated preferred dividend.

CONVERTIBLE PREFERRED

A convertible feature allows the preferred stockholder to convert or exchange their preferred shares for common shares at a fixed price known as the conversion price.

EXAMPLE

TRW has issued a 4% convertible preferred stock, which may be converted into TRW common stock at $20 per share. How many shares may the preferred stockholder receive upon conversion?

Number of shares = par/conversion price (CVP)

$100/$20 = 5

The investor may receive five common shares for every preferred share.

These are some additional concepts regarding convertible securities that will be addressed in the convertible bond section that follows.

CALLABLE PREFERRED

A call feature is the only feature that benefits the company and not the investor. A call feature allows the corporation to call in or redeem the preferred shares at their discretion or after some period of time has expired. Most callable preferred stock may not be called in during the first few years after its issuance. This feature, which does not allow the stock to be called in its early years, is known as call protection. Many callable preferred shares will be called at a premium price above par. For example, a $100 par preferred stock may be called at $103. The main reasons a company would call in their preferred shares would be to eliminate the fixed dividend payment or to sell a new preferred stock with a lower dividend rate when interest rates decline. Preferred stock is more likely to be called by the corporation when interest rates decline.

TYPES OF DIVIDENDS

There are a number of ways in which a corporation may pay a dividend to its shareholders. The type of dividend declared for payment may vary between corporation and economic circumstances.

CASH

A cash dividend is the most common form of dividend and it is one that the test focuses on. A corporation will send out a cash payment (in the form of a check) directly to the stockholders. For those stockholders who have their stock held in the name of the brokerage firm, a check will be sent to the brokerage firm and the money will be credited to the investors account. Securities held in the name of the brokerage firm are said to be held in street name.

To determine the amount that an investor will receive, simply multiply the amount of the dividend to be paid by the number of shares.

EXAMPLE JPF pays a $.10 dividend to shareholders. An investor who owns 1,000 shares of JPF will receive $100.

1,000 shares × $.10 = $100

STOCK

A corporation that wants to reward its shareholders—but also wants to conserve cash for other business purposes—may elect to pay a stock dividend to their shareholders. Each investor will receive an additional number of shares based on the number of shares that they own. The market price of the stock will decline after the stock dividend has been distributed to reflect the fact that there are now more shares outstanding, but the total market value of the company will remain the same.

EXAMPLE If HRT pays a 5% stock dividend to its shareholders, an investor with 500 shares will receive an additional 25 shares. This is determined by multiplying the number of shares owned by the amount of the stock dividend to be paid.

500 × 5% = 25

PROPERTY/PRODUCT

This is the least likely way in which a corporation would pay a dividend, but it is a permissible dividend distribution. A corporation may send out to its shareholders samples of its products or portions of its property.

DIVIDEND DISTRIBUTION

If a corporation decides to pay a dividend to its common stockholders, they may not discriminate as to who receives the dividend. The dividend must be paid to all common stockholders of record. An investor who already owns the stock does not need to notify the company that they are entitled to receive the pending dividend, because it will be sent to them automatically. However, new purchasers of the stock may or may not be entitled to receive the dividend depending on when they purchased the stock relative to when the dividend is going to be distributed. We will now examine the dividend distribution process.

DECLARATION DATE

The declaration date is the day that the board of directors decides to pay a dividend to common stockholders of record. The declaration date is the starting point for the entire dividend process. The company must notify the regulators at the exchange or FINRA (depending where the stock trades) at least 10 business days prior to the record date.

EX-DIVIDEND DATE

The ex-dividend date or the ex date is the first day when purchasers of the security are no longer entitled to receive the dividend that the company has declared for payment. Stated another way, the ex date is the first day when the stock trades without (ex) the dividend attached. The exchange or FINRA set the ex date for the stock, based on the record date determined and announced by the corporation's board of directors. Because it takes three business days for a trade to settle, the ex date is always two business days prior to the record date.

RECORD DATE

This is the day when investors must have their name recorded on the stock certificate in order to be entitled to receive the dividend that was declared by the board of directors. All stockholders whose name is on the stock certificate (owners of record) will be entitled to receive the dividend. The investor would have had to have purchases the stock before the ex-dividend date in order to be an owner of record on the record date. The record date is determined by the corporation's board of directors and is used to determine the shareholders that will receive the dividend.

PAYMENT DATE

This is the day when the corporation actually distributes the dividend to shareholders and it completes the dividend process. The payment date is controlled and set by the board of directors of the corporation and is usually four weeks following the record date.

STOCK PRICE AND THE EX-DIVIDEND DATE

It is important to note that the value of the stock prior to the ex-dividend date reflects the value of the stock with the dividend. On the ex-dividend date, the stock is now trading without the dividend attached and new purchasers will not receive the dividend that had been declared for payment. As a result of this, the stock price will be adjusted down on the ex-dividend date in an amount equal to the dividend.

TESTFOCUS!

TRY declares a $.20 dividend payable to shareholders of record as of Thursday, August 22. The ex-dividend date will be two business days prior to the record date. In this case, the ex date will be Tuesday, August 20. If TRY closed on Monday, August 19, at $24 per share, the stock would open at $23.80 on Tuesday.

Sunday	Monday	Tuesday	Wednesday	Thursday	Friday	Saturday
				1	2	3
4	5	6	7	8	9	10
11	12	13	14	15	16	17
18	19	20	21	22	23	24
25	26	27	28	29	30	31

TAXATION OF DIVIDENDS

All qualified dividends received by investors are taxed at a rate of 15% for the year the dividend is received. The tax rate for dividends is a hotly debated topic and may be subject to change.

SELLING DIVIDENDS

Selling dividends is a violation! A registered representative may not use the pending dividend payment as the sole basis of their recommendation to purchase the stock. Additionally, using the pending dividend as a means to create urgency on the part of the investor to purchase the stock is a prime example of this type of violation. If the investor were to purchase the shares just prior to the ex-dividend date simply to receive the dividend, the investor in many cases would end up worse off. The dividend in this case would actually be a return of the money that the investor used to purchase the stock and then the investor would have a tax liability when they receive the dividend.

DIVIDEND DISBURSEMENT PROCESS

The corporation's dividend disbursement agent is responsible for the distribution of dividends and will send the dividends to the shareholders of record on the record date. For convenience, most investors have their securities held in the name of the broker dealer, also known as street name. As a result, the dividend disbursement agent will send the dividends directly to the broker dealer. The broker dealer's dividend department will collect the dividends and distribute them to the beneficial owners.

WARRANTS

A warrant is a security that gives the holder the opportunity to purchase common stock. Like a right, the warrant has a subscription price. However, the subscription price on a warrant is always above the current market value of the common stock when the warrant is originally issued. A warrant has a much longer life than a right and the holder of a warrant may have up to 10 years to purchase the stock at the subscription price. The long life is what makes the warrant valuable, even though the subscription price is higher than the market price of the common stock when the warrant is issued.

HOW DO PEOPLE GET WARRANTS?

UNITS

Many times, companies will issue warrants to people who have purchased their common stock when it was originally sold to the public during its initial public offering (IPO). A common share that comes with a warrant attached to purchase an additional common share is known as a unit.

ATTACHED TO BONDS

Many times, companies will attach warrants to their bond offerings as a "sweetener" to help market the bond offering. The warrant to purchase the common stock makes the bond more attractive to the investor and may allow the company to issue the bonds with a lower coupon rate.

SECONDARY MARKET

Warrants often will trade in the secondary market just like the common stock. An investor who wishes to participate in the potential price appreciation of the common stock may elect to purchase the corporation's warrant instead of its common shares.

POSSIBLE OUTCOMES OF A WARRANT

A warrant, like a right, may be exercised or sold by the investor. A warrant may also expire if the stock price is below the warrant's subscription price at its expiration.

Rights vs. Warrants

Rights		Warrants
Up to 45 days	**Term**	Up to 10 years
Below the market	**Subscription Price**	Above the market
May trade with or without common stock	**Trading**	May trade with or without common stock or bonds
Issued to existing shareholders to ensure preemptive rights	**Who**	Offered as a sweetener to make securities more attractive

AMERICAN DEPOSITARY RECEIPTS (ADRs)/ AMERICAN DEPOSITARY SHARES (ADSs)

American depositary receipts facilitate the trading of foreign securities in the U.S. markets. An ADR is a receipt that represents the ownership of the foreign shares that are being held abroad in a branch of a U.S. bank. Each ADR represents ownership of between one to 10 shares of the foreign stock and the holder of the ADR may request the delivery of the foreign shares. Holders of ADRs also have the right to vote and the right to receive dividends that the foreign corporation declares for payment to shareholders.

CURRENCY RISKS

The owner of an ADR has currency risk along with the normal risks associated with the ownership of the stock. Should the currency of the country decline relative to the U.S. dollar, the holder of the ADR will receive fewer U.S. dollars when a dividend is paid and less in U.S. dollars when the security is sold. It's important to note that the dividend on the ADR is paid by the corporation to the custodian bank, in the foreign currency. The custodian bank will convert the dividend to U.S. dollars for distribution to the holders of the ADRs.

FUNCTIONS OF THE CUSTODIAN BANK ISSUING ADRs

ADRs are actually issued and guaranteed by the bank that holds the foreign securities on deposit. The custodian bank is the registered owner of the foreign shares and must guarantee that the foreign shares remain in the bank as long as the ADRs remain outstanding. Foreign corporations will often use ADRs as a way of generating U.S. interest in their company. The issuance of the ADR allows them to avoid the long and costly registration process for their securities.

REAL ESTATE INVESTMENT TRUSTS/REITs

A real estate investment trust, or a REIT, is a special type of equity security. REITs are organized for the specific purpose of buying, developing, or managing a portfolio of real estate. REITs are organized as a corporation or as a trust and publicly traded REITs will trade on the exchanges or in the over-the-counter market just like other stocks. A real estate investment trust is organized as a conduit for the investment income generated by the portfolio of real estate. REITs are entitled to special tax treatment under internal revenue code Subchapter M. A REIT will not pay taxes at the corporate level as long as:

- It receives 75% of its income from real estate.
- It distributes at least 90% of its taxable income to shareholders.

As long as the REIT meet these requirements, the income will be allowed to flow through to the shareholders and will be taxed at their rate. Dividends received by REIT shareholders will continue to be taxed as ordinary income.

It is important to note that REITs do not pass through losses or expenses to shareholders, only income. REIT investors own an undivided share of the underlying real estate portfolio. An investor may elect to invest in a REIT rather than directly in real estate ownership because of the greater liquidity provided by the REIT and the quality of the property manager.

DIRECT PARTICIPATION PROGRAMS AND LIMITED PARTNERSHIPS

Direct participation programs and limited partnerships are entities that allow income, expenses, gains, losses, and tax benefits to be passed through to the investors. There is generally no active secondary market for these investments, so it's important that investors understand the risks and can afford the risks associated with direct participation programs and limited partnerships. Series 65 candidates can expect to see several questions on this material on their exam.

LIMITED PARTNERSHIPS

A limited partnership is an entity that allows all of the economic events of the partnership to flow through to the partners. These economic events are:

- Income
- Gains
- Losses
- Tax credits
- Deductions

There are two types of partners in a limited partnership. They are the limited partners and the general partner. The limited partners:

- Put up the investment capital
- Losses are limited to their investment
- Receive the benefits from the operation
- May not exercise management over the operation
- May vote to change the objective of the partnership
- May vote to switch or remove the general partner
- May sue the general partner, if the general partner does not act in the best interest of the partnership

A limited partner may never exercise any management or control over the limited partnership. Doing so would jeopardize their limited status and they may be considered a general partner.

The general partner is the person or corporation that manages the business and has unlimited liability for the obligations of the partnership business. The general partner may also:

- Buy and sell property for the partnership
- Receive compensation for managing the partnership
- Enter into legally binding contracts for the partnership

The general partner also must maintain a financial interest in the partnership of at least 1%. The general partner may not:

- Commingle funds of the general partner with the funds of the partnership
- Compete against the partnership
- Borrow from the partnership

It is important to note that there are no tax consequences at the partnership level. In order to qualify for the preferential tax treatment, a DPP or LP must avoid at least two of the six characteristics of a corporation. These characteristics are:

- Continuity of life
- Profit motive
- Central management
- Limited liability
- Associates
- Freely transferable interest

Several of the characteristics cannot be avoided, such as associates and a profit motive. The easiest two characteristics of a corporation to avoid are continuity of life and freely transferable interest. The LP can put a termination date on the partnership and substitute limited partners may not be accepted or may only be accepted once the general partner has agreed.

STRUCTURING AND OFFERING LIMITED PARTNERSHIPS

The foundation of every limited partnership is the partnership agreement. All limited partners must be given a copy of the partnership agreement. The partnership agreement will spell out all of the terms and conditions, as well as the business purpose for the partnership. The powers and limitations of the general partner's authority will be one of the main points detailed in the partnership agreement. Prior to forming a limited partnership, the general partner will have to file a certificate of limited partnership in the state in which the partnership is formed. The certificate will include:

- Name and address of the partnership
- A description of the partnership's business

- The life of the partnership
- Size of limited partner's investments (if any)
- Conditions for assignment of interest by limited partners
- Conditions for dissolving the partnership
- Conditions for admitting new limited partners
- The projected date for the return of capital if one is set

A material change to any of these conditions must be updated on the certificate within 30 days.

Most limited partnerships will be offered to investors through a private placement. All investors who purchase a limited partnership through a private placement must receive a private placement memorandum. Private placements, with very limited exceptions, may only be offered to accredited investors. However, a few limited partnerships will be offered to the public through a standard public offering. All investors who purchase a limited partnership though a public offering must receive a prospectus. If the partnership is sold through a syndicator, the syndicator is responsible for filing the partnership documents. The maximum fee that may be received by the syndicator is limited to 10% of the offering. If a secondary market develops for a partnership, the partnership will be known as a master limited partnership or MLP. All investors wishing to become a limited partner must complete the partnership's subscription agreement. The subscription agreement will include:

- A power of attorney appointing the general partner
- A statement of the prospective limited partner's net worth
- A statement regarding the prospective limited partner's income
- A statement from the prospective limited partner that they understand and can afford the risks related to the partnership

TYPES OF LIMITED PARTNERSHIPS

A limited partnership may be organized for any lawful purpose. The limited partnerships that are most common are set up to:

- Invest in real estate
- Invest in oil and gas wells
- Engage in equipment leasing

There are several types of real estate partnerships. They are:

- Existing property
- New construction
- Raw land
- Government-assisted housing
- Historic rehabilitation

Type of LP	Risk	Advantages	Disadvantages	Tax Benefits
Existing property Purchase income property	Low	Immediate predictable cash flow	Rental problems and repairs	Deductions for mortgage interest and depreciation
New construction Build units for appreciation or rental	Higher	Potential capital gains low maintenance	No deduction for current expenses and no promise of rental or sale	Deduction of expenses and depreciation only after completion
Raw land Purchase land for appreciation	Highest	Only appreciation potential	No tax deductions or income	No tax benefits
Government-assisted housing Low-income housing	Low	Government rent subsidies and tax credits	High maintenance costs risk of a change in government programs	Tax credits and any losses on the property
Historic Rehabilitation Restore sites for use	Higher	Tax credits	Financing trouble, no rental history	Tax credits deductions and depreciation

TAX REPORTING FOR DIRECT PARTICIPATION PROGRAMS

Direct participation programs are organized as either limited partnerships or as Subchapter S corporations. These entities allow for the flow-through of income and losses and the DPP has no tax consequences. The DPP will only report the results of its operation to the IRS. The responsibility for paying any taxes due rests with the partners or shareholders. DPPs allow the losses to flow through to the investors. Losses from DPPs can only be used to offset the investor's passive income. Investors may not use the losses to shelter or offset the ordinary income. Investors should not purchase DPPs simply for the tax benefits; they should purchase them to earn a return. Any DPP that is found to have been formed simply to create tax benefits may subject the investors to strict penalties. Investors could owe back taxes, fines, or be prosecuted for fraud.

LIMITED PARTNERSHIP ANALYSIS

Before investing in a limited partnership, the investor should analyze the key features of the partnership to ensure that the partnership's objectives meet their investment objectives. The investor should review:

- Economic viability of the program
- Tax considerations
- Management's ability
- Lack of liquidity
- Time horizon
- Whether it is a blind pool or a specified program
- Internal rate of return

A blind pool is a partnership in which less than 75% of the assets that the partnership is going to acquire have been identified. In a specified program, more than 75% of the assets that the partnership is going to acquire have been identified.

A partnership's internal rate of return is the discounted present value of its projected future cash flow.

TAX DEDUCTIONS VS. TAX CREDITS

Tax deductions that are generated by partnerships are used to lower the investor's taxable income. A tax credit results in a dollar-for-dollar reduction in the amount of taxes due from the investor.

OTHER TAX CONSIDERATIONS

If a limited partnership has used up all of its deductions and has a gain on the sale of a depreciated asset, the sale above the asset's depreciated cost basis may subject the limited partners to a taxable recapture. There are two types of loans that a partnership may take out: a nonrecourse loan and a recourse loan. With a nonrecourse loan, if the partnership defaults, the lender has no recourse to the limited partners. With a recourse loan, in the event of the partnership's default, the lender can go after the limited partners for payment. A recourse loan can increase the investor's cost base. Partners must monitor their cost base and adjust it for:

- Cash or property contributions to the partnership
- Recourse loans
- Any cash or property received from the partnership

Investors are responsible for any gain on the sale of their partnership interest in excess of their cost basis.

DISSOLVING A PARTNERSHIP

A partnership will terminate on the date set forth in partnership agreement, unless earlier terminated. A partnership may dissolve if a majority of the limited partners vote for its dissolution. If the partnership terminates its activities, the general partner must cancel the certificate of limited partnership and liquidate the partnership assets. The priority of payment will be as follows:

- Secured lenders
- General creditors
- Limited partners' profits first, then return of investment
- General partner for fees first, then profits, then return of capital

TAKENOTE!

An investor in a limited partnership is subject to both liquidity risk and legislative risk. The investor may not be able to liquidate their interest when they need to and the government may change tax laws relating to their investment. As a result, an investor should not have more than 10% of their portfolio in limited partnerships.

CHAPTER 1

Pretest

EQUITY SECURITIES

1. A company you own common stock in has just filed for bankruptcy. As a shareholder, you will have the right to receive:
   a. The par value of the common shares
   b. New common shares in the reorganized company
   c. A percentage of your original investment
   d. Your proportional percentage of residual assets

2. A corporation may pay a dividend in which of the following ways?
   a. Stock
   b. Cash
   c. Stock of another company
   d. All of the above

3. ABC common stock has declined dramatically in value over the last quarter but the dividend it has declared for payment this quarter has remained the same. The dividend yield on the stock has:
   a. Not changed because the board has to declare the dividend amount
   b. Gone down because the yield is a stated rate
   c. Gone up as the price of ABC has fallen
   d. Been fixed at the time of issuance

4. All qualified dividends are:
   a. Taxed as ordinary income each year
   b. Tax-free income
   c. Taxed as special interest-free income
   d. Taxed at a set rate of 15%

5. All of the following are rights of common stockholders, except:
   a. Right to elect the board of directors
   b. Right to vote for executive compensation
   c. Right to vote for a stock split
   d. Right to maintain their percentage of ownership in the company

6. Which of the following is not true regarding American Depositary Receipts (ADRs)?
   a. They are receipts of ownership of foreign shares being held abroad in a U.S. bank.
   b. Each ADR represents 100 shares of foreign stock, and the ADR holder may request delivery of the foreign shares.
   c. ADR holders have the right to vote and to receive dividends that the foreign corporation declares for shareholders.
   d. The foreign country may issue restrictions on the foreign ownership of stock.

7. An investor buys a 10% preferred stock at 110. What is their current yield?
   a. 10.4%
   b. 9.1%
   c. 10%
   d. 9.5%

8. An investor buys 100 shares of XYZ 7% convertible preferred stock which is convertible into XYZ common at $20 per share. How many shares of common shares upon conversion:
   a. 5
   b. 400
   c. 500
   d. 5,000

9. An investor has purchased shares of a foreign company through an ADR. Which of the following is not true?
   a. The ADR may represent one or more shares of the company's common stock.
   b. The dividend will be paid in U.S. dollars.
   c. The investor may elect to exchange the ADR for the underlying common shares.
   d. The investor is subject to currency risk.

10. An investor owns 100 shares of XYZ 8% participating preferred stock. XYZ's common stock pays a quarterly dividend of $.25. How much will the investor earn each year in dividends?
    a. $825
    b. $90
    c. $180
    d. $900

11. An investor who buys a 7% cumulative preferred stock will receive semi-annual dividends of:
    a. $7 per share
    b. 7% of the corporate profits
    c. $3.50 per share
    d. 3.5% of the corporate profits

12. As the owner of a cumulative preferred stock, an investor would have all of the following rights, except:
    a. Voting if dividends are missed for a significant period of time
    b. Right to receive past dividends not paid by the corporation
    c. Right to exchange the preferred for the underlying common shares
    d. The right to receive the past dividends before common holders receive a dividend

13. Authorized stock is all of the following, except:
    a. The maximum number of shares a company may sell
    b. Arbitrarily determined at the time of incorporation and may not be changed
    c. May be sold in total or in part when the company goes public
    d. Sold to investors to raise operating capital for the company

14. Common stockholders do not have the right to vote on which of the following issues?
    a. Election of the board of directors
    b. Stock splits
    c. Issuance of additional common shares
    d. Bankruptcy

15. Common dividends are all of the following except:
    a. A portion of the earnings of the company
    b. A source of income for the investor
    c. Generally paid quarterly
    d. A figure determined by subtracting the current yield from the current market price

16. If a 5% stock dividend is paid to an investor who owns 800 shares of stock already, the investor will receive how many shares?
    a. 4 shares
    b. 8 shares
    c. 40 shares
    d. 80 shares

17. It may be necessary for a company to repurchase some of its stock, to increase its treasury stock, for which one of the following reasons:
    a. To maintain control of the company
    b. To allow the company to pay out smaller dividends
    c. To increase the funding in the company's treasury
    d. To reassure its investors that all is well

CHAPTER 2

Corporate and Municipal Debt Securities

INTRODUCTION

Many different types of entities issue bonds in an effort to raise working capital. Corporations and municipalities, along with the U.S. government and U.S. government agencies, all issue bonds in order to meet their capital needs. A bond represents a loan to the issuer in exchange for its promise to repay the face amount of the bond known as the principal amount at maturity. On most bonds, the investor receives semiannual interest payments during the bond's term. These semiannual interest payments, along with any capital appreciation or depreciation at maturity, represent the investor's return. A bondholder invests primarily for the interest income that will be generated during the bonds term.

CORPORATE BONDS

Corporations will issue bonds in an effort to raise working capital to build and expand their business. Corporate bondholders are not owners of the corporation; they are creditors of the company. Corporate debt financing is known as leverage financing because the company pays interest only on the loan until maturity. Bondholders do not have voting rights as long as the company pays the interest and principal payments in a timely fashion. If the company defaults, the bondholders may be able to use their position as creditors to gain a voice in the company's management. Bondholders will always be paid before preferred and common stockholders in the event of liquidation. Interest income received by investors on corporate bonds is taxable at all levels, federal, state and local.

TYPES OF BOND ISSUANCE

BEARER BONDS

Bonds that are issued in coupon or bearer form do not record the owner's information with the issuer and the bond certificate does not have the legal owner's name printed on it. As a result, anyone who possesses the bond is entitled to receive the interest payments by clipping the coupons attached to the bond and depositing them in a bank or trust company for payment. Additionally, the bearer is entitled to receive the principal payment at the bond's maturity. Bearer bonds are no longer issued within the United States; however, they are still issued outside the country.

REGISTERED BONDS

Most bonds now are issued in registered form. Bonds that have been issued in registered form have the owner's name recorded on the books of the issuer and the buyer's name will appear on the bond certificate.

PRINCIPAL-ONLY REGISTRATION

Bonds that have been registered as to principal only have the owner's name printed on the bond certificate. The issuer knows who owns the bond and who is entitled to receive the principal payment at maturity. However, the bondholder will still be required to clip the coupons to receive the semiannual interest payments.

FULLY REGISTERED

Bonds that have been issued in fully registered form have the owner's name recorded for both the interest and principal payments. The owner is not required to clip coupons and the issuer will send out the interest payments directly to the holder on a semiannual basis. The issuer will also send the principal payment along with last semiannual interest payment directly to the owner at maturity. Most bonds in the United States are issued in fully registered form.

BOOK ENTRY/JOURNAL ENTRY

Bonds that have been issued in book entry or journal entry form have no physical certificate issued to the holder as evidence of ownership. The bonds are fully registered and the issuer knows who is entitled to receive the semiannual interest payments and the principal payment at maturity. The investor's only evidence of ownership is the trade confirmation, which is generated by the brokerage firm, when the purchase order has been executed.

BOND CERTIFICATE

If a bond certificate is issued, it must include:

- Name of issuer
- Principal amount
- Issuing date
- Maturity date
- Interest payment dates
- Place where interest is payable (paying agent)
- Type of bond
- Interest rate
- Call feature (if any or noncallable)
- Reference to the trust indenture

BOND PRICING

Once issued, corporate bonds trade in the secondary market between investors similar to the way equity securities do. The price of bonds in the secondary market depends on all of the following:

- Rating
- Interest rates
- Term
- Coupon rate
- Type of bond
- Issuer

- Supply and demand
- Other features, i.e., callable, convertible

Corporate bonds are always priced as a percentage of par and par value for all bonds is always $1,000, unless otherwise stated.

PAR VALUE

Par value of a bond is equal to the amount that the investor has loaned to the issuer. The terms par value, face value, and principal amount are synonymous and are always equal to $1,000. The principal amount is the amount that will be received by the investor at maturity, regardless of the price the investor paid for the bond. An investor who purchases a bond in the secondary market for $1,000 is said to have paid par for the bond.

DISCOUNT

In the secondary market, many different factors affect the price of the bond. It is not at all unusual for an investor to purchase a bond at a price that is below the bond's par value. Anytime an investor buys a bond at a price that is below the par value, they are said to be buying the bond at a discount.

PREMIUM

Often market conditions will cause the price of existing bonds to rise and make it attractive for the investors to purchase a bond at a price that is greater than its par value. Anytime an investor buys a bond at a price that exceeds its par value, the investor is said to have paid a premium.

CORPORATE BOND PRICING

All corporate bonds are priced as a percentage of par into fractions of a percent. For example, a quote for a corporate bond reading 95 actually translates into:

95% × $1,000 = $950

A quote for a corporate bond of $97^{1}/4$ translates into:

97.25% × $1,000 = $972.50

BOND YIELDS

A bond's yield is the investor's return for holding the bond. Many factors affect the yield that an investor will receive from a bond such as:

- Current interest rates
- Term of the bond
- Credit quality of the issuer
- Type of collateral
- Convertible or callable
- Purchase price

An investor who is considering investing in a bond needs to be familiar with the bond's nominal yield, current yield, and yield to maturity.

NOMINAL YIELD

A bond's nominal yield is the interest rate that is printed or "named" on the bond. The nominal yield is always stated as a percentage of par. It is fixed at the time of the bond's issuance and never changes. The nominal yield may also be called the coupon rate. For example, a corporate bond with a coupon rate of 8% will pay the holder $80.00 per year in interest.

8% × $1,000 = $80. The nominal yield is 8%.

CURRENT YIELD

The current yield is a relationship between the annual interest generated by the bond and the bond's current market price. To find any investment's current yield, use the following formula:

Annual income/current market price

For example, let's take the same 8% corporate bond used in the previous example on nominal yield and see what its current yield would be if we paid $1,100 for the bond.

Annual income = 8% × $1,000 = $80

Current market price = 110% × $1,000 = $1,100

Current yield = $80/$1,100 = 7.27%

In this example, we have purchased the bond at a premium or a price that is higher than par and we see that the current yield on the bond is lower than the nominal yield.

Let's take a look at the current yield on the same bond if we were to purchase the bond at a discount or a price which is lower than par. Let's see what the current yield for the bond would be if we pay $900 for the bond.

Annual income = 8% × $1,000 = $80

Current market price = 90% × $1,000 = $900

Current yield = $80/$900 = 8.89%

In this example we see that the current yield is higher than the nominal yield. By showing examples calculating the current yield for the same bond purchased at both a premium and a discount, we have demonstrated the inverse relationship between prices and yields. That is to say, prices and yields on income-producing investments move in the opposite direction. As the price of an investment rises, the investment's yield falls. Conversely, as the price of the investment falls, the investment's yield will rise.

YIELD TO MATURITY

A bond's yield to maturity is the investor's total annualized return for investing in the bond. A bond's yield to maturity takes into consideration the annual income received by the investor along with any difference between the price the investor paid for the bond and the par value that will be received at maturity. It also assumes that the investor is reinvesting the semiannual interest payments at the same rate. The yield to maturity is the most important yield for an investor who purchases the bond.

YIELD TO MATURITY: PREMIUM BOND

The yield to maturity for a bond purchased at a premium will be the lowest of all the investor's yields. Although an investor may purchase a bond at a price that exceeds the par value of the bond, the issuer is only obligated to pay the bondholder the par value upon maturity. For example: An investor who purchases a bond at 110 or for $1,100 will receive only $1,000 at maturity and, therefore, will lose the difference of $100. This loss is what causes the yield to maturity to be the lowest of the three yields for an investor who purchases a bond at a premium.

YIELD TO MATURITY: DISCOUNT BOND

The yield to maturity for a bond purchased at a discount will be the highest of all of the investor's yields. In this case, the investor has purchased the bond at a price that is less than the par value of the bond. In this example, even though the investor paid less than the par value for the bond, the issuer is still obligated to pay them the full par value of the bond at maturity or the full $1,000. For example: An investor who purchases a bond at 90 or for $900 will still be entitled to receive the full par amount of $1,000 at maturity, therefore, gaining $100. This gain is what causes the yield to maturity to be the highest of the three yields for an investor who purchases a bond at a discount.

CALCULATING THE YIELD TO MATURITY

When an investor purchases a bond in the secondary market at a discount, the discount must be accreted over the remaining life of the bond. The accretion of the discount will result in a higher yield to maturity. When an investor purchases a bond in the secondary market at a premium, the premium must be amortized over the remaining life of the bond. The amortization of the premium will result in a lower yield to maturity.

In order to calculate the bonds approximate yield to maturity, use the following formulas:

For a bond purchased at a discount use:

$$\frac{\textbf{(Annual interest + annualized discount)}}{\dfrac{\textbf{(Price paid + PAR)}}{\textbf{2}}}$$

The annualized discount is found by taking the total discount and dividing it by the number of years remaining until maturity. For example, let's assume an investor purchased a 10% bond at $900 with 10 years until maturity. The bonds approximate yield to maturity would be found as follows:

$$\frac{\textbf{(\$100 + \$10)}}{\dfrac{\textbf{(\$900 + \$1,000)}}{\textbf{2}}}$$

In this case, the bond's approximate yield to maturity is 11.57%.

For a bond purchased at a premium use:

$$\frac{\text{(Annual interest} - \text{annualized premium)}}{\frac{\text{(Price paid} + \text{PAR)}}{2}}$$

The annualized premium is found by taking the total premium and dividing it by the number of years remaining until maturity. For example, let's assume an investor purchased a 10% bond at $1,100 with 10 years until maturity.

The bond's approximate yield to maturity would be found as follows:

$$\frac{(\$100 - \$10)}{\frac{(\$1{,}100 + \$1{,}000)}{2}}$$

In this case, the bond's approximate yield to maturity is 8.57%.

CALCULATING THE YIELD TO CALL

In the event that the bond may be called in or redeemed by the issuer under a call feature, an investor may calculate the approximate yield to call by using the approximate number of years left until the bond may be called.

> **TAKENOTE!**
>
> The yield to call will always extend past the yield to maturity. The yield to call will always be the highest yield on a bond purchased at a discount and it will always be the lowest yield for a bond purchased at a premium.

REALIZED COMPOUND YIELD RETURNS

Portfolio managers can determine how changing interest rates will affect a bond's yield to maturity by calculating its realized compound yield. A bond's realized compound yield measures a bond's annual return based on the semiannual compounding of coupon payments. The bond's realized compound yield will largely depend on the purchase price of the bond and the rate at which the interest payments are reinvested. Investors with longer holding periods will have higher total dollar and percentage returns.

YIELD SPREADS

Investors must look at the competing yields that are offered by a wide variety of bonds. The difference in the yields offered by two bonds is known as the yield spread. Many bonds are measured by the relationship between the bond's yield and the yield offered by similar term Treasury securities. This is known as the spread over Treasuries. As perceptions about the issuer and the economy change, yield spreads will change. During times of uncertainty, investors will be less likely to hold more risky debt securities. As a result, the yield spread between Treasuries and more risky corporate debt will widen.

THE REAL INTEREST RATE

Investors must calculate the effect inflation will have on the interest they receive on fixed-income securities. The interest rate received by an investor, before the effects of inflation are considered, is known as the nominal interest rate. The real interest rate is what the investor will receive after inflation is factored in. For example, if an investor is receiving an 8% interest rate on a corporate bond when inflation is running at 2%, the investor's real interest rate would be 6%. The investor's nominal interest rate consists of the real interest rate plus an inflation premium. The inflation premium factors in the expected rate of inflation during various bond maturities.

BOND MATURITIES

When a bond matures, the principal payment and the last semiannual interest payment are due. Corporations will select to issue bonds with the maturity type that best fits their needs, based on the interest rate environment and marketability.

TERM MATURITY

A term bond is the most common type of corporate bond issue. With a term bond, the entire principal amount becomes due on a specific date. For example, if XYZ corporation issued $100,000,000 worth of 8% bonds due June 1, 2025, the entire $100,000,000 would be due to bondholders on June 1, 2025. On June 1, bondholders would also receive their last semiannual interest payment and their principal payment.

SERIAL MATURITY

A serial bond issue is one that has a portion of the issue maturing over a series of years. Traditionally, serial bonds have larger portions of the principal maturing in later years. The portion of the bonds maturing in later years will carry a higher yield to maturity because investors who have their money at risk longer will demand a higher interest rate.

BALLOON MATURITY

A balloon issue contains a maturity schedule that repays a portion of the issue's principal over a number of years, just like a serial issue. However, with a balloon maturity, the largest portion of the principal amount is due on the last date.

SERIES ISSUE

With a series issue, corporations may elect to spread the issuance of the bonds over a period of several years. This will give the corporation the flexibility to borrow money to meet its goals as its needs change.

TYPES OF CORPORATE BONDS

A corporation will issue or sell bonds as a means to borrow money to help the organization meet its goals. Corporate bonds are divided into two main categories: secured and unsecured.

SECURED BONDS

A secured bond is one that is backed by a specific pledge of assets. The assets that have been pledged become known as collateral for the bond issue or the loan. A trustee will hold the title to the collateral and, in the event of default, the bondholders may claim the assets that have been pledged. The trustee then will attempt to sell off the assets in an effort to pay off the bondholders.

MORTGAGE BONDS

A mortgage bond is a bond that has been backed by a pledge of real property. The corporation will issue bonds to investors and the corporation will pledge real estate, owned by the company, as collateral. A mortgage bond works in a similar fashion to a residential mortgage. In the event of default, the bondholders take the property.

EQUIPMENT TRUST CERTIFICATES

An equipment trust certificate is backed by a pledge of large equipment that the corporation owns. Airlines, railroads, and large shipping companies often will borrow money to purchase the equipment that they need through the sale of equipment trust certificates. Airplanes, railroad cars, and ships are all good examples of the types of assets that might be pledged as collateral. In the event of default, the equipment will be liquidated by the trustee in an effort to pay off the bondholders.

COLLATERAL TRUST CERTIFICATES

A collateral trust certificate is a bond that has been backed by a pledge of securities that the issuer has purchased for investment purposes or they could be backed by shares of a wholly owned subsidiary. Both stocks and bonds are acceptable forms of collateral as long as another issuer has issued them. Securities that have been pledged as collateral are generally required to be held by the trustee for safekeeping. In the event of a default, the trustee will attempt to liquidate the securities, which have been pledged as collateral, and divide the proceeds among the bondholders.

It's important to note that while having a specific claim against an asset that has been pledged as collateral benefits the bondholder, bondholders do not want to take title to the collateral. Bondholders invest for the semiannual interest payments and the return of their principal at maturity.

UNSECURED BONDS

Unsecured bonds are known as debentures and have no specific asset pledged as collateral for the loan. Debentures are only backed by the good faith and credit of the issuer. In the event of a default, the holder of a debenture is treated like a general creditor.

SUBORDINATED DEBENTURES

A subordinated debenture is an unsecured loan to the issuer that has a junior claim on the issuer in the event of default relative to the straight debenture. Should the issuer default, the holders of the debentures and other general creditors will be paid before the holders of the subordinate debentures will be paid anything.

INCOME/ADJUSTMENT BONDS

Corporations, usually in severe financial difficulty, issue income or adjustment bonds. The bond is unsecured and the investor is only promised to be paid interest if the corporation has enough income to do so. As a result of the large risk that the investor is taking, the interest rate is very high and the bonds are issued at a deep discount to par. An income bond is never an appropriate recommendation for an investor seeking income or safety of principal.

ZERO-COUPON BONDS

A zero-coupon bond is a bond that pays no semiannual interest. It is issued at a deep discount from the par value and appreciates up to par at maturity. This appreciation represents the investor's interest for purchasing the bond. Corporations, the U.S. government, and municipalities will all issue zero-coupon bonds in an effort to finance their activities. An investor might be able to purchase the $1,000 principal payment in 20 years for as little as $300 today. Because zero-coupon bonds pay no semiannual interest and the price is so deeply discounted from par, the price of the bond will be the most sensitive to a change in the interest rates. Both corporate and U.S. government zero-coupon bonds subject the investor to federal income taxes on the annual appreciation of the bond. This is known as phantom income.

GUARANTEED BONDS

A guaranteed bond is a bond whose interest and principal payments are guaranteed by a third party such as a parent company. The higher the credit rating of the company who is guaranteeing the bonds the better the guarantee.

CONVERTIBLE BONDS

A convertible bond is a corporate bond that may be converted or exchanged for common shares of the corporation at a predetermined price known as the conversion price. Convertible bonds have benefits to both the issuer and the investor. Because the bond is convertible, it usually will pay a lower rate of interest than nonconvertible bonds. This lower interest rate can save the corporation an enormous amount of money in interest expense over the life of the issue. The convertible feature will also benefit the investor if the common stock does well. If the shares of the underlying common stock appreciate, the investor could realize significant capital appreciation in the price of the bond and may also elect to convert the bond into common stock in the hopes of realizing additional appreciation. As an investor in the bond, they maintain a senior position as a creditor while enjoying the potential for capital appreciation.

CONVERTING BONDS INTO COMMON STOCK

All Series 65 candidates must be able to perform the conversion calculations for both convertible bonds and preferred stock. It is essential that perspective representatives are able to determine the following:

Number of shares: To determine the number of shares that can be received upon conversion, use the following formula:

Par value/conversion price

TESTFOCUS!

XYZ has a 7% subordinated debenture trading in the market place at 120. The bonds are convertible into XYZ common stock at $25 per share. How many shares can the investor receive upon conversion?

$1,000/$25 = 40 shares

The investor is entitled to receive 40 shares of XYZ common stock for each bond that they own.

PARITY PRICE

A stock's parity price determines the value at which the stock must be priced in order for the value of the common stock to be equal to the value of the bond that the investor already owns. The value of the stock that can be received by the investor upon conversion must be equal to, or at parity with, the value of the bond. Otherwise, converting the bonds into common stock would not make economic sense. Determining parity price is a two-step process. First, one must determine the number of shares that can be received by using the formula: par value/conversion price. Then it is necessary to calculate the price of each share at the parity price.

To determine parity price, use the following formula:

$$\frac{\textbf{Current market value of the convertible bond}}{\textbf{Number of shares to be received}}$$

In this example, the convertible bond was quoted at 120, which equals a dollar price of $1,200. We determined that the investor could receive 40 shares of stock for each bond so the parity price equals:

$1,200/40 = $30

If the question is looking for the number of shares or the parity price for a convertible preferred stock, the formulas are the same and the only thing that changes is the par value. Par value for all preferred stocks is $100 instead of $1,000 par value for bonds.

ADVANTAGES OF ISSUING CONVERTIBLE BONDS

Only corporations may issue convertible bonds. Some of the advantages of issuing convertible bonds to the company are:

- Makes the issue more marketable
- Can offer a lower interest rate
- If the bonds are converted, the debt obligation is eliminated.
- The issuance of the convertible bonds does not immediately dilute ownership or earnings per share.

DISADVANTAGES OF ISSUING CONVERTIBLE BONDS

There are some disadvantages to issuing convertible for the company such as:

- Reduced leverage upon conversion
- Conversion causes the loss of tax-deductible interest payments
- Conversion dilutes shareholder's equity
- Conversion by a large holder may shift control of the company

CONVERTIBLE BONDS AND STOCK SPLITS

If a corporation declares a stock split or a stock dividend, the conversion price of the bond will be adjusted accordingly. The trust indenture of a convertible bond will state the maximum number of shares that the corporation may issue while the bonds are outstanding, as well as the minimum price at which the additional shares may be issued.

THE TRUST INDENTURE ACT OF 1939

The Trust Indenture Act of 1939 requires that corporate bond issues in excess of $5,000,000, that are to be repaid during a term in excess of one year, issue a trust indenture for the issue. The trust indenture is a contract between the issuer and the trustee. The trustee acts on behalf of all of the bondholders and ensures that the issuer is in compliance with all of the promises and covenants made to the bondholders. The trustee is appointed by the corporation and is usually a bank or a trust company. The Trust Indenture Act of 1939 only applies to corporate issuers. Both federal and municipal issuers are exempt.

BOND INDENTURE

Corporate bonds may be issued with either an open-end or closed-end indenture. Bonds issued with an open-end indenture allow the corporation to issue additional bonds secured by the same collateral and whose claim on the collateral is equal to the original issue. A closed-end indenture does not allow the corporation to issue additional bonds having an equal claim on the collateral. If the corporation wants to issue new bonds, their claim must be subordinate to the claim of the original issue or secured by other collateral.

RATINGS CONSIDERATIONS

When the rating agencies assign a rating to a debt issue, they must look at many factors concerning the issuer's financial condition such as:

- Cash flow
- Total amount and type of debt outstanding
- Ability to meet interest and principal payments
- Collateral
- Industry and economic trends
- Management

S&P and Moody's are the two biggest ratings agencies. In order for a corporation to have their debt rated by one of these agencies, the issuer must request it and pay for the service. One of the main reasons a corporation would want to have their debt rated is because many investors will not purchase bonds that have not been rated. Additionally, if the issuer receives a higher rating, they will be able to sell the bonds with a lower interest rate.

FOCUSPOINT

Standard & Poor's		Moody's
AAA		Aaa
	Investment grade or high grade	
BBB		Baa
	Speculative high-yield junk bonds	

EXCHANGE TRADED NOTES (ETNs)

Exchange-traded notes sometimes known as equity-linked notes or index-linked notes are debt securities that base a maturity payment on the performance of an underlying security or group of securities such as an index. ETNs do not make coupon or interest payments to investors during the time the investor owns the ETN. ETNs may be purchased and sold at any time during the trading day and may be purchased on margin and sold short. One very important risk factor to consider when evaluating an ETN is the fact that ETNs are unsecured and carry the credit risk of the issuing bank or broker dealer. Similarly, principal protected notes (PPNs), which are structured products that guarantee the return of the investor's principal if the note is held until maturity, carry a principal guarantee that is only as good as the issuer's credit rating and therefore are never 100% guaranteed.

EURO AND YANKEE BONDS

A Eurobond is a bond issued in domestic currency of the issuer but sold outside of the issuer's country. For example, if Virgin Plc sold bonds to investors in Japan with the principal and interest payable in British pounds, this would be an example of a Eurobond. A Eurobond carries significant currency risk should the value of the foreign currency fall relative to the domestic currency of the purchaser. If the foreign currency fell, the interest and principal payments to be received in the foreign currency would result in the receipt of fewer units of the domestic currency upon conversion. A Eurodollar bond is bond issued by a foreign issuer denominated in U.S. dollars and sold to investors outside of the U.S. and outside of the issuer's country. Eurodollar bonds are issued in barer form by foreign corporations, federal governments, and municipalities. Eurobonds trade with accrued interest and interest is paid annually.

A Yankee bond is similar to a Eurodollar bond, except, Yankee bonds are dollar denominated bonds issued by a foreign issuer and sold to U.S. investors. If Virgin sold the same bonds to U.S. investors but the bond's interest and principal were denominated in U.S. dollars rather than in British pounds, the bonds would be a Yankee bond. The advantage of a Yankee bond over a Eurobond for U.S. investors is that the Yankee bond does not have any currency risk.

VARIABLE RATE SECURITIES

The two main types of variable rate securities are Auction Rate Securities and Variable Rate Demand Obligations (VRDO). Auction Rate Securities are long term securities that are traded as short term securities. The interest rate paid will be reset at regularly scheduled auctions for the securities every 7, 28, or 35 days. Investors who buy or who elect to hold the securities will have the interest rate paid on the securities reset to the clearing rate until the next auction. Should the auction fail due to a lack of demand, investors who were looking to sell the securities may not have immediate access to their funds. VRDOs have the interest rate reset at set intervals daily, weekly, or monthly. The interest rate set on the VRDO is set by the dealer to a rate that will allow the instruments to be priced at par. Investors may elect to put the securities back to the issuer or a third party on the reset date. Variable rate securities may be issued as debt securities or as preferred stock offerings.

RETIRING CORPORATE BONDS

The retirement of a corporation's debt may occur under any of the following methods:

- Redemption
- Refunding
- Prerefunding

- Exercise of a call feature by the company
- Exercise of a put feature by the investor
- Tender offering
- Open market purchases

REDEMPTION

Bonds are redeemed upon maturity and the principal amount is repaid to investors. At maturity, investors also will receive their last semiannual interest payment.

REFUNDING

Many times corporations will use the sale of new bonds to pay off the principal of their outstanding bonds. Corporations will issue new bonds to refund their maturing bonds or call the outstanding issue in whole or in part under a call feature. This is known as refunding corporate debt. Refunding corporate debt is very similar to refinancing a home mortgage.

PREREFUNDING

A corporation may seek to take advantage of a low interest rate environment by prerefunding their outstanding bonds prior to being able to retire them under a call feature. The proceeds from the new issue of bonds are placed in an escrow account and invested in government securities. The interest generated in the escrow account is used to pay the debt service of the outstanding or prerefunded issue. The prerefunded issue will be called in by the company on the first call date. Because the prerefunded bonds are now backed by the government securities held in the escrow account, they are automatically rated AAA. Once an issue has been prerefunded (or advance refunded), the issuer's obligations under the indenture are terminated. This is known as defeasance.

CALLING IN BONDS

Many times corporations will attach a call feature to their bonds that will allow them to call in and retire the bonds, either at their discretion or on a set schedule. The call feature gives the corporation the ability to manage the amount of debt outstaying, as well as the ability to take advantage of favorable interest rate environments. Most bonds are not callable in the first several years after issuance. This is known as call protection. A call feature on a bond benefits the company, not the investor.

PUTTING BONDS TO THE COMPANY

As a way to make a bond issue more attractive to investors, a company may attach a put feature or put option on their bonds. Under a put option, the holder of the bonds may tender the bonds to the company for redemption. Some put features will allow the bondholders to put the bonds to the company for redemption if their rating falls to low or if interest rates rise significantly. A put option on a bond benefits the bondholder.

TENDER OFFERS

A company may make a tender offer in an effort to reduce its outstanding debt or as a way to take advantage of low interest rates. Tender offers may be made for both callable and noncallable bonds. Companies usually will offer a premium for the bonds in order to make the offer attractive to bondholders.

OPEN-MARKET PURCHASES

Issuers, in an effort to reduce the amount of their outstanding debt, may simply repurchase the bonds in the marketplace.

MUNICIPAL BONDS

State and local governments will issue municipal bonds in order to help local governments meet their financial needs. Most municipal bonds are considered to be almost as safe as Treasury securities issued by the federal government. However, unlike the federal government, from time to time an issuer of municipal securities does default. The degree of safety varies from state to state and from municipality to municipality. Municipal securities may be issued by:

- States
- Territorial possessions of the United States, such as Puerto Rico
- Legally constituted taxing authorities and their agencies
- Public authorities that supervise ports and mass transit

TYPES OF MUNICIPAL BONDS

GENERAL OBLIGATION BOND

General obligation bonds (also known as GOs) are full faith and credit bonds. The bonds are backed by the full faith and credit of the issuer and by their ability to raise and levy taxes. In essence, tax revenues back the bonds. GOs often will be issued to fund projects that benefit the entire community and the financed projects generally do not produce revenue of any kind. General obligation bonds would be issued, for example, to fund a local park, a new school building, or a new police station. General obligation bonds that have been issued by the state are backed by income and sales taxes while GOs that have been issued by local governments or municipalities are backed by property taxes.

VOTER APPROVAL

General obligation bonds are a drain on the tax revenue of the state or municipality that issues them. The amount of general obligation bonds that may be issued must be within certain debt limits and requires voter approval. The maximum amount of general obligation debt that may be issued is known as the statutory debt limit. State and municipal governments may not issue general obligation debt in excess of their statutory limit.

PROPERTY TAXES

General obligation bonds issued at the local level are mostly supported by property tax revenue received from property owners. A property owner's taxes are based on the assessed value of the property, not on its actual market value. Towns will periodically send an assessor to inspect properties and determine what the properties' assessed values are.

EXAMPLE A homeowner whose home has a market value of $100,000 will not be taxed on the entire market value of the home. If the town uses a 75% assessment rate, the home's assessed value would be $75,000.

OVERLAPPING DEBT

Taxpayers are subject to the taxing authority of various municipal authorities. Municipal debt that is issued by different municipal authorities that draws revenue from the same base of taxpayers is known as overlapping debt or coterminous debt.

EXAMPLE The county water authority issued bonds that are supported by the property taxes levied in the county. The water authority's debt overlaps the towns' and county's other general obligation debt by drawing support from the same tax revenue. State issues are not included when determining overlapping debt because they are supported by other revenue sources such as state sales taxes and income taxes.

REVENUE BONDS

A revenue bond is a municipal bond that has been issued to finance a revenue-producing project such as a toll bridge. The proceeds from the issuance of the bond will construct or repair the facility, and the debt payments will be supported by revenue generated by the facility. Municipal revenue bonds are exempt from the Trust Indenture Act of 1939, but all revenue bonds must have an indenture that spells out the following:

- Rate covenant
- Maintenance covenant
- Additional bond test
- Catastrophe clause
- Call or put features
- Flow of funds
- Outside audit
- Insurance covenant
- Sinking fund

INDUSTRIAL DEVELOPMENT BONDS/ INDUSTRIAL REVENUE BONDS

An industrial revenue bond or an industrial development bond is a municipal bond issued for the benefit of a private corporation. The proceeds from the issuance of the bond will go toward building a facility or toward purchasing equipment for the corporation. The facility or equipment then will be leased back to the corporation and the lease payments will support the debt service on the bonds. Interest earned by some high-income earners on industrial development bonds may be subject to the investor's alternative minimum tax. States are limited as to the amount of industrial revenue bonds that may be issued, based on the population of the state.

LEASE RENTAL BONDS

A lease-back arrangement is created when a municipality issues a municipal bond to build a facility for an authority or agency such as a school district. The proceeds of the issue would be used to build the facility that is then leased to the agency and the lease payments will support the bond's debt service.

SPECIAL TAX BONDS

A special tax bond is issued to meet a specific goal. The bond's debt service is paid only by revenue generated from specific taxes. The debt service on special tax bonds is, in many cases, supported by "sin" taxes, such as taxes on alcohol, tobacco, gasoline, hotel and motel fees, and business licenses. Keep in mind that special tax bonds are revenue bonds, not general obligation bonds.

SPECIAL ASSESSMENT BONDS

A special assessment bond will be issued in order to finance a project that benefits a specific geographic area or portion of a municipality. Sidewalks and reservoirs are examples of projects that may be financed through issuance of special assessment bonds. The homeowners in the area that benefit from the project will be subject to a special tax assessment. The assessment then will be used to support the debt service of the bonds. Homeowners that do not benefit from the project are not subject to the tax assessment.

DOUBLE-BARRELED BONDS

Double-barreled bonds are bonds that have been issued to build or maintain a revenue-producing facility such as a bridge or a roadway. The initial debt service is supported by the user fees generated by the facility. However, if the revenue generated by the facility is insufficient to support the bond's interest and principal payments, the payments will be supported by the general tax revenue of the state or municipality. The debt service on double-barreled bonds is backed by two sources of revenue. Because the tax revenue of the state or municipality also backs them, revenue bonds are rated and trade like general obligation bonds.

MORAL OBLIGATION BONDS

A moral obligation bond is issued to build or maintain a revenue-producing facility such as a park that charges an entrance fee or a tunnel that charges a toll. If the revenue generated by the facility is insufficient to cover the debt service, the state legislature may vote to allocate tax revenue to cover the short fall. A moral obligation bond does not require that the state cover any shortfall; it merely gives them the option to. Some reasons why a state may elect to cover a shortfall are to:

- Keep a high credit rating on all municipal issues
- Ensure that interest rates on their municipal issues do not rise

NEW HOUSING AUTHORITY/ PUBLIC HOUSING AUTHORITY

New housing authority (NHA) and public housing authority (PHA) bonds are issued to build low-income housing. The initial debt service for the bonds is the rental income received from the project's tenants. Should the rental income be insufficient to cover the bond's debt service, the U.S. government will cover any shortfall. Because the payments are guaranteed by the federal government, NHA/PHA bonds are considered to be the safest type of municipal bond. NHA/PHA bonds are not considered to be double-barreled bonds because any shortfall will be covered by the federal government, not the state or municipal government.

SHORT-TERM MUNICIPAL FINANCING

States and municipalities, like other issuers, need to obtain short-term financing to manage their cash flow and will sell both short-term notes and tax-exempt commercial paper. Short-term notes are sold in anticipation of receiving other revenue and are issued an MIG rating by Moody's investor service. The MIG ratings range from 1 to 4, with a rating of MIG 1 being the highest and a rating of MIG 4 being the lowest. The types of short-term notes a state or municipality may issue are:

- Tax anticipation notes (TANs)
- Revenue anticipation notes (RANs)
- Bond anticipation notes (BANs)
- Tax and revenue anticipation notes (TRANs)

Municipal tax-exempt commercial paper matures in 270 days or less and usually will be backed by a line of credit at a bank.

TAXATION OF MUNICIPAL BONDS

The interest earned by investors from municipal bonds is free from federal income taxes. The doctrine of reciprocal immunity, established by the Supreme Court in 1895, sets forth that the federal government will not tax the interest earned by investors from municipal securities and that the states will not tax interest earned by investors on federal securities. The decision that established this doctrine was repealed in 1986 and allows for the federal taxation of municipal bond interest. This, however, is highly unlikely.

TAX-EQUIVALENT YIELD

It's important for investors to consider the tax implications of investing in municipal bonds. Because the interest earned from municipal bonds is federally tax free, municipal bonds will offer a lower rate than other bonds of similar quality. Even though the rate is oftentimes much lower, the investor may still be better off with the lower rate municipal than with a higher rate corporate bond. Investors in a higher tax bracket will realize a greater benefit from the tax exemption than investors in a lower tax bracket. To determine where an investor would be better off after taxes, look to the tax equivalent yield that is found by using the following formula:

Tax-free yield (100% – investor's tax bracket)

For example, take an investor considering purchasing a municipal bond with a coupon rate of 7%. The investor is also considering investing in a corporate bond instead. The investor is in the 30% federal tax bracket and wants to determine which bond is going to give the greatest return after taxes.

Tax equivalent yield = 7%/(100% – 30%) = 7%/.7 = **10%**

In this example, if the corporate bond of similar quality does not yield more than 10%, then the investor will be better off with the municipal bond. However, if the corporate bond yields more than 10%, the investor will be better off with the corporate bond.

PURCHASING A MUNICIPAL BOND ISSUED IN THE STATE IN WHICH THE INVESTOR RESIDES

If an investor purchases a municipal bond issued within the state in which he or she resides, then the interest earned on the bond will be free from federal, state, and local income taxes.

TRIPLE TAX FREE

Municipal bonds that have been issued by a territory such as Puerto Rico or Guam are given tax-free status for the interest payments from federal, state, and local income taxes.

ORIGINAL ISSUE DISCOUNT (OID) AND SECONDARY MARKET DISCOUNTS

Purchasers of original issue discount bonds, as well as those that have been purchased in the secondary market, are required to accrete the discount over the number of years remaining to maturity. That is to say, the investor must step up their cost base by the annualized discount each year.

EXAMPLE If an investor purchases a municipal bond in the secondary market at $900 with 10 years remaining to maturity, the investor would be required to step up their cost base each year by the annualized discount. The annualized discount is found by:

$$\frac{\textbf{Total discount}}{\textbf{No. of years to maturity}}$$

$100/10 years = $10 per year

The investor in this example would have to step up their cost base $10 per year. So in the third year, if the investor sold the bond at $925, they would have a $5 loss because their cost base would be $930.

If an investor purchases a municipal bond and sells it at a profit at some time in the future, the capital gain is taxable as ordinary income for the investor.

AMORTIZATION OF A MUNICIPAL BOND'S PREMIUM

Investors who purchase municipal bonds at a premium are required to amortize the premium over the number of years remaining to maturity. That is to say that the investor must step down their cost base by the annualized premium each year.

EXAMPLE If an investor purchases a municipal bond in the secondary market at $1,100 with 10 years remaining to maturity, the investor would be required to step down their cost base each year by the annualized premium. The annualized premium is found by:

$$\frac{\textbf{Total premium}}{\textbf{No. of years to maturity}}$$

$100/10 years = $10 per year

The investor in this example would have to step down their cost base $10 per year. So in the third year, if the investor sold the bond at $1,075, they would have a $5 gain because their cost base would be $1,070.

BOND SWAPS

An investor from time to time may wish to sell a bond at a loss for tax purposes. The loss will be realized when the investor sells the bond. The investor may not repurchase the bond, or a bond that is substantially the same, for 30 days after the sale is made. The investor may purchase bonds that differ as to the issuer, the coupon, or maturity, thus creating a bond swap and not a wash sale. A wash sale would result in the loss being disallowed by the IRS, because a bond swap does not affect the investor's ability to claim the loss.

ANALYZING MUNICIPAL BONDS

The quality and safety of municipal bonds vary from issuer to issuer. Investors who purchase municipal securities need to be able to determine the risk that may be associated with a particular issuer or with a particular bond.

ANALYZING GENERAL OBLIGATION BONDS

The quality of a general obligation bond is largely determined by the financial health of the issuing state or municipality. General obligation bonds are supported through the tax revenue that has been received by the issuer. The ability of the issuer to levy and collect tax revenue varies from state to state and from municipality to municipality. It is important that the fundamental health of the issuer be examined before investing in municipal bonds. Just as an investor would read a company's financial reports before purchasing their stock or bonds, an investor should read a state or municipality's reports before purchasing their bonds.

DURATION

In a normal interest rate environment, longer-term bonds will pay investors a higher interest rate than short-term bonds of equal quality. As interest rates change, the price of existing bonds will move inversely to the change in interest rates. A bond's duration is a measure of the bond's price sensitivity to a small change in interest rates and is stated in years. Longer term bonds and bonds with low coupons will generally have a higher duration than shorter term or higher yielding bonds. The higher the bond's duration, the greater the bond's interest rate risk and the greater its price volatility. Duration allows investors to compare the interest rate risk associated with bonds of different maturities, quality, and coupons. The bond's duration may be stated as either modified duration or effective duration. Modified duration assumes that a change in interest rates will not affect the bond's expected cash flow. Effective or call-adjusted duration assumes that a change in interest rates may affect the bond's cash flow if the bonds are callable or have other options for early retirement. Call-adjusted duration is lower than the bond's duration to maturity. All bonds that make regular interest payments will have a duration that is lower than the number of years to the bond's maturity. Because a zero-coupon bond does not provide any cash flow other than its principal payment at maturity, a zero-coupon bond's duration will be equal to the number of years to maturity. For example, a 20-year zero-coupon bond would have a duration of 20. To determine a bond's duration, use the following formula:

Bond price change percentage = duration × (change in yield in basis points/100)

EXAMPLE If a bond portfolio has an average duration of 7 years and interest rates rise by 1% or 100 basis points, the portfolio manager can expect the price of the bonds in the portfolio to fall by 7%.

CONVEXITY

A bond's convexity measures its price volatility to large changes in interest rates. A bond's price will not respond equally to both an increase and decrease in interest rates. As interest rates fall, bonds tend to increase in price more than they would fall if interest rates were to rise by an equal amount. Bond prices tend to rise faster in response to a fall in interest rates and fall slower in response to a rise in interest rates. Bonds whose prices react in this way are said to have positive convexity. Mortgage-backed and callable bonds tend to have negative convexities. A fall in interest rates increases both mortgage prepayments and the likelihood that the bonds will be called. Convexity is a better risk management tool than duration in volatile interest rate environments or when interest rates are low.

TAKENOTE!

Convexity is only important when comparing two investments with similar durations.

BOND PORTFOLIO MANAGEMENT

Bond portfolios may be either actively or passively managed to meet the needs of different investors. Active portfolio management tends to seek an above-average total return for the portfolio. The portfolio's total return includes:

- Coupon return: the total of all interest payments received by the portfolio plus accrued interest earned during a specific holding period
- Reinvestment return: the total interest earned from the reinvestment of interest payments during a specific holding period
- Price return: the total of the portfolio's appreciation or depreciation during a specific holding period

For long-term holding periods, the portfolio's reinvestment return will be the most important factor when determining the portfolio's return. For holding periods between two to 10 years, the coupon return and reinvestment return will be the most important factors. For short-term holding periods, the price return will be the most important factor.

Passive bond portfolio management includes both indexing and buy-and-hold strategies. Portfolio managers who use indexing try to match the performance of a given bond index by purchasing bonds that are included in the index. Advantages of indexing include lower management fees, diversification, and more predictable performance. Buy-and-hold managers tend to purchase bonds in the primary market and hold them for long periods of time or until maturity. By consistently purchasing new issues of bonds, the portfolio manager can maintain diversification of terms and coupon rates.

Pension and insurance company portfolio managers often will try to manage the portfolio's income to meet the current cash obligations of the pension plan or the insurance company's guaranteed investment contracts. Two methods used to match the portfolio's income with current cash liabilities are dedicated portfolio management and bond immunization. Dedicated portfolio management matches the portfolio's monthly income with the monthly cash liabilities. Bond immunization creates a portfolio designed to generate a specific return during a known time horizon. Portfolio managers using bond immunization will match the bonds' maturity dates with the known time when a lump sum payment is due. Because the portfolio's maturity dates match the time when the payment is due, the portfolio is said to be immunized from interest rate risk.

CHAPTER 2

Pretest

CORPORATE AND MUNICIPAL DEBT SECURITIES

1. An investor has purchased 10 corporate bonds at a price of 135. At the end of the day, the bonds are quoted at 136.25. How much have the bonds risen in dollars?
   - **a.** $125
   - **b.** $12.50
   - **c.** $1.25
   - **d.** $.125

2. Which type of bonds require the investor to deposit coupons to receive their interest payments but have the owner's name recorded on the books of the issuer?
   - **a.** Registered bonds
   - **b.** Bearer bonds
   - **c.** Book entry/journal entry bonds
   - **d.** Principal-only bonds

3. In response to a customer's request for information on how inflation will affect their return realized from their semiannual coupon payments, you would look at the:
   - **a.** real interest rate.
   - **b.** adjusted interest rate.
   - **c.** interest conversion rate.
   - **d.** current interest rate.

4. Which bonds are issued as a physical certificate without the owner's name on them and require whoever possesses these bonds to clip the coupons to receive their interest payments and to surrender the bond at maturity in order to receive the principal payment?
   a. Registered bonds
   b. Book entry/journal entry bonds
   c. Principal-only registered bonds
   d. Bearer bonds

5. All of the following are reasons a corporation would attach a warrant to their bond, except to:
   a. save money.
   b. make the bond more attractive.
   c. increase the number of shares outstanding when the warrants are exercised.
   d. lower the coupon.

6. The type of bond that is secured by real estate is called:
   a. Real estate trust certificates
   b. Mortgage bond
   c. Equipment trust certificates
   d. Collateral trust certificates

7. Collateral trust certificates use which of the following as collateral?
   a. Real estate
   b. Mortgage
   c. Stocks and bonds issued by the same company
   d. Stocks and bonds issued by another company

8. An investor holding an 8% subordinated debenture will receive how much at maturity?
   a. $1,000
   b. $1,080
   c. $1,040
   d. Depends on the purchase price

9. An ABC corporate bond is quoted at 110 and is convertible into ABC common at 20 per share parity. Price for the stock is:
   a. 21
   b. 22
   c. 23
   d. 24

10. An investor buys $10,000 of 10% corporate bonds with 5 years left to maturity. The investor pays 120 for the bonds. The approximate yield to maturity is:
   a. 5.45%
   b. 11.1%
   c. 6%
   d. 9.2%

11. XYZ has 8% subordinated debentures trading in the market place at $120. They are convertible into XYZ common stock at $25 per share. What is the parity price of the common stock?
   a. 29
   b. 31
   c. 30
   d. 28

12. Which one of the following debt securities pays interest?
   a. Commercial paper
   b. T-bill
   c. Industrial revenue bond
   d. Banker's acceptance

13. An investor would expect to realize the largest capital gain by buying bonds that are:
   a. long term when rates are high.
   b. short term when rates are low.
   c. short term when rates are high.
   d. long term when rates are low.

CHAPTER 3

Government and Government Agency Issues

INTRODUCTION

The U.S. government is the largest issuer of debt. It is also the issuer with the least amount of default risk. Default risk is also known as credit risk and is the risk that the issuer will not be able to meet its obligations under the terms of the bond in a timely fashion. The U.S. government issues debt securities with maturities ranging from one month up to 30 years. The treasury department issues the securities on behalf of the federal government and they are a legally binding obligation of the federal government. Interest earned by the investors from U.S. government securities is only taxed at the federal level. The state and local governments do not tax the interest income.

SERIES EE BONDS

The series EE bonds are commonly known as savings bonds. They are purchased directly from the U.S. government at a discount from their face value, typically 50%. The Series EE bonds pay no semiannual interest and may be redeemed at maturity for the face value. The investor's interest is earned through the bonds' appreciation toward the face value. The interest earned through this appreciation is taxable by the federal government and the investor may pay taxes on this money each year or may wait until the bond matures. The investor also may elect to roll the matured Series EE bonds into Series HH bonds and continue to defer taxes.

SERIES HH BONDS

A Series HH bond may only be purchased by trading in matured Series EE bonds. They may not be purchased for cash. Series HH bonds, unlike EEs, pay semiannual interest and are available in denominations of $500 to $10,000 and mature in 10 years. Series HH bonds may be redeemed at their face value at any time.

TREASURY BILLS, NOTES, AND BONDS

The most widely held U.S. government securities are Treasury bills, notes, and bonds. These direct obligations of the U.S. government range from one month up to 30 years.

PURCHASING TREASURY BILLS

Treasury bills range in maturity from four to 52 weeks and are auctioned off by the treasury department through a weekly competitive auction. Large banks and broker dealers, known as primary dealers, submit competitive bids or tenders for the bills being sold. The Treasury awards the bills to the bidders who submitted the highest bid and work their way down to lower bids until all of the bills are sold. Treasury bills pay no semiannual interest and are issued at a discount from par. The bill appreciates up to par at maturity and the appreciation represents the investor's interest. Because bills are priced at a discount from par, a higher dollar price represents a lower interest rate for the purchaser.

All noncompetitive tenders are filled before any competitive tenders are filled. A bidder who submits a noncompetitive tender agrees to accept the average of all the yields accepted by the treasury and does not try to get the best yield. All competitive tenders are limited to a maximum amount of $500,000. All bids that are accepted and filled by the treasury are settled in fed funds. Treasury bills range in denominations from $100 up to $1,000,000.

> **TAKENOTE!**
>
> A quote for a Treasury bill has a bid that appears to be higher than the offer, but remember that the bills are quoted on a discounted yield basis. The higher bid actually represents a lower dollar price than the offer.

Example

Bid	Ask
2.91	2.75

TREASURY NOTES

Treasury notes are the U.S. government's intermediate-term security and range in term from one year up to 10 years. Treasury notes pay semiannual interest and are auctioned off by the treasury every four weeks. Treasury notes are issued in denominations ranging from $100 up to $1,000,000 and may be refunded by the government. If a Treasury note is refunded, the government will offer the investor a new Treasury note with a new interest rate and maturity. The investor may always elect to receive their principal payment instead of accepting the new note.

TREASURY BONDS

Treasury bonds are the U.S. government's long-term bonds. Maturities on Treasury bonds range from 10 years up to 30 years. Treasury bonds, like Treasury notes, pay semiannual interest and are issued in denominations ranging from $100 up to $1,000,000. Some Treasury bonds may be called in at par by the treasury. If the treasury department calls in a bond issue, they must give holders four months' notice before calling the bonds.

TREASURY BOND AND NOTE PRICING

Treasury notes and bonds are quoted as a percentage of par. However, unlike their corporate counterparts, Treasury notes and bonds are quoted as a percentage of par down to 32nds of 1%. For example, a Treasury bond quote of 92.02 translates into:

92 2/32% × $1,000 = $920.625

A quote of 98.04 translates into:

98.125% × $1,000 = $981.25

It is important to remember that the number after the decimal points represents 32nds of a percent.

Treasury Security	Type of Interest	Term	Priced
Bill	None	4, 13, 26, 52 weeks 1, 3, 6, 12 months	At a discount from par
Note	Semiannual	1–10 years	As a percentage of par to 32nds of 1%
Bond	Semiannual	10–30 years	As a percentage of par to 32nds of 1%

The minimum denomination for purchasing a Treasury bill, note, or bond from TreasuryDirect.gov is $100. All quotes in the secondary market are based on $1,000 par value.

TAKENOTE!

The treasury does not currently sell one-year bills. However, this is a policy decision and the treasury may at any time elect to issue one-year bills just as it recently decided to reissue 30-year bonds.

TREASURY STRIPs

The term Treasury STRIPs actually stands for separate trading of registered interest and principal securities. The treasury securities are separated into two parts: a principal payment and semiannual interest payments. A Treasury STRIP is a zero-coupon bond that is backed by U.S. government securities. An investor may purchase the principal payment component of $1,000 due on a future date at a discount. An investor seeking some current income may wish to purchase the semiannual coupon payments due over the term of the treasury securities.

A STRIP may be purchased by an investor who needs to have a certain amount available on a known date in the future (like the time when a child is going to college). By purchasing the STRIP, the investor will be guaranteed to have $1,000 on that date in the future for each STRIP purchased.

TREASURY RECEIPTS

Treasury receipts are similar to Treasury STRIPs, except that broker dealers and banks create them. Broker dealers and banks will purchase large amounts of treasury securities, place them in a trust, and sell off the interest and principal payments to different investors.

TREASURY INFLATION PROTECTED SECURITIES (TIPS)

Treasury inflation protected securities, or TIPS, offer the investor protection from inflation. The TIPS are sold with a fixed interest rate and their principal is adjusted semiannually to reflect changes in the consumer price index. During times of inflation, the principal amount of the TIP will be increased and the investor's interest payments will rise, while during times of falling prices, the principal amount of the bond will be adjusted down and the investor will receive a lower interest payment.

EXAMPLE

A conservative investor purchases a TIP with a coupon rate of 4 percent. Prior to taking inflation into consideration the investor will receive 4% × $1,000 or $40 per year paid $20 or 2 percent every 6 months. TIPS pay interest every 6 months based on the adjusted principal amount. If Inflation is running at 6 percent per year over the next 2 years the investor's principal and interest payments will be as follows:

Year	Semi Annual Adjustment	Adjusted Principal	Adjusted Payment
1	Number 1	$1,030	$20.60
1	Number 1	$1,60.90	$21.22
2	Number 2	$1,092.73	$21.85
2	Number 2	$1,125.51	$22.51

Because inflation was running at 6 percent per year the principal was increased by 3 percent every 6 months. The adjustment to the principal and interests compounds semiannually and results in the continued increase in the principal amount and payment received. To determine the amount of the payment take half of the coupon rate and multiply it by the adjusted principal. In our example the TIP paid interests at a rate of 2 percent of the adjusted principal every 6 months. If on your test you cannot remember how to calculate compound interest over time you may approximate it by simply taking the inflation rate over a given period and multiply it by the principal. In our case 6 percent per year for two years = 12 percent. 12 percent of $1,000 = $120. The adjusted principal would be approximately $1,120. On the exam round up to the next nearest answer as you can see the approximate method gets you within about $5 of the compounded principal.

> **TAKENOTE!**
>
> Because the principal amount of the TIP is adjusted every 6 months to account for inflation the real return or the inflation adjusted return will always be equal to the coupon rate.

AGENCY ISSUES

The federal government has authorized certain agencies and certain quasi agencies to issue debt securities that are collectively referred to as agency issues. Revenues generated through taxes, fees, and interest income back these agency securities. Investors who purchase agency securities are offered interest rates that generally fall in between the rates offered by similar term treasury and corporate securities. Investors who purchase agency issues in the secondary market will be quoted prices for the agency issues that are based on a percentage of par just like corporate issue.

GOVERNMENT NATIONAL MORTGAGE ASSOCIATION (GNMA)

The Government National Mortgage Association often referred to as Ginnie Mae is a wholly owned government corporation and is the only agency whose securities are backed by the full faith and credit of the U.S. government. The purpose of Ginnie Mae is to provide liquidity to the mortgage markets. Ginnie Mae buys up pools of mortgages that have been insured by the Federal Housing Administration (FHA) and the Department of Veteran Affairs (VA). The ownership in these pools of mortgages then is sold off to private investors in the form of pass-through certificates. Investors in Ginnie Mae pass-through certificates receive monthly interest and principal payments based on their investment. As people pay down their mortgages, part of each payment is interest and part of each payment is principal and both portions flow through to the investor on a monthly basis. The only real risk in owning a Ginnie Mae is the risk of early refinancing. As the interest rates in the marketplace fall, people are more likely to refinance their homes and, as a result, the investor will not receive the higher interest rates for as long as they had hoped. Ginnie Mae pass-through certificates are issued with a minimum denomination of $1,000 and the interest earned by investors is taxable at all levels: federal, state, and local. Yield quotes on Ginnie Maes are based on a 12-year prepayment assumption because most mortgages are repaid early as a result of refinancing, moving, or a homeowner simply paying off their mortgage.

FEDERAL NATIONAL MORTGAGE ASSOCIATION (FNM)

The Federal National Mortgage Association, also known as Fannie Mae, is a public for-profit corporation. Fannie Mae's stock trades publicly and is in business to realize a profit by providing mortgage capital. It's called an agency security because Fannie Mae has a credit facility with the government and receives certain favorable tax considerations. Fannie Mae purchases mortgages and, in turn, packages them to create mortgage-backed securities. These mortgage-backed notes are issued in denominations from $5,000 to $1,000,000 and pay interest semiannually. Fannie Mae also issues debentures with a minimum denomination of $10,000 that mature in three to 25 years. Interest is paid semiannually and the interest earned by investors from Fannie Mae securities is taxable at all levels: federal, state, and local.

FEDERAL HOME LOAN MORTGAGE CORPORATION (FHLMC)

The Federal Home Loan Mortgage Corporation also known as Freddie Mac is a publicly traded company in business to earn a profit on its loans. Freddie Mac purchases residential mortgages from lenders and, in turn, packages them into pools and sells off interests in those pools to investors. Interest earned by investors from FHLMC-issued securities is taxable at all levels: federal, state, and local.

TAKENOTE!

Both Fannie Mae and Freddie Mac have been placed in receivership by the U.S. government.

FEDERAL FARM CREDIT SYSTEM

The Federal Farm Credit System is a group of privately owned lenders that provide different types of financing for farmers. The FFCS sells off farm credit securities in order to obtain the funds to provide to the farmers. The securities are the obligations of all the lenders in the system and are not backed by the U.S. government. The securities pay interest every six months and are only available in book-entry form. There are several lenders of which you need to be aware:

- Federal Land Bank provides mortgage money.
- Bank of the Cooperatives provides money for feed and grain.
- Federal Intermediate Credit Bank provides money for tractors and equipment.

COLLATERALIZED MORTGAGE OBLIGATION (CMO)

A collateralized mortgage obligation is a mortgage-backed security issued by private finance companies, as well as by FHLMC and FNMA. The securities are structured much like a pass-through certificate and their term is set into different maturity schedules, known as tranches. Pools of mortgages on one-family to four-family homes collateralize CMOs. Because CMOs are backed by mortgages on real estate, they are considered relatively safe investments and are given an AAA rating. The only real risk that the owner of a CMO faces is the risk of early refinance. CMOs pay interest and principal monthly. However, they pay the principal to only one tranche at a time in $1,000 payments. The CMO pays off each tranche until the final tranche known as a Z tranche is paid off. The Z tranche is the most volatile CMO tranche.

CMOs AND INTEREST RATES

CMOs, like other interest-bearing investments, will be affected by a change in the interest-rate environment. CMOs may experience the following if interest rates change:

- If interest rates fall, homeowners will refinance more quickly and the holder of the CMO will be paid off more quickly than they hoped.
- The rate of principal payments may vary.

- If interest rates rise, refinancing may slow down and the investors will be paid off more slowly than they hoped.

Most CMOs have an active secondary market and are considered relatively liquid securities. However, the more complex CMOs may not have an active secondary market and may be considered illiquid. Interest earned by investors from CMOs is taxable at all levels: federal, state, and local.

TYPES OF CMOs

Like many other investments there are several different types of CMOs. They are:

- Principal only (PO)
- Interest only (IO)
- Planned amortization class (PAC)
- Targeted amortization class (TAC)

PRINCIPAL-ONLY CMOs

Principal-only CMOs, as the name suggests, receives only the principal payments made on the underlying mortgage. Principal-only CMOs receive both the scheduled principal payments as well as any prepayments made by the home owners in the pool. Because the principal-only CMO does not receive any interest payments, it is sold at a discount to its face value. The appreciation of the CMO, up to its face value, represents the investor's return. The price of a principal-only CMO will be sensitive to a change in interest rates. As interest rates fall, the value of the CMO will rise as prepayments accelerate. A rise in interest rates will have the opposite effect.

INTEREST-ONLY CMOs

Interest-only CMOs receive the interest payments made by homeowners in the pool of underlying mortgages. Interest-only CMOs also will sell at a discount to their face value due to the amortization of the underlying mortgages. Interest-only CMOs will increase in value as interest rates rise and decrease in value as interest rates fall, as a result of the changes in prepayments on the underlying pool of mortgages. The changes in the prepayments on the underlying mortgages will affect the number of interest payments the holder of the CMO will receive. As interest rates rise, prepayments will slow, thus increasing the number of interest payments the investor receives. The more interest payments the CMO holder receives, the more valuable the CMO becomes.

PLANNED AMORTIZATION CLASS (PAC) CMO

Planned amortization class CMOs are paid off first and offer the investor the most protection against prepayment risk and extension risk. If prepayments come in too quickly, those principal payments will be deferred to another CMO known as a support class to protect the owner of the PAC from prepayment risk. If principal payments are made more slowly, principal payments will be taken from a support class to protect the investor against extension risk.

TARGETED AMORTIZATION CLASS (TAC) CMOs

Targeted amortization class CMOs only offer the investor protection from prepayment risk. If principal payments are made more quickly, they will be transferred to a support class. However, if principal payments come in more slowly, payments will not be taken from a support class and will be subject to extension risk.

TAKENOTE!

More complex CMOs are not suitable for all investors and investors should sign a suitability statement before investing. The secondary market for complex CMOs may also be very illiquid.

PRIVATE-LABEL CMOs

Private-label CMOs are issued by investment banks and the payment of interest and principal payments are the responsibility of the issuing investment bank. The payments due to a holder of a private-label CMO are not guaranteed by any government agency. The credit ratings of the private-label CMOs are based on the collateral that backs the CMO and the credit rating of the issuer. If the private-label CMO uses agency issues as collateral for the CMO, those agency issues still carry the guarantee of the issuing government agency.

CHAPTER 3

Pretest

GOVERNMENT AND GOVERNMENT AGENCY ISSUES

1. Your customer wants to invest in a conservative income-producing investment and is inquiring about GNMAs. She wants to know the minimum dollar amount required to purchase a pass-through certificate. You should tell her:
   - **a.** $1,000
   - **b.** $10,000
   - **c.** There is no minimum; you can invest almost any sum.
   - **d.** $5,000

2. Your customer buys a U.S. T-bond at 103.16. How much did he pay for the bond?
   - **a.** $1,031.60
   - **b.** $103.16
   - **c.** $1,035.00
   - **d.** $10,316.00

3. When is the interest on an EE savings bond paid?
   - **a.** When redeemed
   - **b.** Annually
   - **c.** Quarterly
   - **d.** Monthly

4. All of the following are true regarding the Federal National Mortgage Association (Fannie Mae) except:
   a. It purchases mortgages and packages them to create mortgage-backed securities that pay interest semiannually.
   b. It provides an investment free of federal, state, and local taxes.
   c. It is a public for-profit corporation.
   d. Its purpose is to earn a profit by providing mortgage capital.

5. An investor purchased a treasury bond at 95.03. How much did he pay for the bond?
   a. $ 9,530.00
   b. $ 9,500.9375
   c. $ 950.9375
   d. $ 953.00

CHAPTER 4

Investment Companies

INTRODUCTION

We examined many of the different types of securities that an investment company may purchase in order to achieve its objectives. In this chapter, we will look at how an investment company pools investors' funds in order to purchase a diversified portfolio of securities. It is imperative that all candidates have a complete understanding of how an investment company operates. Some of the test focus points will be on:

- Types of investment companies
- Investment company structure
- Investment company registration
- Investment company taxation
- Investment strategies and recommendations
- Investor benefits

INVESTMENT COMPANY PHILOSOPHY

An investment company is organized as either a corporation or as a trust. Individual investor's money then is pooled together in a single account and used to purchase securities that will have the greatest chance of helping the investment company reach its objectives. All investors jointly own the portfolio that is created through these pooled funds and each investor has an undivided interest in the securities. No single shareholder has any right or claim that exceeds the rights or claims of any other shareholder regardless of the size of the investment. Investment companies offer individual investors the opportunity to have their money managed by professionals that may otherwise only offer their services to large institutions. Through diversification, the investor may participate in the future growth or income generated from the large number of different securities contained in the portfolio. Both diversification and professional management should contribute significantly to the attainment of the objectives set forth by the investment company. There are many other features and benefits that may be offered to investors that will be examined later in this chapter.

TYPES OF INVESTMENT COMPANIES

All investment company offerings are subject to the Securities Act of 1933 that requires the investment company to register with the Securities Exchange Commission and to give all purchasers a prospectus. Investment companies also are all subject to the Investment Company Act of 1940 that sets forth guidelines on how investment companies operate. The Investment Company Act of 1940 breaks down investment companies into three different types:

1. Face-amount company (FAC)
2. Unit investment trust (UIT)
3. Management investment company (mutual funds)

FACE-AMOUNT COMPANY/ FACE-AMOUNT CERTIFICATES

An investor may enter into a contract with an issuer of a face-amount certificate to contract to receive a stated or fixed amount of money (the face amount) at a stated date in the future. In exchange for this future sum, the investor must deposit an agreed lump sum or make scheduled installment payments. Face-amount certificates are rarely issued today as most of the tax advantages that the investment once offered have been lost through changes in the tax laws.

UNIT INVESTMENT TRUST (UIT)

A unit investment trust will invest either in a fixed portfolio of securities or in a nonfixed portfolio of securities. A fixed UIT traditionally will invest in a large block of government or municipal debt. The bonds will be held until maturity and the proceeds will be distributed to investors in the UIT. Once the proceeds have been distributed to the investors, the UIT will have achieved its objective and will cease to exist. A nonfixed UIT will purchase mutual fund shares in order to reach a stated objective. A nonfixed UIT is also known as a contractual plan. Both types of UITs are organized as a trust and operate as a holding company for the portfolio. UITs are not actively managed and they do not have a board of directors or investment advisers. Both types of UITs issue units or shares of beneficial interest to investors which represent as undivided interest in the underlying portfolio of securities. UITs must maintain a secondary market in the units or shares to offer some liquidity to investors.

MANAGEMENT INVESTMENT COMPANIES (MUTUAL FUNDS)

A management investment company employs an investment adviser to manage a diversified portfolio of securities designed to obtain its stated investment objective. The management company may be organized as either an open-end company or as a closed-end company. The main difference between an open-end company and a closed-end company is how the shares are purchased and sold. An open-end company offers new shares to any investor who wants to invest. This is known as a continuous primary offering. Because the offering of new shares is continuous, the capitalization of the open-end fund is unlimited. Stated another way, an open-end mutual fund may raise as much money as investors are willing to put in. An open-end fund must repurchase its own shares from investors who want to redeem them. There is no secondary market for open-end mutual fund shares. The shares must be purchased from the fund company and redeemed to the fund company. A closed-end fund offers common shares to investors through an initial public offering (IPO) just like a stock. Its capitalization is limited to the number of authorized shares that have been approved for sale. Shares of the closed-end fund will trade in the secondary market in investor-to-investor transactions on an exchange or in the over-the-counter market (OTC), just like common shares.

OPEN END VS. CLOSED END

Although both open-end and closed-end funds are designed to achieve their stated investment objective, the manner in which they operate is different. The following is a side-by-side comparison of the important features of both open-end and closed-end funds and shows how those features differ between the fund types.

Feature	Open End	Closed End
Capitalization	Unlimited continuous primary offering	Single fixed offering through IPO
Investor may purchase	Full and fractional shares	Full shares only
Securities offered	Common shares only	Common and preferred shares and debt securities
Shares purchased and sold	Shares purchased from the fund company and redeemed to the fund company	Shares may be purchased only from the fund company during IPO, then secondary market transactions between investors
Share pricing	Shares priced by formula NAV + SC = POP	Shares priced by supply and demand
Shareholder rights	Dividends and voting	Dividends, voting, and preemptive

DIVERSIFIED VS. NONDIVERSIFIED

Investors in a mutual fund will achieve diversification through their investment in the fund. However, in order to determine if the fund itself is a diversified fund, the fund must meet certain requirements. The Investment Company Act of 1940 laid out an asset allocation model that must be followed in order for the fund to call itself a diversified mutual fund. It is known as the 75-5-10 test and the requirements are as follows:

75%: 75% of the fund's assets must be invested in securities of other issuers. Cash and cash equivalents are countered as part of the 75%. A cash equivalent may be a T-bill or a money market instrument.

5%: The investment company may not invest more than 5% of its assets in any one company.

10%: The investment company may not own more than 10% of any company's outstanding voting stock.

EXAMPLE

XYZ fund markets itself as a diversified mutual fund. It has $10,000,000,000 in net assets and the investment adviser thinks that the ABC Company would be a great company to acquire for $300,000,000. Since XYZ markets itself as a diversified mutual fund, they would not be allowed to purchase the company even though the price of $300,000,000 would be less than 5% of the fund's assets. The investment company must meet both the diversification requirements of 5% of assets and 10% of ownership in order to continue to market itself as a diversified mutual fund.

INVESTMENT COMPANY REGISTRATION

Investment companies are regulated by both the Securities Act of 1933 and by the Investment Company Act of 1940. An investment company must register with the SEC if the company operates to own, invest, reinvest, or trade in securities. A company also must register with the SEC as an investment company if the company has 40% or more of its assets invested in securities other than those issued by the U.S. government or one of the company's subsidiaries.

REGISTRATION REQUIREMENTS

Before an investment company may register with the SEC, it must meet certain minimum requirements. An investment company may not register with the SEC unless it has the following:

- Minimum net worth of $100,000
- At least 100 shareholders
- Clearly defined investment objectives

An investment company may be allowed to register without having 100 shareholders and without a net worth of $100,000 if it can meet these requirements within 90 days.

Investment companies must file a full registration with the SEC before the offering becomes effective. The investment company is considered to have registered when the SEC receives its notice of registration. The investment company's registration statement must contain:

- Type of investment company (open-end, closed-end, etc.)
- Biographical information on the officers and directors of the company
- Name and address of each affiliated person

- Plans to concentrate investments in any one area (i.e., sector fund)
- Plans to invest in real estate or commodities
- Borrowing plans
- Conditions under which investment objective may be changed through a vote of shareholders

Once registered, the investment company may:

- Raise money through the sale of shares
- Lend money to earn interest
- Borrow money on a limited basis

An investment company obtains its investment capital from shareholders through the sale of shares. Once it's operating, it may lend money to earn interest such as by purchasing bonds or notes. An investment company, however, may not lend money to employees. An investment company may borrow money for such business purposes as to redeem shares. If the investment company borrows money, it must have $3 in equity for every dollar that it wants to borrow. Another way of saying that is that the investment company must maintain an asset-to-debt ratio of at least three-to-one or of at least 300%.

An investment company is prohibited from:

- Taking over or controlling other companies
- Acting as a bank or a savings and loan
- Receiving commission for executing orders or for acting as a broker
- Continuing to operate with less than 100 shareholders or less than $100,000 net worth

Unless the investment company meets strict capital and disclosure requirements, it may not engage in any of the following:

- Selling securities short
- Buying securities on margin
- Maintaining joint accounts
- Distributing its own shares

Regardless of the makeup of their investment holdings, all of the following are exempt from the registration requirements of an investment company:

- Broker dealers
- Underwriters
- Banks and savings and loans
- Mortgage companies
- Real estate investment trusts (REITs)
- Security holder protection committees

INVESTMENT COMPANY COMPONENTS

Investment companies have several different groups that serve specialized functions. Each of these groups plays a key role in the investment company's operation. They are the:

- Board of directors
- Investment adviser
- Custodian bank
- Transfer agent

BOARD OF DIRECTORS

Management companies have an organizational structure that is similar to that of other companies. The board of directors oversees the company's president and other officers who run the day-to-day operations of the company. The board and the corporate officers concern themselves with the business and administrative functions of the company. They do not manage the investment portfolio. The board of directors:

- Defines investment objectives.
- Hires the investment adviser, custodian bank, and transfer agent.
- Determines what type of funds to offer, i.e., growth, income, etc.

The board of directors is elected by a vote of the shareholders. The Investment Company Act of 1940 governs the makeup of the board. The Investment

Company Act of 1940 requires that a majority or at least 51% of the board be noninterested persons. A noninterested person is a person whose only affiliation with the fund is as a member of the board. Therefore, a maximum of 49% of the board may hold another position within the fund company or may otherwise be interested in the fund. An affiliated person is anyone who could exercise control over the company, such as an accountant. An affiliated person may also include:

- Broker dealer
- Attorney
- Immediate family of an affiliated person
- Anyone else the SEC designates

Both affiliated and interested parties are prohibited from selling securities or property to the investment company or any of its subsidiaries. Anyone who has been convicted of any felony or securities-related misdemeanor or who has been barred from the securities business may not serve on the board of directors.

BONDING OF KEY EMPLOYEES

The investment company is required to obtain a bond to cover itself and each officer, director, and employee with access to the investment company's assets. The company may obtain a bond for each employee or may obtain a blanket bond for all employees that are required to be bonded. In the case of a blanket bond, the company must list the names of the employees to be covered. The bond only covers the employees for negligence. Any criminal acts or acts of bad faith are not covered.

INVESTMENT ADVISER

The investment company's board of directors hires the investment adviser to manage the fund's portfolio. The investment adviser is a company, not a person, which must also determine the tax consequences of distributions to shareholders and ensure that the investment strategies are in line with the fund's stated investment objectives. The investment adviser's compensation is a percentage of the net assets of the fund, not a percentage of the profits, although performance bonuses are allowed. The investment adviser's fee is typically the largest expense of the fund and the more aggressive the objective, the higher the fee. The investment adviser may not borrow from the fund and may not have any security-related convictions.

CUSTODIAN BANK

The custodian bank or the exchange member broker dealer that has been hired by the investment company physically holds all of the fund's cash and securities. The custodian holds all of the fund's assets for safekeeping and provides other bookkeeping and clerical functions for the investment company, such as maintaining books and records for accumulation plans for investors. All fund assets must be kept segregated from other assets. The custodian must ensure that only approved persons have access to the account and that all distributions are done in line with SEC guidelines.

TRANSFER AGENT

The transfer agent for the investment company handles the issuance, cancellation, and redemption of fund shares. The transfer agent also handles name changes and may be part of the fund's custodian or a separate company. The transfer agent receives an agreed fee for its services.

MUTUAL FUND DISTRIBUTION

Most mutual funds do not sell their own shares directly to investors. The distribution of the shares is the responsibility of the underwriter. The underwriter for a mutual fund is also known as the sponsor or distributor. The underwriter is selected by the fund's board of directors and receives a fee in the form of a sales charge for the shares it distributes. As the underwriter receives orders for the mutual fund shares, it purchases the shares directly from the fund at the net asset value (NAV). The sales charge then is added to the NAV as the underwriter's compensation. This process of adding the sales charge to the NAV is responsible for the mutual fund pricing formula, which is NAV + SC = POP.

The underwriter may purchase shares from the mutual fund only to fill customer orders. They may not hold mutual fund shares in inventory in anticipation of receiving future customer orders.

SELLING GROUP MEMBER

Most brokerage firms maintain selling agreements with mutual fund distributors, which allow them to purchase mutual fund shares at a discount from the public offering price (POP). Selling group members may then sell the mutual fund shares to investors at the POP and earn part of the sales charge.

In order to purchase mutual fund shares at a discount from the POP, the selling group member must be a member of FINRA. All non-FINRA members and suspended members must be treated as members of the general public and pay the public offering price.

DISTRIBUTION OF NO-LOAD MUTUAL FUND SHARES

No-load mutual funds do not charge a sales charge to the investors who invest in the mutual fund. Because there is no sales charge, the mutual fund may sell the shares directly to investors at the NAV.

DISTRIBUTION OF MUTUAL FUND SHARES

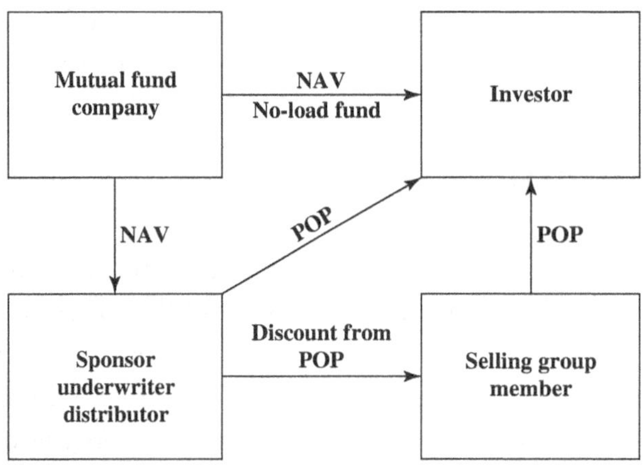

MUTUAL FUND PROSPECTUS

The prospectus is the official offering document for open-end mutual fund shares. The prospectus must be presented to all purchasers of the fund either before or during the sales presentation. The prospectus is the fund's full-disclosure document and provides details regarding:

- Fund's investment objectives
- Sales charges
- Management expenses
- Fund services
- Performance data for the past 1, 5, and 10 years or for the life of the fund

The prospectus, which is given to most investors, is the summary prospectus. If the investor wants additional information regarding the mutual fund, they may request a statement of additional information. The statement of additional information will include details regarding the following as of the date it was published:

- Fund's securities holdings
- Balance sheet
- Income statement
- Portfolio turnover data
- Compensation paid to the board of directors and investment advisory board

A summary prospectus that contains past performance data is known as an advertising prospectus. Requirements regarding updating and using a mutual fund prospectus are as follows:

A mutual fund prospectus:

- Should be updated by the fund every 12 months
- Must be updated by the fund every 13 months
- May be used by a representative for up to 16 months
- Should be discarded after 16 months from publication

Mutual funds also are required to disclose either in the prospectus or in its annual report to shareholders:

- A performance comparison graph showing the performance of the fund
- Names of the officers and directors who are responsible for the portfolio's day-to-day management
- Disclosure of any factors that materially affected performance over the latest fiscal year

CHARACTERISTICS OF OPEN-END MUTUAL FUND SHARES

All open-end mutual fund shares are sold through a continuous primary offering and each new investor receives new shares from the fund company. The new shares are created for investors as their orders are received by the fund. Investors purchase shares from the fund company at the public offering price and redeem them to the fund company at the net asset value. The mutual fund has seven calendar days to forward the proceeds to an investor after receiving a redemption request. If the investor has possession of the mutual fund certificates, the fund then has seven calendar days from the receipt of the certificate by the custodian to forward the proceeds. Suspension of the seven-day rule may be allowed only if:

- The NYSE is closed for an extraordinary reason.
- The NYSE's trading is restricted or limited.
- The liquidation of the securities would not be practical.
- An SEC order has been issued.

ADDITIONAL CHARACTERISTICS OF OPEN-END MUTUAL FUNDS

- Diversification
- Professional management
- Low minimum investment
- Easy tax reporting, Form 1099
- Reduction of sales charges through breakpoint schedule, letter of intent, and rights accumulation
- Automatic reinvestment of dividends and capital gains distributions
- Structured withdrawal plans

MUTUAL FUND INVESTMENT OBJECTIVES

EQUITY FUNDS

The only investment that will meet a growth objective is common stock. Growth funds seeking capital appreciation will invest in the common stock of corporations whose business is growing more rapidly than other companies and more rapidly than the economy as a whole. Growth funds seek capital gains and do not produce significant dividend income.

EQUITY INCOME FUND

An equity income fund will purchase both common and preferred shares that have a long track record of paying consistent dividends. Preferred shares are purchased by the fund for their stated dividend. Utility stocks also are purchased because utilities traditionally pay out the highest percentage of their earnings to shareholders in the form of dividends. Other common shares of blue-chip companies also may be purchased.

SECTOR FUNDS

Mutual funds that concentrate 25% or more of their assets in one business area or region are known as sector funds. Technology, biotech, and gold funds would all be examples of sector funds that concentrate their investments in one business area. A Northeast growth fund would be an example of a sector fund that concentrates its assets geographically. Sector funds traditionally carry higher risk reward ratios. If the sector does well, the investor may enjoy a higher rate of return. If, however, the sector performs poorly, the investor may suffer larger losses. The high-risk reward ratio is due to the funds concentration in one area.

INDEX FUNDS

An index fund is designed to mirror the performance of a large market index such as the S&P 500 or the Dow Jones Industrial Average. An index fund's portfolio is comprised of the stocks that are included in the index that the fund is designed to track. The fund manager does not actively seek out which stocks to buy or sell, making an index fund an example of a fund that is passively managed. If the stock is in the index, it will usually be in the portfolio. Portfolio turnover for an index fund is generally low, which helps keep the fund's expenses down.

GROWTH AND INCOME (COMBINATION FUND)

A growth and income fund, as the name suggests, invests to achieve both capital appreciation and current income. The fund will invest a portion of its assets in shares of common stock that offer the greatest appreciation potential and will invest a portion of its assets in preferred and common shares that pay high dividends, in order to produce income for investors.

BALANCED FUNDS

A balanced fund invests in both stocks and bonds, according to a predetermined formula. For example, the fund may invest 70% of its assets in equities and 30% of its assets in bonds.

ASSET ALLOCATION FUNDS

Asset allocation funds invest in stocks, bonds, and money market instruments, according to the expected performance for each market. For example, if the portfolio manager feels that equities will do well, they may invest more money in equities. Alternatively, if they feel that the bond market will outperform equities, they may shift more money into the debt markets.

OTHER TYPES OF FUNDS

There are other types of equity funds, such as foreign stock funds that invest outside the United States, and special situation funds that invest in takeover candidates and restructuring companies. A final type of fund is a an option income fund that purchases shares of common stock and sells call options against the portfolio in order to generate premium income for investors. Because the fund has sold call options on the shares it owns, it will limit the capital appreciation of the portfolio.

BOND FUNDS

Investors who invest in bond funds are actually purchasing an equity security that represents their undivided interest in a portfolio of debt. Corporations, U.S. government, or state and local municipalities may have issued the debt in the portfolio. Bond funds invest mainly to generate current income for investors through interest payments generated by the bonds in the portfolio.

CORPORATE BOND FUNDS

Corporate bond funds invest in debt securities that have been issued by corporations. The debt in the portfolio could be investment grade or it could be speculative, such as in a high-yield or junk-bond fund. Dividend income that is generated by the portfolio's interest payments is subject to all taxes.

GOVERNMENT BOND FUNDS

Government bond funds invest in debt securities issued by the U.S. government such as Treasury bills, notes, and bonds. Many funds also invest in the debt of government agencies such as those issued by the Government National Mortgage Association also known as Ginnie Mae. Government bond funds provide current income to investors, along with a high degree of safety of principal. Dividends based upon the interest payments received from direct treasury obligations are only subject to federal taxation.

MUNICIPAL BOND FUNDS

Municipal bond funds invest in portfolios of municipal debt. Investors in municipal bond funds receive dividend income, which is free from federal taxes because the dividends are based on the interest payments received from the municipal bonds in the portfolio. Investors are still subject to taxes for any capital gains distributions or for any capital gains realized through the sale of the mutual fund shares.

MONEY MARKET FUNDS

Money market funds invest in short-term money market instruments such as banker's acceptances, commercial paper, and other debt securities with less than one year remaining to maturity. Money market funds are no-load funds that offer the investor the highest degree of safety of principal along with current income. The NAV for money market funds is always equal to $1, however, this is not guaranteed. Investors use money market funds as a place to hold idle funds and to earn current income. Interest is earned by investors daily and is credited to their accounts monthly. Most money market funds offer check writing privileges and investors must receive a prospectus prior to investing or opening an account.

MONEY MARKET GUIDELINES

Money market funds must adhere to certain guidelines in order to qualify as a money market fund, such as:

- The prospectus must clearly state on its cover that the fund is not insured or guaranteed by the U.S. government and that the fund's net asset value may fall below $1.
- Securities in the portfolio may have a maximum maturity of 13 months.

- The average maturity for securities in the portfolio may not exceed 90 days.
- No more than 5% of the fund's assets may be invested in any one issuer's debt securities.
- Investments are limited to the top two ratings awarded by a nationally recognized ratings agency, i.e., S&P and Moody's.
- 95% of the portfolio must be in the top ratings category with no more than 5% being invested in the second tier.

VALUING MUTUAL FUND SHARES

Mutual funds must determine the net asset value of the fund's shares at least once per business day. Most mutual funds will price their shares at the close of business of the NYSE (4:00 PM EST). The mutual fund prospectus will provide the best answer as to when the fund calculates the price of its shares. The calculation is required to determine both the redemption price and the purchase price of the fund's shares. The price, which is received by an investor who is redeeming shares, and the price that is paid by an investor who is purchasing shares, will be based upon the price, which is next calculated after the fund has received the investor's order. This is known as forward pricing. To calculate the fund's NAV, use the following formula:

Assets – liabilities = net asset value

To determine the NAV per share, simply divide the total net asset value by the total number of outstanding shares.

$$\frac{\textbf{Total NAV}}{\textbf{Total no. of shares}}$$

TESTFOCUS!

If XYZ mutual fund has $10,000,000 in assets and $500,000 in liabilities, what is the fund's NAV?

Assets – liabilities = NAV

$10,000,000 – $500,000 = $9,500,000

If XYZ has 1,000,000 shares outstanding, its NAV per share would be:

$$\frac{\textbf{Total NAV}}{\textbf{Total no. of shares}} \qquad \frac{\$9{,}500{,}000}{1{,}000{,}000}$$

NAV per share = $9.50

CHANGES IN THE NAV

The net asset value of a mutual fund is constantly changing as security prices fluctuate and as the mutual fund conducts its business. The following illustrates how the NAV per share will be affected given certain events.

INCREASES IN THE NAV

The net asset value of the mutual fund will increase if the:

- Value of the securities in the portfolio increase
- Portfolio receives investment income, such as interest payments from bonds

DECREASES IN THE NAV

The net asset value will decrease if the:

- Value of the securities in the portfolio fall in value
- Fund distributes dividends or capital gains

NO EFFECT ON THE NAV

The following will have no effect on the net asset value of the mutual fund share:

- Investor purchases and redemptions
- Portfolio purchases and sales of securities
- Sales charges

SALES CHARGES

The maximum allowable sales charge that an open-end fund may charge is 8.5% of the POP. The sales charge that may be assessed by a particular fund will be detailed in the fund's prospectus. It is important to note that the sales charge is not an expense of the fund; it is a cost of distribution, which is born by the investor. The sales charges pay for all of the following:

- Underwriters commission
- Commission to brokerage firms and registered representatives

CLOSED-END FUNDS

Closed-end funds do not charge a sales charge to invest. An investor who wants to purchase a closed-end fund will pay the current market price plus the commission their brokerage firm charges them to execute the order.

EXCHANGE TRADED FUNDS (ETFs)

In recent years, exchange-traded funds or ETFs have gained a lot of popularity. ETFs are created through the purchase of a basket of securities that are designed to track the performance of an index or sector. ETFs are not actively managed, provide investors with lower costs and the ability to buy, sell, and sell short the ETF at any point during the trading day, and may be purchased on margin. Certain types of ETFs are designed to provide returns and performance characteristics of positions that take on the leverage. Such ETFs are often known as "ultra" or double ETFs. These ETF may provide returns that are double or more of the return of an index, or double or more the inverse return of an index.

FRONT-END LOADS

A front-end load is a sales charge that the investor pays when they purchase shares. The sales charge is added to the NAV of the fund and the investor purchases the shares at the POP. The sales charge, in essence, is deducted from the gross amount invested and the remaining amount is invested in the portfolio at the NAV. Shares that charge a front-end load are known as "A" shares.

EXAMPLE

XYZ mutual fund has a NAV of $9.50 and a POP of $10 and a sales charge percentage of 5%. How much in sales charges would an investor pay if they were to invest $10,000 in the fund?

$10,000	**$10,000**
× 5%	**– $500**
$500 = sales charge	**$9,500 invested in the portfolio at NAV**

BACK-END LOADS

A back-end load is also known as a contingent differed sales charge (CDSC). An investor in a fund that charges a back-end load will pay the sales charge at the time of redemption of the fund shares. The sales charge will be assessed on the value of the shares that have been redeemed and the amount of the sales charge will decline as the holding period for the investor increases. The following is a hypothetical back-end load schedule:

Years Money Left in Portfolio	Sales Charge
1	8.5%
2	7%
3	5%
4	3%
5	1.5%
5 years or more	0%

The mutual fund prospectus will detail the particular schedule for back-end load sales charges. Mutual fund shares that charge a back-end load are also known as "B" shares.

OTHER TYPES OF SALES CHARGES

There are other ways in which a mutual fund assesses a sales charge. Shares, which charge a level load based on the NAV, are known as level-load funds or "C" shares. Shares, which charge an asset-based fee and a back-end load, are known as "D" shares.

CALCULATING A MUTUAL FUND'S SALES CHARGE PERCENTAGE

There are many times when an investor may know only the NAV and the POP for a given mutual fund and not the sales charge percentage that is charged by the fund. To determine the sales charge percentage given the NAV and the POP, use the following formula.

$$SC\% = \frac{(POP - NAV)}{POP}$$

FOCUSPOINT

$$SC\% = \frac{(POP - NAV)}{POP} = \frac{10 - 9.50}{10} = \frac{\$.50}{\$10} = 5\%$$

FINDING THE PUBLIC OFFERING PRICE

There also will be times when an investor knows the NAV of a fund and the sales charge percentage but does not know the POP that they must pay to invest in the fund. To calculate the POP given the sales charge percentage and the NAV, use the following formula:

$$POP = \frac{NAV}{(100\% - SC\%)}$$

FOCUSPOINT

Using the same fund once again, XYZ (which has an NAV of \$9.50 and a sales charge percentage of 5%), to determine the POP, simply plug the numbers into the formula as follows:

$$POP = \frac{9.50}{(100\% - SC\%)} = \frac{9.50}{(100\% - 5\%)} = \frac{9.50}{.95} = \$10.00$$

SALES CHARGE REDUCTIONS

The maximum allowable sales charge that may be assessed by an open-end mutual fund is 8.5% of the public offering price. If a mutual fund charges 8.5%, they must offer the following three privileges to investors:

1. Breakpoint sales charge reductions that reduce the amount of the sales charge based on the dollar amount invested
2. Rights of accumulation that will reduce the sales charge on subsequent investments based on the value of the investor's account
3. Automatic reinvestment of dividends and capital gains at the NAV

If a mutual fund does not offer all three of these benefits to investors, the maximum allowable sales charge that may be charged drops to 6.25%. Although a mutual fund that charges 8.5% must offer these features, most mutual funds that charge less than 8.5% also offer them.

BREAKPOINT SCHEDULE

As an incentive for investors to invest larger sums of money into a mutual fund, the mutual fund will reduce the sales charge based upon the dollar amount of the purchase. Breakpoint sales charge reductions are available to any person including corporations, trusts, couples, and accounts for minors. Breakpoint sales charge reductions are not available to investment clubs or to parents and their adult children investing in separate accounts. The following is an example of a breakpoint schedule that a family of funds might use:

Dollar Amount Invested	Sales Charge
$1–$24,999	8.5%
$25,000–$74,999	7%
$75,000–$149,999	5%
$150,000–$499,999	3%
$500,000 or greater	1%

A breakpoint schedule benefits all parties, the fund company, the investor, and the representative.

LETTER OF INTENT

An investor who might not be able to reach a breakpoint with a single purchase may qualify for a breakpoint sales charge reduction by signing a letter of intent. A letter of intent will give the investor up to 13 months to reach the dollar amount to which they subscribed. The letter of intent is binding only on the fund company, not on the investor. The additional shares that will be purchased as a result of the lower sales charge will be held by the fund company in an escrow account. If the investor fulfills the letter of intent, the shares are released to them. Should the investor fail to reach the breakpoint to which they subscribed, they will be charged an adjustment to their sales charge. The investor may choose to pay the adjusted sales charge by either sending a check or by allowing some of the escrowed shares to be liquidated.

BACKDATING A LETTER OF INTENT

An investor may backdate a letter of intent up to 90 days to include a prior purchase and the 13-month window starts from the back date. For example, if an investor backdates a letter of intent by the maximum of 90 days allowed, then the investor has only 10 months to complete the letter of intent.

BREAKPOINT SALES

A breakpoint sale is a violation committed by a registered representative who is trying to earn larger commissions by recommending the purchase of mutual fund shares in a dollar amount that is just below the breakpoint that would allow the investor to qualify for a reduced sales charge. A breakpoint violation also may be considered to have been committed if a representative spreads out a large sum of money over different families of funds. A registered representative must always notify an investor of the availability of a sales charge reduction, especially when the investor is depositing a sum of money that is close to the breakpoint.

RIGHTS OF ACCUMULATION

Rights of accumulation allow the investor to qualify for reduced sales charges on subsequent investments by taking into consideration the value of the investor's account, including the growth. Unlike a letter of intent, there is no time limit and, as the investor's account grows over time, they can qualify for lower sales charges on future investments. The sales charge reduction is not retroactive and does not reduce the sales charges on prior purchases. To qualify for the breakpoint, the dollar amount of the current purchase is calculated into the total value of the investor's account.

TESTFOCUS!

Using the earlier breakpoint schedule, let's look at an investor's account over the last three years:

	Deposit	Sales Charge
Year 1	$5,000	8.5%
Year 2	$5,000	8.5%
Year 3	$5,000	8.5%

Let's assume that the investor's account has increased in value by $6,000, making the total current value of the account $21,000. The investor has another $5,000 to invest this year and, because there is a sales charge reduction available at the $25,000 level, based on the breakpoint schedule on page 99, the investor will pay a sales charge of 7% on the new $5,000.

AUTOMATIC REINVESTMENT OF DISTRIBUTIONS

Investors may elect to have their distributions automatically reinvested in the fund and use the distributions to purchase more shares. Most mutual funds will allow the investor to purchase the shares at the NAV when they reinvest distributions. This feature has to be offered by mutual funds charging a sales charge of 8.5%. However, it is offered by most other mutual funds as well.

OTHER MUTUAL FUND FEATURES

COMBINATION PRIVILEGES

Most mutual fund companies offer a variety of portfolios to meet different investment objectives. The different portfolios become known as a family of funds. Combination privileges allow an investor to combine the simultaneous purchases of two different portfolios to reach a breakpoint sales charge reduction.

EXAMPLE An investor purchases $15,000 worth of an income fund and, at the same time, invests $40,000 into a growth portfolio offered by the same fund company. If the fund company offers a breakpoint sales charge reduction at $50,000, the investor would qualify for the lower sales charge under combination privileges.

CONVERSION OR EXCHANGE PRIVILEGES

Most mutual fund families will offer its investors conversion or exchange privileges that allow the investor to move money from one portfolio to another offered by the same fund company without paying another sales charge. Another way of looking at this is that the fund company allows the investor to redeem the shares of one portfolio at the NAV and use the proceeds to purchase shares of another portfolio at the NAV. The IRS sees this as a purchase and a sale and the investor will have to pay taxes on any gain on the sale of portfolio shares. Other exchange conditions are as follows:

- Dollar value of purchase may not exceed sales proceeds
- Purchase of new portfolio must occur within 30 days
- Sale may not include a sales charge refund
- No commission may be paid to a registered representative of broker dealer

FOCUSPOINT

An aggressive investor has $20,000 invested in the ABC high-growth fund that has an NAV of $12 and a POP of $12.60. They want to move the money into the ABC biotech fund that has a NAV of $17.20 and a POP of $17.90. ABC offers conversion privileges, so the investor will redeem the shares of the growth portfolio at $12 and will purchase 1162.79 shares of the biotech portfolio at $17.20.

30-DAY EMERGENCY WITHDRAWAL

Many mutual funds will provide investors with access to their money in a time of unexpected financial need. If the investor needs to liquidate mutual fund shares for emergency purposes, the investor will be able to reinvest an equal sum of money at the portfolio's NAV if they reinvest the money within 30 days. This is usually a one-time privilege and the NAV used to purchase the shares is the NAV on the day of the reinvestment.

TAKENOTE!

If a client redeems their shares within seven business days of purchase, the sales charge earned by the broker dealer and the representative is returned to the fund company.

DOLLAR COST AVERAGING

One of the more popular methods to accumulate mutual fund shares is through a process known as dollar cost averaging. An investor purchases mutual fund shares through regularly scheduled investments of a fixed dollar amount. An investor may elect to invest $100 a month into a mutual fund by having the fund company debit their checking account. As the share price of the mutual fund fluctuates, the investor's $100 investment will purchase fewer shares when the market price of the mutual fund share is high and will purchase more shares when the market price is low. As the market price of the mutual fund share continues to fluctuate over time, the investor's average cost per share should always be lower than their average price per share, allowing the investor to liquidate the shares at a profit. Dollar cost averaging does not, however, guarantee a profit because a mutual fund share could continue to decline until the share price hits zero. All Series 6 candidates should be able to determine an investor's average cost and average price per share.

TESTFOCUS!

Let's look at the dollar cost averaging results for an investor who is depositing $100 a month into a mutual fund whose share price has been fluctuating widely over that time.

Investment	Share Price	Number of Shares Purchased
$100	$20	5
$100	$12.5	8
$100	$10	10
$100	$25	4
$400	$67.5	27 total shares

In order to calculate the investor's average cost per share use the following formula:

$$\text{average cost} = \frac{\text{total dollars invested}}{\text{total \# of shares invested}}$$

Using the numbers from the example we get:

$$\text{average cost} = \frac{\$400}{27} = \$14.81$$

In order to determine the average price that the investor paid per share use the following formula:

$$\text{average price} = \frac{\text{total of purchase prices}}{\text{number of purchases}}$$

Using the numbers from the example we get:

$$\text{average price} = \frac{67.5}{4} = \$16.875$$

The example illustrates the effects of dollar cost averaging in a mutual fund with a fluctuating market price. The result is an average cost per share that is significantly lower than the investor's average price per share. The change in the mutual fund share price is more dramatic than will usually be experienced in real life and the investor would normally have to invest in the fund for a longer period of time before achieving similar results.

MUTUAL FUNDS VOTING RIGHTS

Mutual fund investors have the right to vote on major issues regarding the fund. All votes are won by a simple majority; that is, 51% of the outstanding shares will win the vote. It is important to distinguish that shares vote, not shareholders. An investor with 5,000 shares has five times as many votes as an investor with 1,000 shares, even though they are both shareholders. Among the major issues to be voted on are:

- Changing capitalization (going from an open-end to a closed-end fund)
- Changing sales load (going from a loaded fund to a no-load fund)
- Changing or terminating business
- Changing investment objectives
- Lending money
- Entering into real estate transactions
- Issuing or underwriting other securities
- Changing in borrowing policies
- Electing the board of directors

- Electing the investment adviser
- 12B-1 fees

MUTUAL FUND YIELDS

A mutual fund's current yield is found by dividing its annual dividends by its current market price or POP. The higher the yield, the more income the fund produces for every dollar invested. A mutual fund's current yield may be based on dividends only, not on capital gains distributions.

Annual income/POP = current yield

PORTFOLIO TURNOVER

Portfolio turnover rates will tell you how long the fund holds its securities. The higher the rate, the shorter the fund's holding period. Higher portfolio turnover causes the fund to incur additional expenses in the form of execution charges. A turnover rate of 100% means that the fund replaces its portfolio annually.

CHAPTER 4

Pretest

INVESTMENT COMPANIES

1. An investor with $20,000 invested in the XYZ growth fund is:
   a. A stockholder in XYZ
   b. An owner of XYZ
   c. An owner of an undivided interest in the XYZ growth portfolio
   d. Both an owner of XYZ and an owner of an undivided interest in the XYZ growth portfolio

2. All of the following benefit an investor, except:
   a. Combination privileges
   b. Emergency withdrawal privileges
   c. Breakpoint sale
   d. Form 1099

3. A mutual fund investor has 500 shares of XYZ growth fund, which has an NAV of 22.30 and a POP of 23.05. The investor wants to invest the money in the biotech fund offered by XYZ, which has an NAV of 17.10 and a POP of 18. If XYZ offers conversion privileges, how many shares will the investor be able to purchase of the biotech fund?
   a. 652
   b. 619
   c. 640
   d. 605

4. A mutual fund's custodian bank does which of the following?
   a. Holds customer's securities
   b. Cancels certificates
   c. Maintains records for accumulation plans
   d. Issues certificates

5. A no-load mutual fund may charge a 12B-1 fee that is:
   a. Up to .25 of 1% of the NAV
   b. Less than .25 of 1% of the NAV
   c. Up to .25 of 1% of the POP
   d. Less than .25 of 1% of the POP

6. The ex-dividend date on a closed-end mutual fund is set by the:
   a. Board of directors
   b. SEC
   c. Board of governors
   d. FINRA/NYSE

7. A mutual fund has been seeking to attract new customers to invest in its growth fund. They have been running an advertising campaign that markets them as a diversified mutual fund. How much of any one company may they own?
   a. 15%
   b. 5%
   c. 10%
   d. 9%

8. An investor wires $10,000 into his mutual fund on Tuesday, March 11, and the money is credited to his account at 3 pm. He will be the owner of record on:
   a. Friday, March 14
   b. Wednesday, March 12
   c. Tuesday, March 11
   d. Tuesday, March 18

9. As it relates to the bonding of mutual fund employees, which of the following is true?
   a. All fund employees are required to be listed on the bond coverage.
   b. Only key employees are required to be listed on the bond coverage.
   c. All employees must have an individual bond posted for them.
   d. All employees with access to assets must be listed on the bond coverage.

10. A long-term growth fund has a portfolio turnover ratio of 25%. How often does the fund replace its total holdings?
   a. Every four years
   b. Once a year
   c. Every four months
   d. Every six months

CHAPTER 5

Variable Annuities and Retirement Plans

INTRODUCTION

This chapter will cover a variety of important topics relating to annuity products and retirement plans. For most people, saving for retirement has become an important investment objective for at least part of their portfolio Many investors chose to purchase annuities to help plan for retirement. Over the years a wide range of annuity products have been developed to meet different investment objectives and risk profiles. Candidates will need to fully understand how annuities and retirement plans function in order to successfully complete the exam.

ANNUITIES

An annuity is a contract between an individual and an insurance company. Once the contract is entered into, the individual becomes known as the annuitant. There are three basic types of annuities that are deigned to meet different objectives. They are:

1. Fixed annuity
2. Variable annuity
3. Combination annuity

Although all three types allow the investor's money to grow tax deferred, the type of investments made and how the money is invested varies according to the type of annuity.

FIXED ANNUITY

A fixed annuity offers investors a guaranteed rate of return regardless of whether the investment portfolio can produce the guaranteed rate. If the performance of the portfolio falls below the rate that was guaranteed, the insurance company owes investors the difference. Because the purchaser of a fixed annuity does not have any investment risk, a fixed annuity is considered to be an insurance product, not a security. Representatives who sell fixed annuity contracts must have an insurance license. Because fixed annuities offer investors a guaranteed return, the money invested by the insurance company will be used to purchase conservative investments like mortgages and real estate. These are investments whose historical performance is predictable enough so that a guaranteed rate can be offered to investors. All of the money invested into fixed annuity contracts is held in the insurance company's general account. Because the rate that the insurance company guarantees is not very high, the annuitant may suffer a loss of purchasing power due to inflation risk.

VARIABLE ANNUITY

An investor seeking to achieve a higher rate of return may elect to purchase a variable annuity. Variable annuities seek to obtain a higher rate of return by investing in stocks, bonds, or mutual fund shares. These securities traditionally offer higher rates of return than more conservative investments. A variable annuity does not offer the investor a guaranteed rate of return and the investor may lose all or part of their principal. Because the annuitant bears the investment risk associated with a variable annuity, the contract is considered to be both a security and an insurance product. Representatives who sell variable annuities must have both their securities license and their insurance license. The money and securities contained in a variable annuity contract are held in the insurance company's separate account. The separate account was named this because the variable annuity's portfolio must be kept separate from the insurance company's general funds. The insurance company must have a net worth of $1,000,000, or the separate account must have a net worth of $1,000,000, in order for the separate account to begin operating. Once the separate account begins operations, it may invest in one of two ways:

1. Directly
2. Indirectly

DIRECT INVESTMENT

If the money in the separate account is invested directly into individual stocks and bonds, the separate account must have an investment adviser to actively manage the portfolio. If the money in the separate account is actively managed and invested directly, then the separate account is considered to be an open-end investment company under the Investment Company Act of 1940 and must register as such.

INDIRECT INVESTMENT

If the separate account uses the money in the portfolio to purchase mutual fund shares, it is investing in the equity and debt markets indirectly and no investment adviser is required to actively manage the portfolio. If the separate account purchases mutual fund shares, then the separate account is considered to be a unit investment trust under the Investment Company Act of 1940 and must register as such.

COMBINATION ANNUITY

For investors who feel that a fixed annuity is too conservative and that a variable annuity is too risky, a combination annuity offers the annuitant features of both a fixed and variable contract. A combination annuity has a fixed portion that offers a guaranteed rate and a variable portion that tries to achieve a higher rate of return. Most combination annuities will allow the investor to move money between the fixed and variable portions of the contract. The money invested in the fixed portion of the contract is invested in the insurance company's general account and used to purchase conservative investment like mortgages and real estate. The money invested in the variable side of the contract is invested in the insurance company's separate account and used to purchase stocks, bonds, or mutual fund shares. Representatives who sell combination annuities must have both their securities license and their insurance license.

BONUS ANNUITY

An insurance company that issues annuity contracts may offer incentives to investors who purchase their annuities. Such incentives are often referred to as bonuses. One type of bonus is known as premium enhancement. Under a premium enhancement option, the insurance company will make an additional contribution to the annuitant's account based on the premium paid by the annuitant. For example, if the annuitant is contributing $1,000 per month, the insurance company may offer to contribute an additional 5% or $50 per month to the account. Another type of bonus offered to annuitants is the ability to withdraw the greater of the account's earnings or up to 15% of the total premiums paid without a penalty. Although the annuitant will not have to pay a penalty to the insurance company, there may be income taxes and a 10% penalty tax owed to the IRS. Bonus annuities often have higher expenses and longer surrender periods than other annuities and these additional costs and surrender periods need to be clearly disclosed to perspective purchasers.

EQUITY-INDEXED ANNUITY

Equity-indexed annuities offer investors a return that varies according to the performance of a set index such as the S&P 500. Equity-indexed annuities will credited additional interest to the investor's account based on the contract's participation rate. If a contract sets the participation rate at 70% of the return for the S&P 500 index, and the index returns 5%, the investor's account will be credited for 70% of the return or 3.5%. Equity-index annuities may also set a floor rate and a cap rate for the contract. The floor rate is the minimum interest rate that will be credited to the investor's account. The floor rate may be zero or it may be a positive number, depending on the specific contract. The contract's cap rate is the maximum rate that will be credited to the contract. If the return of the index exceeds the cap rate, the investor's account will only be credited up to the cap rate. If the S&P 500 index returns 11% and the cap rate set in the contract is 9%, the investor's account will only be credited 9%.

Most equity indexed annuities combine the guarantee features of a fixed annuity with the potential for additional returns like that of a variable annuity. Equity indexed annuities may also be referred to as equity indexed contracts or EICs.

The following table compares the features of fixed and variable annuities:

Feature	Fixed Annuity	Variable Annuity
Payment received	Guaranteed/fixed	May vary in amount
Return	Guaranteed minimum	No guarantee/return may vary in amount
Investment risk	Assumed by insurance co.	Assumed by investor
Portfolio	Real estate, mortgages, and fixed income securities	Stocks, bonds, or mutual fund shares
Portfolio held in	General account	Separate account

Feature	Fixed Annuity	Variable Annuity
Inflation	Subject to inflation risk	Resistant to inflation
Representative registration	Insurance license	Insurance and securities license

ANNUITY PURCHASE OPTIONS

An investor may purchase an annuity contract in one of three ways. They are:

1. Single payment deferred annuity
2. Single payment immediate annuity
3. Periodic payment deferred annuity

SINGLE PAYMENT DEFERRED ANNUITY

With a single payment deferred annuity, the investor funds the contract completely with one payment and defers receiving payments from the contract until some point in the future, usually after retirement. Money being invested in a single payment deferred annuity is used to purchase accumulation units. The number and value of the accumulation units varies as the distributions are reinvested and the value of the separate account's portfolio changes.

SINGLE PAYMENT IMMEDIATE ANNUITY

With a single payment immediate annuity, the investor funds the contract completely with one payment and begins receiving payments from the contract immediately, normally within 60 days. The money that is invested in a single payment immediate annuity is used to purchase annuity units. The number of annuity units remains fixed and the value changes as the value of the securities in the separate accounts portfolio fluctuates.

PERIODIC PAYMENT DEFERRED ANNUITY

With a periodic payment annuity, the investor purchases the annuity by making regularly scheduled payments into the contract. This is known as the accumulation stage. During the accumulation stage, the terms are flexible and, if the investor misses a payment, there is no penalty. The money invested in a periodic payment deferred annuity is used to purchase accumulation units. The number and value of the accumulation units fluctuate with the securities in the separate account's portfolio.

TAKENOTE!

The suitability obligation for variable annuities covers the initial purchase and subaccount allocation as well as the exchange one annuity contact for any other contract. Exempt from suitability determination are any changes made to the allocation of assets among the available sub accounts.

ACCUMULATION UNITS

An accumulation unit represents the investor's proportionate ownership in the separate account's portfolio during the accumulation or differed stage of the contract. The value of the accumulation unit will fluctuate as the value of the securities in the separate account's portfolio changes. As the investor makes contributions to the account or as distributions are reinvested, the number of accumulation units will vary. An investor will only own accumulation units during the accumulation stage when money is being paid into the contract or when receipt of payments is being deferred by the investor, such as with a single payment deferred annuity.

TAKENOTE!

Most annuities allow the investor to designate a beneficiary who will receive the greater of the value of the account or the total premiums paid if the investor dies during the accumulation stage.

ANNUITY UNITS

When an investor changes from the pay-in or deferred stage of the contract to the payout phase, the investor is said to have annuitized the contract. At this point, the investor trades in their accumulation units for annuity units. The number of annuity units is fixed and represents the investor's proportional ownership of the separate accounts portfolio during the payout phase. The number of annuity units that the investor receives when they annuitize a contract is based upon the payout option selected, the annuitant's age, sex, the value of the account, and the assumed interest rate.

ANNUITY PAYOUT OPTIONS

An investor in an annuity has the choice of taking a lump sum distribution or receiving scheduled payments from the contract. If the investor decides to annuitize the contract and receive scheduled payments, once the payout option is selected, it may not be changed. The following is a list of typical payout options in order from the largest monthly payment to the smallest. They are:

- Life only/straight life
- Life with period certain
- Joint with last survivor

LIFE ONLY/STRAIGHT LIFE

This payout option will give the annuitant the largest periodic payment from the contract and the investor will receive payments from the contract for their entire life. However, when the investor dies, there are no additional benefits paid to their estate. If an investor has accumulated a large sum of money in the contract and dies unexpectedly shortly after annuitizing the contract, the insurance company keeps the money in their account.

LIFE WITH PERIOD CERTAIN

A life with period certain payout option will pay out from the contract to the investor or to their estate for the life of the annuitant or for the period certain, whichever is longer. If an investor selects a 10-year period certain when they annuitize the contract and the investor lives for 20 years, payments will cease upon the death of the annuitant. However, if the same investor died only two years after annuitizing the contract, payments would go to their estate for another eight years.

JOINT WITH LAST SURVIVOR

When an investor selects a joint with last survivor option, the annuity is jointly owned by more than one party and payments will continue until the last owner of the contract dies. For example, if a husband and wife are receiving payments from an annuity under a joint with last survivor option and the husband dies, payments will continue to the wife for the rest of her life. The payments received by the wife could be at the same rate as when the husband was alive or at a reduced rate, depending upon the contract. The monthly payments will initially be based on the life expectancy of the youngest annuitant.

FACTORS AFFECTING THE SIZE OF THE ANNUITY PAYMENT

All of the following determine the size of the annuity payments:

- Account value
- Payout option selected
- Age
- Sex
- Account performance vs. the assumed interest rate (AIR)

THE ASSUMED INTEREST RATE (AIR)

When an investor annuitizes a contract, they trade their accumulation units in for annuity units. Once the contract has been annuitized, the insurance company sets a benchmark for the separate account's performance known as the assumed interest rate or AIR. The AIR is not a guaranteed rate of return; it is only used to adjust the value of the annuity units up or down, based upon the actual performance of the separate account. The assumed interest rate is an earnings target that the insurance company sets for the separate account. The separate account must meet this earnings target in order to keep the annuitant's payments at the same level. As the value of the annuity unit changes, so does the amount of the payment that is received by the investor. If the separate account outperforms the AIR, an investor would expect their payments to increase. If the separate account's performance fell below the AIR, the investor could expect their payment to decrease. The separate account's performance is always measured against the AIR, never against the previous month's performance. An investor's annuity payment is based on the number of annuity units owned by the investor multiplied by the value of the annuity unit. When the performance of the separate account equals the AIR, the value of the annuity unit will remain unchanged and so will the investor's payment. Selecting an AIR that is realistic is important. If the AIR is too high and the separate account's return cannot equal the assumed rate, the value of the annuity unit will continue to fall and so will the investor's payment. The opposite is true if the AIR is set too low. As the separate account outperforms the AIR, the value of the annuity unit will continue to rise and so will the investor's payment. The AIR is only relevant during the payout phase of the contract when the investor is receiving payments and owns annuity units. The AIR does not concern itself with accumulation units during the accumulation stage or when benefits are being deferred.

TAXATION

Contributions made to an annuity are made with after-tax dollars. The money the investor deposits becomes their cost base and is allowed to grow tax deferred. When the investor withdraws money from the contract, only the growth is taxed. Their cost base is returned to them tax free. All money in excess of the investor's cost base is taxed as ordinary income.

TYPES OF WITHDRAWALS

An investor may begin withdrawing money from an annuity contract through any of the following options:

- Lump sum
- Random
- Annuitizing

Both lump sum and random withdrawals are done on a last in, first out (LIFO) basis. The growth portion of the contract is always considered to be the last money that was deposited and is taxed at the ordinary income rate of the annuitant. If the annuitant is under age 59.5 and takes a lump sum or random withdrawal, the withdrawal will be subject to a 10% tax penalty, as well as ordinary income taxes.

ANNUITIZING THE CONTRACT

When an investor annuitizes the contract and begins to receive monthly payments, part of each payment is the return of the investor's cost base and a portion of each payment is the distribution of the account's growth. To determine how much of each payment is taxable and how much is the return of principal, the investor would look at the exclusion ratio.

Contracts that are annuitized prior to age 59.5 under a life-income option are not subject to the 10% tax penalty nor are withdrawals due to disability or death.

SALES CHARGES

There is no maximum sales charge for an annuity contract. The sales charge that is assessed must be reasonable in relation to the total payments over the life of the contract. Most annuity contracts have backend sales charges or surrender charges similar to a contingent deferred sales charge.

INVESTMENT MANAGEMENT FEES

The individuals running the separate account are professionals and are compensated for their management of the account through a fee-based agreement. A fee is deducted from the separate account to cover this management expense. The more aggressive the portfolio, the larger the management fee will be. The management fee, sales charges, and other expenses and fees will all reduce the return.

VARIABLE ANNUITY VS. MUTUAL FUND

Feature	Variable Annuity	Mutual Fund
Maximum sales charge	No max	8.5%
Investment adviser	Yes	Yes
Custodian bank	Yes	Yes
Transfer agent	Yes	Yes
Voting	Yes	Yes
Management	Board of managers	Board of directors
Taxation of growth and reinvestments	Tax-deferred	Currently taxed

RETIREMENT PLANS

For most people, saving for retirement has become an important investment objective for at least part of their portfolio. Investors may participate in retirement plans that have been established by their employers, as well as those they have established for themselves. Both corporate and individual plans may be qualified or nonqualified, and it is important for an investor to understand the difference before deciding to participate. Series 65 candidates will see a fair number of questions on the exam dealing with retirement plans. The following table compares the key features of qualified and nonqualified plans.

Feature	Qualified	Nonqualified
Contributions	Pretax	After-tax
Growth	Tax-deferred	Tax-deferred
Participation must be allowed	For everyone	Corporation may choose who gets to participate
IRS approval	Required	Not required
Withdrawals	100% taxed as ordinary income	Growth in excess of cost base is taxed as ordinary income

INDIVIDUAL PLANS

Individuals may set up a retirement plan for themselves that are qualified and allow contributions to the plan to be made with pretax dollars. Individuals also may purchase investment products such as annuities that allow their money to grow tax deferred. The money used to purchase an annuity has already been taxed, making an annuity a nonqualified product.

INDIVIDUAL RETIREMENT ACCOUNTS (IRAs)

All individuals with earned income may establish an IRA for themselves. Contributions to traditional IRAs may or may not be tax deductible, depending on the individual's level of adjusted gross income and whether the individual is eligible to participate in an employer-sponsored plan. Individuals who do not qualify to participate in an employer-sponsored plan may deduct their IRA contributions, regardless of their income level. The level of adjusted gross income that allows an investor to deduct their IRA contributions has been increasing since 1998. These tax law changes occur too frequently to make them a practical test question. Our review of IRAs will focus on the four main types, which are:

1. Traditional
2. Roth

3. SEP
4. Educational

TRADITIONAL IRA

A traditional IRA allows an individual to contribute a maximum of 100% of earned income or $5,500 per year or up to $11,000 per couple. If only one spouse works, the working spouse may contribute $5,500 to an IRA for themselves and $5,500 to a separate IRA for their spouse, under the nonworking spousal option. Investors over 50 may contribute up to $6,500 of earned income to their IRA. Regardless of whether the IRA contribution was made with pretax or after-tax dollars, the money is allowed to grow tax deferred. All withdrawals from an IRA are taxed as ordinary income regardless of how the growth was generated in the account. Withdrawals from an IRA prior to age 59.5 are subject to a 10% penalty tax as well as ordinary income taxes. The 10% penalty will be waived for first-time homebuyers or educational expenses for the taxpayer's child, grandchildren, or spouse. The 10% penalty will also be waived if the payments are part of a series of substantially equal payments. Withdrawals from an IRA must begin by April 1 of the year following the year in which the taxpayer reaches 70.5. If an individual fails to make withdrawals that are sufficient in size and frequency, the individual will be subject to a 50% penalty on the insufficient amount. An individual who makes a contribution to an IRA that exceeds 100% of earned income or $5,500, whichever is less, will be subject to a penalty of 6% per year on the excess amount for as long as the excess contribution remains in the account.

ROTH IRA

A Roth IRA is a nonqualified account. All contributions made to a Roth IRA are made with after-tax dollars. The same contribution limits apply for Roth IRAs. An individual may contribute the lesser of 100% of earned income to a maximum of $5,500 per person or $11,000 per couple. Any contribution made to a Roth IRA reduces the amount that may be deposited in a traditional IRA and vice versa. All contributions deposited in a Roth IRA are allowed to grow tax deferred and all of the growth may be taken out of the account tax free provided that the individual has reached age 59.5 and the assets have been in the account for at least five years. A 10% penalty tax will be charged on any withdrawal of earnings prior to age 59.5, unless the owner is purchasing a home, has become disabled, or has died. There are no requirements for an individual to take distributions from a Roth IRA by a certain age.

The following table details contribution limits that have been in place for IRA contributions for the last several years:

Year	Age 49 & Below	Age 50 & Above
2012	$5,000	$6,000
2013	$5,500	$6,500
2014	$5,500	$6,500

TAKENOTE!

Individuals and couples who are eligible to open a Roth IRA may convert their traditional IRA to a Roth IRA. The investor will have to pay income taxes on the amount converted, but will not be subject to the 10% penalty.

SIMPLIFIED EMPLOYEE PENSION (SEP) IRA

A SEP IRA is used by small corporations and self-employed individuals to plan for retirement. A SEP IRA is attractive to small employers because it allows them to set up a retirement plan for their employees rather quickly and inexpensively. The contribution limit for a SEP IRA far exceeds that of traditional IRAs. The contribution limit is the lesser of 25% of the employee's compensation or $52,000 per year. Should the employee wish to make their annual IRA contribution to their SEP IRA, they may do so or they may make their standard contribution to a traditional or Roth IRA.

PARTICIPATION

All eligible employees must open an IRA to receive the employer's contribution to the SEP. If the employee does not open an IRA account, the employer must open one for them. The employee must be at least 21 years old, have worked during three of the last five years for the employer, and have earned at least $550. All eligible employees must participate as well as the employer.

EMPLOYER CONTRIBUTIONS

The employer may contribute between 0% to 25% of the employee's total compensation to a maximum of $52,000. Contributions to all SEP IRAs, including the employer's SEP IRA must be made at the same rate. An employee who is over 70.5 must also participate and receive a contribution. All eligible employees are immediately vested in the employer's contributions to the plan.

SEP IRA TAXATION

Employer's contributions to a SEP IRA are immediately tax deductible by the employer. Contributions are not taxed at the employee's rate until the employee withdraws the funds. Employees may begin to withdraw money from the plan at age 59.5. All withdrawals are taxed as ordinary income and withdrawals prior to age 59.5 are subject to a 10% penalty tax.

IRA CONTRIBUTIONS

Contributions to IRs must be made by April 15 of the following calendar year, regardless of whether an extension has been filed by the taxpayer. Contributions may be made between January 1 and April 15 for the previous year, the current year, or both. All IRA contributions must be made in cash.

IRA ACCOUNTS

All IRA accounts are held in the name of the custodian for the benefit of the account holder. Traditional custodians include banks, broker dealers, and mutual fund companies.

IRA INVESTMENTS

Individuals who establish IRAs have a wide variety of investments to choose from when deciding how to invest the funds. Investors should always choose investments that fit their investment objectives. The following is a comparison of allowable and nonallowable investments:

Allowable	Nonallowable
Stocks	Margin accounts
Bonds	Short sales
Mutual funds /ETFs/ETNs	Tangibles/collectibles/art
Annuities	Speculative option trading
UITs	Term life insurance
Limited partnerships	Rare coins
U.S. minted coins	Real estate

IT IS NOT WISE TO PUT A MUNICIPAL BOND IN AN IRA

Municipal bonds or municipal bond funds should never be placed in an IRA, because the advantage of those investments is that the interest income is free from federal taxes. Because their interest is free from federal taxes, the interest rate that is offered will be less than the rates offered by other alternatives. The advantage of an IRA is that money is allowed to grow tax deferred; therefore, an individual would be better off with a higher yielding taxable bond of the same quality.

ROLLOVER VS. TRANSFER

An individual may want or need to move their IRA from one custodian to another. There are two ways by which this can be accomplished. An individual may rollover their IRA or they may transfer their IRA.

ROLLOVER

With an IRA rollover, the individual may take possession of the funds for a maximum of 60 calendar days prior to depositing the funds into another qualified account. An investor may only rollover their IRA once every 12 months. The investor has 60 days from the date of the distribution to deposit 100% of the funds into another qualified account or they must pay ordinary income taxes on the distribution and a 10% penalty tax, if the investor is under 59.5.

TRANSFER

An investor may transfer their IRA directly from one custodian to another by simply signing an account transfer form. The investor never takes possession of the assets in the account and the investor may directly transfer their IRA as often as they like.

DEATH OF AN IRA OWNER

Should the owner of an IRA die, the account will become the property of the beneficiary named on the account by the owner. If the beneficiary is the spouse of the owner special rules apply. The spouse may elect to rollover the IRA in to their own IRA or retirement plan such as a 401k. If this is elected there will be no tax presently due on the money. However, the spouse is still subject to the required minimum distribution rule at age 70½. The surviving spouse may also elect to cash in the IRA. The distributions will be subject to income tax but will not be subject to the 10 percent penalty tax. If the beneficiary is not the spouse the money may not be rolled in to another IRA or retirement account. If the account owner died prior to age 70½ when the required distributions need to be made the money must all be distributed prior to the end of the fifth year or the money may be distributed in equal installments based upon the beneficiary's life expectancy. If the account owner has died after the start of the required minimum distributions the payment schedule of distributions will now be based on the life expectancy of the beneficiary.

EDUCATIONAL IRA/COVERDELL IRA

An educational IRA allows individuals to contribute up to $2,000 in after-tax dollars to an educational IRA for each student who is under the age of 18 years of age. The money is allowed to grow tax deferred and the growth may be withdrawn tax free, as long as the money is used for educational purposes. If all of the funds have not been used for educational purposes by the time the student reaches 30 years of age, the account must be rolled over to another family member who is under 30 years of age or distributed to the original student and is subject to a 10% penalty tax as well as ordinary income taxes.

529 PLANS

A 529 plan may be set up either as a prepaid tuition plan or as a college savings plan. With the prepaid tuition plan, the plan locks in a current tuition rate at a specific school.

The prepaid tuition plan can be set up as an installment plan or one where the contributor funds the plan with a lump sum deposit. Many states will guarantee the plans but may require that either the contributor or the beneficiary to be a state resident. The plan covers only tuition and mandatory fees. A room and board option is available for some plans. A college cost-savings account may be opened by any adult and the donor does not have to be related to the child. The assets in the college savings plan can be used to cover all costs of qualified higher education including tuition, room and board, books, computers and mandatory fees. College savings accounts are not guaranteed by the state and the value of the account may decline in value depending on the investment results of the account. Collage savings account are not state specific and do not lock in a tuition rate. Contributions to a 529 plan are made with after-tax dollars and are allowed to grow tax deferred. The assets in the account remain under the control of the donor, even after the student reaches the age of majority. The funds may be used to meet the student's educational needs and the growth may be withdrawn federally tax-free. Most states also allow the assets to be withdrawn tax free. There are no income limits for the donors and contribution limits vary from state to state.

KEOGH PLANS (HR-10)

A Keogh is a qualified retirement plan set up by self-employed individuals, sole proprietors, and unincorporated businesses. If the business is set up as a corporation, a Keogh may not be used.

KEOGH CONTRIBUTIONS

Keoghs may only be funded with earned income during a period when the business shows a gross profit. If the business realizes a loss, no Keogh contributions are allowed. A self-employed person may contribute the lesser of 25% of their post-contribution income or $51,000. If the business has eligible employees, the employer must make a contribution for the employees at the same rate as their own contribution. Employee contributions are based on the employee's gross income and are limited to $51,000 per year. All money placed in a Keogh plan is allowed to grow tax deferred and is taxed as ordinary income when distributions are made to retiring employees and plan participants. From time to time, a self-employed person may make a nonqualified contribution to their Keogh plan; however, the total of the qualified and nonqualified contributions may not exceed the maximum contribution limit. Any excess contribution may be subject to a 10% penalty tax.

An eligible employee is defined as one who:

- Works full time (at least 1,000 hours per year)
- Is at least 21 years old
- Has worked at least one year for the employer

Employees who participate in a Keogh plan must be vested after five years. Withdrawals from a Keogh may begin when the participant reaches 59.5. Any premature withdrawals are subject to a 10% penalty tax. Keoghs, like IRAs, may be rolled over every 12 months. In the event of a participant's death, the assets will go to the individual's beneficiaries.

TAX-SHELTERED ANNUITIES (TSAs) AND TAX-DEFERRED ACCOUNTS (TDAs)

Tax-sheltered annuities and tax-deferred accounts are established as retirement plans for employees of nonprofit and public organizations such as:

- Public schools (403B)
- Nonprofit organizations (IRC 501C3)

- Religious organizations
- Nonprofit hospitals

TSAs and TDAs are qualified plans and contributions are made with pretax dollars. The money in the plan is allowed to grow tax deferred until it is withdrawn. TSAs and TDAs offer a variety of investment vehicles for participants to choose from such as:

- Stocks
- Bonds
- Mutual funds
- CDs

PUBLIC EDUCATIONAL INSTITUTIONS (403B)

In order for a school to be considered a public school and qualify to establish a TSA/TDA for their employees, the school must be supported by the state, the local government, or by a state agency. State-supported schools are:

- Elementary schools
- High schools
- State colleges and universities
- Medical schools

Any individual who works for a public school, regardless of their position, may participate in the school's TSA or TDA.

NONPROFIT ORGANIZATIONS/TAX-EXEMPT ORGANIZATIONS (501C3)

Organizations, which qualify under the Internal Revenue Code 501C3 as a nonprofit or tax-exempt entity may set up a TSA or TDA for their employees. Examples of nonprofit organizations are:

- Private hospitals
- Charitable organizations
- Trade schools
- Private colleges
- Parochial schools

- Museums
- Scientific foundations
- Zoos

All employees of organizations that qualify under the Internal Revenue Code 501C3 or 403B are eligible to participate as long as they are at least 21 years old and have worked full time for at least one year.

TSA/TDA CONTRIBUTIONS

In order to participate in a TSA or TDA, the employees must enter into a contract with their employer agreeing to make elective deferrals into the plan. The salary reduction agreement will state the amount and frequency of the elective deferral to be contributed to the TSA. The agreement is binding on both parties and covers only one year of contributions. Each year, a new salary reduction agreement must be signed to set forth the contributions for the new year. The employee's elective deferral is limited to a maximum of $17,500 per year. Employer contributions are limited to the lesser of 25% of the employee's earnings or $52,000.

TAX TREATMENT OF TSA/TDA DISTRIBUTIONS

All distributions for TSAs and TDAs are taxed as ordinary income in the year in which the distribution is made. Distributions from a TSA or TDA prior to age 59.5 are subject to a 10% penalty tax, as well as ordinary income taxes. Distributions from a TSA/TDA must begin by age 70.5 or be subject to an excess accumulation tax.

CORPORATE PLANS

A corporate retirement plan can be qualified or nonqualified. We will first review the nonqualified plans.

NONQUALIFIED CORPORATE RETIREMENT PLANS

Nonqualified corporate plans are funded with after-tax dollars and the money is allowed to grow tax deferred. If the corporation makes a contribution to the plan, they may not deduct the contribution from their corporate earnings until the plan participant receives the money. Distributions from a nonqualified plan, which exceed the investors cost base, are taxed as ordinary income.

All nonqualified plans must be in writing and the employer may discriminate as to who may participate.

PAYROLL DEDUCTIONS

The employee may set up a payroll deduction plan by having the employer make systematic deductions from the employee's paycheck. The money, which has been deducted from the employee's check, may be invested in a variety of ways. Mutual funds, annuities, and savings bonds are all usually available for the employee to choose from. Contributions to a payroll deduction plan are made with after-tax dollars.

DEFERRED COMPENSATION PLANS

A deferred compensation plan is a contract between an employee and an employer. Under the contract, the employee agrees to defer the receipt of money owed to the employee from the employer until after the employee retires. After retirement, the employee will traditionally be in a lower tax bracket and will be able to keep a larger percentage of the money for themselves. Deferred compensation plans are traditionally unfunded and, if the corporation goes out of business, the employee becomes a creditor of the corporation and may lose all of the money due under the contract. The employee may only claim the assets if they retire, become disabled, or, in the case of death, their beneficiaries may claim the money owed. Money due under a deferred compensation plan is paid out of the corporation's working funds when the employee or their estate claims the assets. Should the employee leave the corporation and go to work for a competing company, they may lose the money owed under a noncompete clause. Money owed to the employee under a deferred compensation agreement is traditionally not invested for the benefit of the employee and, as a result, does not increase in value over time. The only product that traditionally is placed in a deferred compensation plan is a term life policy. In the case of the employee's death, the term life policy will pay the employee's estate the money owed under the contract.

QUALIFIED PLANS

All qualified corporate plans must be in writing and set up as a trust. A trustee or plan administrator will be appointed for the benefit of all plan holders.

TYPES OF PLANS

There are two main types of qualified corporate plans: a defined benefit plan and a defined contribution plan.

DEFINED BENEFIT PLAN

A defined benefit plan is designed to offer the participant a retirement benefit that is known or defined. Most defined benefit plans are set up to provide employees with a fixed percentage of their salary during their retirement, such as 74% of their average earnings during their five highest paid years. Other defined benefit plans are structured to pay participants a fixed sum of money for life. Defined benefit plans require the services of an actuary to determine the employer's contribution to the plan, based upon the participant's life expectancy and benefits promised.

DEFINED CONTRIBUTION PLAN

With a defined contribution plan, only the amount of money that is deposited into the account is known, such as 6% of the employee's salary. Both the employee and the employer may contribute a percentage of the employee's earnings into the plan. The money is allowed to grow tax deferred until the participant withdraws it at retirement. The ultimate benefit under a defined contribution plan is the result of the contributions into the plan, along with the investment results of the plan. The employee's maximum contribution to a defined contribution plan is $17,500 per year. Some types of defined contribution plans are:

- 401K
- Money purchase plan
- Profit sharing
- Thrift plans
- Stock bonus plans

All withdrawals from pension plans are taxed as ordinary income in the year in which the distribution is made.

PROFIT-SHARING PLANS

Profit-sharing plans let the employer reward the employees by letting them "share" in a percentage of the corporation's profits. Profit-sharing plans are based on a preset formula and the money may be paid directly to the employee or placed in a retirement account. In order for a profit-sharing plan to be qualified, the corporation must have substantial and recurring profits. The maximum contribution to a profit sharing plan is the lesser of 15% of the employee's compensation or $52,000.

401K AND THRIFT PLANS

401K and thrift plans allow the employee to contribute a fixed percentage of their salary to their retirement account and have the employer match some or all of their contributions. A "self-directed 401K plan" is one where the individual or plan participant selects the investments to be made in the account from a list of investment choices. The plan participant is the person who owns the account and is making contributions to the account to "plan" for their retirement. The employer, investment adviser, and plan administrator or trustee all have important roles in the creation and administration of a 401K plan.

The employer is the entity that creates the plan for its employees and is known as the creator or plan sponsor.

The investment adviser is the company who determines what investment choices will be offered to the participants and who executes the orders entered by the plan participants.

The plan administrator/trustee also known as a third-party administrator is the company that has physical custody the plan's assets and provides communication to the participants regarding the plan.

ROLLING OVER A PENSION PLAN

An employee who leaves an employer may move their pension plan to another company's plan or to another qualified account. This may be accomplished by a direct transfer or by rolling over the plan. With a direct transfer, the assets in the plan go directly to another plan administrator and the employee never has physical possession of the assets. When the employee rolls over their pension plan, they take physical possession of the assets. The plan administrator is required to withhold 20% of the total amount to be distributed and the employee has 60 calendar days to deposit 100% of the assets into another qualified plan. The employee must file with the federal government at tax time to receive a return of the 20% of the assets that were withheld by the plan administrator.

EMPLOYEE STOCK OPTIONS

Employers may establish stock option plans that allow employees to purchase shares of the employer's stock. Employees who operate in certain functions or who meet the criteria for inclusion in the plan may be granted stock options to purchase the common stock of the employer at a stated exercise price. Employee stock option plans may be established as nonqualified stock option plans or as incentive stock option plans. Under a nonqualified stock option plan, the employee may exercise the options at the stated exercise price and sell the shares at the higher market price. The difference between the cost or the exercise price and the sales proceeds for the stock under the plan will be treated as compensation and taxed as earned income. If certain plan requirements are met under an incentive stock option plan, any gain on the sale of the stock may be treated as a capital gain. If the employee has held the stock purchased under an ISO for at least two years from the grant date of the options and at least one year from the purchase/exercise date of the options, any appreciation will be treated as a capital gain. Incentive stock option plans must be approved by the board of directors and by the shareholders. Employee stock option plans may set any criteria the employer wishes to determine who may participate in the plan.

EMPLOYEE RETIREMENT INCOME SECURITY ACT OF 1974 (ERISA)

The Employee Retirement Income Security Act of 1974 (ERISA) is a federal law that establishes legal and operational guidelines for private pension and employee benefit plans. Not all decisions directly involving a plan, even when made by a fiduciary, are subject to ERISA's fiduciary rules. These decisions are business judgment type decisions and are commonly called "settlor" functions. This caveat is sometimes referred to as the "business decision" exception to ERISA's fiduciary rules. Under this concept, even though the employer is the plan sponsor and administrator, it will not be considered as acting in a fiduciary capacity when creating, amending or terminating a plan. Among the decisions which would be considered settlor functions are:

- Choosing the type of plan, or options in the plan;
- Amending a plan, including changing or eliminating plan options;
- Requiring employee contributions or changing the level of employee contributions;
- Terminating a plan, or part of a plan, including terminating or amending as part of a bankruptcy process.

ERISA also regulates all of the following:

- Pension plan participation
- Funding
- Vesting

- Communication
- Beneficiaries

PLAN PARTICIPATION

All plans governed by ERISA may not discriminate among who may participate in the plan. All employees must be allowed to participate if:

- They are at least 21 years old.
- They have worked at least one year full time (1,000 hours).

FUNDING

Plan funding requirements set forth guidelines on how the money is deposited into the plan and how the employer and employee may contribute to the plan.

VESTING

Vesting refers to the process of how the employer's contribution becomes the property of the employee. An employer may be as generous as they like but may not be more restrictive than either one of the following vesting schedules:

- 3- to 6-year gradual vesting schedule
- 3-year cliff; the employee is not vested at all until three years when they become 100% vested

COMMUNICATION

All corporate plans must be in writing at inception and the employee must be given annual updates.

BENEFICIARIES

All plan participants must be allowed to select a beneficiary who may claim the assets in case of the plan participant's death.

ERISA 404C SAFE HARBOR

All individuals and entities acting in a fiduciary capacity must act solely in the interest of the plan participants. Investment advisers, trustees and all individuals who exercise discretion over the plan including those who select the administrative personnel or committee are considered to be fiduciaries. ERISA Rule 404C provides an exemption from liability or a "safe harbor" for plan fiduciaries and protects them from liabilities that may arise from investment losses that result from the participant's own actions. This safe harbor is available so long as:

- The participant exercises control over the assets in their account.
- Participants have ample opportunity to enter orders for their account and to provide instructions regarding their account.
- A broad range of investment options is available for the participant to choose from and the options offer suitable investments for a variety or investment objectives and risk profiles.
- Information regarding the risks and objective of the investment options is readily available to plan participants.

LIFE INSURANCE

Life insurance is a contract between an individual and an insurance company that is designed to provide financial compensation to the policyholder's beneficiaries in the event of the policyholder's death. There are several different types of life insurance policies, and it is important that the individual chooses a policy that best fits his or her needs. The types of life insurance covered on the Series 6 exam are:

- Whole life
- Variable life
- Universal life
- Variable universal life

WHOLE LIFE

A whole life insurance policy provides the insured with a guaranteed death benefit that is equal to the face amount of the policy as well as a guaranteed cash value that the policyholder may borrow against. The cash value of the policy is held in the insurance company's general account and is invested in conservative investments such as mortgages and real estate. The policy's cash value increases each year as the premiums are paid and invested. The death benefit and the premium payments are fixed by the insurance company at the time of issuance and remain constant for the life of the policy. The policyholder is covered from the date of issuance to the date of death, as long as the premiums are paid.

VARIABLE LIFE

A variable life insurance contract is both an insurance policy and a security because of the way the insurance company invests the cash reserves. A variable life policy is a fixed-premium plan that offers the contract holder a minimum death benefit. The holder of a variable life insurance policy may choose how the cash reserves are invested. A variable life policy typically offers stocks, bonds, mutual funds, and other portfolios as investment options. Although the performance of these investments may tend to outperform the performance of more conservative alternatives, the cash value of the policy is not guaranteed. The cash and securities held by the insurance company are invested in the insurance company's separate account and are kept segregated from the insurance company's general account. The separate account is required to register as either an open-end investment or as a UIT under The Investment Company Act of 1940. Representatives who sell these policies must have both a securities license and an insurance license. The insured is covered from the date of issuance to the date of death, as long as the premiums are paid.

UNIVERSAL LIFE

A universal life insurance policy, unlike whole and variable life policies, has no scheduled premium payments and a face amount that can be adjusted according to the policyholder's needs. A universal life policy allows the policyholder to decide when premiums are paid and to determine how large those payments will be. Should the insured determine that he or she needs to change the amount of the insurance, the face amount of the policy may be adjusted up or down. The policyholder has no scheduled premium payments, but the insured must make payments frequently enough to support the policy. The policy will stay in effect as long as there is enough cash value in the policy to support the payment of mortality and expense costs. The net premium payments are invested in the insurance company's general account, and a universal life policy is considered an insurance product. Representatives who sell universal life insurance policies must have their insurance licenses.

VARIABLE UNIVERSAL LIFE/ UNIVERSAL VARIABLE LIFE

A variable universal life policy allows the policyholder the ability to determine when premiums are paid and to decide how large those payments are. The net premium is invested in the insurance company's separate account, and the policy's cash value and variable death benefit are determined by the investment experience of the separate account. A variable universal life insurance policy will remain in effect as long as there is enough cash value in the policy to support the cost of insurance. A variable universal life insurance policy may have a minimum guaranteed death benefit but does not have to. Representatives who sell variable universal life polices must have both insurance and securities licenses.

CHAPTER 5

Pretest

VARIABLE ANNUITIES AND RETIREMENT PLANS

1. A doctor makes the maximum contribution to his Keogh plan while earning $300,000 per year. How much can he contribute to an IRA?
   a. $51,000
   b. $17,000
   c. $9,000
   d. $5,500

2. An individual owns a variable life insurance policy with an assumed interest rate of 5%. If the separate account earns 4%, the individual would expect the:
   I. Death benefit to go up
   II. Death benefit to go down
   III. Cash value to go up
   IV. Cash value to go down

   a. II and IV
   b. I and III
   c. I and II
   d. II and III

3. A school principal has deposited $15,000 in a tax-deferred annuity through a payroll deduction plan. The account has grown in value to $22,000. The principal plans to retire and take a lump sum distribution. On what amount does he pay taxes?
   a. $22,000
   b. $15,000
   c. $7,000
   d. $0

4. The maximum amount that a couple may contribute to their IRAs at any one time is:
   a. 100% of the annual contribution limit
   b. 200% of the annual contribution limit
   c. 300% of the annual contribution limit
   d. 400% of the annual contribution limit

5. An investor has deposited $100,000 into a qualified retirement account over a 10-year period. The value of the account has grown to $175,000 and the investor plans to retire and take a lump sum withdrawal. The investor will pay:
   a. Capital gains tax on $75,000 only
   b. Ordinary income taxes on the $75,000 only
   c. Ordinary income taxes on the whole $175,000
   d. Ordinary income taxes on the $100,000 and capital gains on the $75,000

6. A 42-year-old investor wants to put $20,000 into a plan to help meet the educational expenses of his 12-year-old son. He wants to make a lump sum deposit. Which would you recommend?
   a. 529 plan
   b. Coverdell IRA
   c. Roth IRA
   d. Growth mutual fund

7. A client who is 65 years old has invested $10,000 in a Roth IRA. It has now grown to $14,000. He plans to retire and take a lump sum distribution. He will pay taxes on:
   a. $0
   b. $14,000
   c. $4,000
   d. $10,000

8. A fixed annuity guarantees all of the following except:
   a. Income for life
   b. Protection from inflation
   c. Rate of return
   d. Protection from investment risk

9. A self-employed individual may open a SEP IRA to plan for his retirement. The maximum contribution to the plan is:
   a. $4,000
   b. $8,000
   c. $16,000
   d. The lesser of 25% of the post-contribution income, up to $51,000

CHAPTER 6

Fundamental and Technical Analysis

INTRODUCTION

Fundamental analysis and technical analysis are the two methods that an investor may use to analyze a potential equity investment. Fundamental analysis is concerned with the financial performance of the company. A fundamental analyst will investigate the company's financial picture to determine if an investment should be made. Technical analysis uses the past price performance of the stock to predict the stock's future price performance. A technical analyst is not concerned with the company's finances. They are only concerned with the price patterns of the stock.

FUNDAMENTAL ANALYSIS

Fundamental analysts examine the company's financial statements and financial ratios to ascertain the company's overall financial performance. The analyst will use the following to determine a value for the company's stock:

- Balance sheet
- Income statement
- Footnotes to financial statements
- Financial ratios
- Liquidity ratios
- Valuation ratios

BALANCE SHEET

The balance sheet will show an investor everything that the corporation owns (assets) and everything that the corporation owes (liabilities) at the time the balance sheet was prepared. A balance sheet is a snapshot of the company's financial health on the day it was created. The difference between the company's assets and its liabilities is the corporation's net worth. The corporation's net worth is the shareholders' equity. Remember that the shareholders own the corporation. The basic balance sheet equation is:

Assets – liabilities = net worth

The balance sheet equation also may be presented as follows:

Assets = liabilities + shareholder's equity

The two columns on the balance sheet contain the company's assets on the left and its liabilities and shareholder's equity on the right. The total dollar amount of both sides must be equal or must balance. The entries on a balance sheet look as follows:

Assets	Liabilities
Current assets	Current liabilities
Fixed assets	Long-term liabilities
Other assets	Equity/net worth
	Preferred stock par value
	Common stock par value
	Additional paid in surplus
	Treasury stock
	Retained earnings

The assets are listed in order of liquidity. Current assets include cash and assets that can be converted into cash within 12 months. Current assets include:

- Money market instruments
- Marketable securities
- Accounts receivable net of any delinquent accounts
- Inventory including work in progress
- Prepaid expenses

Fixed assets are assets that have a long useful life and are used by the company in the operation of its business. Fixed assets include:

- Plant and equipment
- Property and real estate

Other assets are intangible/non-physical assets that belong to the company. Other assets include:

- Goodwill
- Trademarks
- Patents
- Contract rights

Intangible assets generally have significant value to the corporation, but are difficult to place a hard value on by outside companies.

The liabilities of the corporation are listed in the order in which they become due. Current liabilities are obligations that must be paid within 12 months. Current liabilities include:

- Wages payable, including salaries and commissions owed to employees
- Accounts payable to vendors and suppliers
- Current portion of long-term debt; that is, any portion of the company's long term
- Debt due within 12 months
- Taxes due within 12 months
- Short-term notes due within 12 months

Long-term liabilities are debts that will become due after 12 months. Long-term liabilities include:

- Bonds
- Mortgages
- Notes

TAKENOTE!

The corporation's debt, which comes due in five years or more, is known as funded debt.

Stockholders' equity is the net worth of the company. Stockholders' equity is broken up into the following categories:

- Capital stock at par: the aggregate par for both common and preferred stock
- Additional paid in surplus: sometimes known as capital in excess of par is any sum paid over par by investors when the shares were issued by the company
- Retained earnings: profits that have been kept by the corporation, sometimes known as earned surplus

CAPITALIZATION

The term capitalization refers to the sources and makeup of the company's financial picture. The following are used to determine the company's capitalization:

- Long-term debt
- Equity accounts, including par value of common and preferred and paid in and earned surplus

A company that borrows a large portion of its capital though the issuance of bonds is said to be highly leveraged. Raising money through the sale of common stock is considered to be a more conservative method for a corporation to raise money because it does not require the corporation to pay the money back. When a company borrows funds, it is trying to use that borrowed capital to increase its return on equity.

CHANGES IN THE BALANCE SHEET

As a business conducts its operations, its daily transactions will affect the balance sheet. Every transaction requires an offsetting transaction to the appropriate account. This is known as double-entry bookkeeping. For example, if ABC Mills wrote a check to a large vendor for $1,000,000, the company's cash would be reduced by $1,000,000 and the company's accounts payable would be reduced by $1,000,000. Transactions that affect the balance sheet include:

- Purchasing equipment for cash
- Depreciation
- Issuing securities
- Declaring a dividend
- Conversion of convertible securities

Balance Sheet ABC MILLS, Inc., as of December 31			
Assets			
Current assets	Cash and equivalents	$ 6,000,000	
	Accounts receivable	$ 12,000,000	
	Inventory	$ 20,000,000	
	Prepaid expenses	$ 500,000	
	Total current assets		**$ 38,500,000**
Fixed assets	Buildings, furniture, & fixtures (including $5,000,000 depreciation)	$ 50,000,000	
	Land	$ 20,000,000	
	Total fixed assets		**$ 70,000,000**
Other assets (goodwill, intangibles)			**$ 2,000,000**
Total assets			**$110,500,000**
Liabilities and Net Worth			
Current liabilities	Accounts payable	$ 3,000,000	
	Accrued wages payable	$ 1,500,000	
	Current portion of long-term debt	$ 1,500,000	
	Total current liabilities		**$ 6,000,000**
Long-term liabilities			
	7% 30-year convertible debentures		**$ 40,000,000**
Total liabilities			**$ 46,000,000**
Net worth	Preferred stock $100 par 7% convertible noncumulative 250,000 shares issued	$ 25,000,000	
	Common stock $1 par 2,000,000 shares issued	$ 2,000,000	
	Capital paid in excess of par	$ 22,000,000	
	Retained earnings	$ 15,500,000	
Total net worth			**$ 64,500,000**
Total liabilities and net worth			**$ 110,500,000**

- Bond redemption
- Stock splits

Purchasing Equipment for Cash: If the company purchases a piece of industrial equipment for cash, its long-term assets will increase and its cash and current assets will be decreased by the amount of the purchase.

Depreciation: This allows companies to amortize the cost of capital goods over their estimated useful life. As fixed assets wear out, their value declines. Companies may reduce the value of their assets through depreciation and may use the amount of the depreciation to offset taxes owed. Depreciation is a noncash charge that lowers a company's tax liability. Depending on the type of asset involved, depreciation may be taken as either straight line depreciation or as accelerated depreciation. Straight line deprecation is taken in equal amounts over the estimated useful life of the asset. A piece of heavy equipment costing $10,000,000 with a useful life of 10 years would be depreciated at $1,000,000 per year for 10 years. Accelerated depreciation depreciates most of the value of the asset in the first few years of useful life and by lesser amounts during the remaining years. Depreciation impacts both the income statement and balance sheet of a corporation. A company's taxable income is reduced by the amount of the depreciation taken in the current period and accumulated depreciation reduces the value of the asset on the company's balance sheet.

Issuing Securities: If the company were to issue additional shares of $1 par common stock, the net worth of the company would increase by the amount of the par value sold, plus any paid in surplus. As a result of the issuance of the securities, the corporation's cash position would also be increased by the net proceeds of the offering.

Declaring a Dividend: When a cash dividend is declared, the corporation's retained earnings are reduced by the amount of the dividend and the company's current liabilities are increased by the amount of the dividend payable. Once the dividend is paid, the company's cash and current assets are reduced by the amount of the dividend paid. The payment of the dividend also eliminates the current liability that resulted from the declaration of the dividend.

Conversion of Convertible Securities: If the holder of a convertible bond converts the bonds into common stock, the par value of the bonds will be eliminated as a long-term liability and the par value will be credited to the equity account on the balance sheet.

Bond Redemption: Bonds are redeemed at maturity. If the corporation uses cash to pay off the principal amount of the bonds, then the long-term liabilities and the cash and current assets of the corporation will be reduced by an equal amount.

Stock Splits: A forward stock split will increase the number of shares outstanding and reduce the par value of the shares. A reverse stock split will reduce the number of outstanding shares and increase the par value. Shareholders' equity is not affected as a result of a stock split.

A fundamental analyst may look at the balance sheet to determine the following financial information:

- Net worth
- Working capital
- Current ratio
- Quick assets
- Acid test ratio/quick ratio
- Cash assets ratio
- Debt-to-equity ratio
- Common stock ratio
- Preferred stock ratio
- Bond ratio

The following table details fundamental valuation ratios and formulas used by analysts and their purpose.

Measure	Formula	Purpose
Book value per share	Assets – liabilities – intangibles – par value of preferred/no. of outstanding common shares	To determine the value of the company's common stock
Working capital	Current assets – current liabilities	To determine the company's liquidity
Current ratio	Current assets/current liabilities	A relationship between current assets and liabilities
Quick assets	Current assets – inventory	To determine highly liquid assets
Acid test/quick ratio	Quick assets/current liabilities	To determine the company's liquidity
Cash assets ratio	Cash & equivalents/current liabilities	The most stringent liquidity measure
Debt-to-equity ratio	Total long-term debt/total shareholders' equity	To examine the company's capital structure
Common stock ratio	Common shareholders' equity/total capitalization	To examine the company's capital structure
Preferred stock ratio	Preferred stock/total capitalization	To examine the company's capital structure
Bond ratio	Total long-term debt/total capitalization	To examine the company's capital structure

THE INCOME STATEMENT

The income statement details a corporation's revenue and expenses for the period for which it was produced. Income statements are usually prepared on a quarterly and annual basis. A fundamental analyst will use the income statement to determine a corporation's profitability. The three levels of earnings listed on the income statement are:

1. Operating income
2. Net income after taxes
3. Earnings available to common

Operating Income: Is the business profit or loss from operations and is also known as earnings before interest and taxes (EBIT).

Net Income After Taxes: Is the corporation's earnings after all federal and state taxes have been paid. Dividends to shareholders will be paid from net income after taxes.

Earnings Available to Common: Is what is left from the corporation's net income after taxes, after the corporation has paid preferred dividends. If the corporation wants to pay a dividend to common shareholders, then the preferred dividends must have already been paid.

Income Statement ABC Mills, Inc. January 1–December 31			
Net sales			$ 100,000,000
	Cost of goods sold	$ 45,000,000	
	General operating expenses (including $5,000,000 depreciation)	$ 32,000,000	
			$ 77,000,000
Operating income			$ 23,000,000
	Interest expense		$ 2,800,000
Pretax income			$ 20,200,000
	Taxes at 36%		$ 7,272,000
Net income after taxes			$ 12,928,000
	Preferred dividends		$ 1,750,000
Earnings available to common			$ 11,178,000

By combining the information contained in the balance sheet and the income statement, an analyst can determine:

- Earnings per share primary
- Earnings per share fully diluted
- Price earnings ratio
- Dividend payout ratio
- Debt service ratio

Earnings per share primary: Will tell the analyst how much of the company's earnings are credited to each common share.

Earnings per share fully diluted: Will tell the analyst how much of the company's earnings are credited to each common share after all convertible securities and all rights and warrants have been exchanged for common stock.

Price earnings ratio: Will tell the analyst the relationship between the earnings per share and the common stock price.

Dividend payout ratio: Will tell the analyst how much of the earnings per share were paid out to shareholders as dividends.

Debt service ratio: Will tell the analyst the ability of the company to meet their debt service obligations.

Measure	Formula	Purpose
Earnings per share primary	Earnings available to common/no. of common shares	To determine the amount of the company's earnings for each share outstanding
Earnings per share fully diluted	Earnings available to common/no. of common shares	To determine the amount of the company's earnings for each share outstanding after all conversions
Price earnings ratio	Stock price/EPS	To determine a relationship between the stock price and the earnings per share
Dividend payout ratio	Annual dividends per common share/EPS	To determine how much of the company's EPS are paid out in dividends
Debt service ratio	EBIT/annual interest and principal payments	To determine the company's ability to meet its debt service needs

TAKENOTE!

Most balance sheets and income statements will include footnotes which give additional details regarding the items contained in the reports. These footnotes will detail the impact potential events may have on the financial information contained in the statements as well as any assumptions or calculations used to arrive at the information.

INDUSTRY FUNDAMENTALS

There are fundamental economic factors that affect different industries. Analysts must be able to determine how susceptible the company's earnings are to a change in the economy. There are three industry categories. They are:

1. Growth industries
2. Cyclical industries
3. Defensive industries

Growth Industries: The earnings of companies in a growth industry will grow faster than the overall growth of the economy as whole. Growth industries include computers and technology.

Cyclical Industries: The earnings of a company in a cyclical industry are highly susceptible to the condition of the overall economy. As the economy improves, the company will do well. If the economy does poorly, the company will perform poorly. Cyclical industries include manufacturing, raw materials, and automobiles.

Defensive Industries: The earnings of a company in a defensive industry will be the least susceptible to the changes in the overall economy. Defensive industries include food and pharmaceuticals. These are things that people will buy no matter how the economy is performing. It is important to note that a manufacturer of military equipment is not considered to be in a defensive industry.

TOP DOWN AND BOTTOM UP ANALYSIS

Rather than simply zeroing in on the financial picture of a given company many analysts will include an evaluation of the industry or sector and the economy as a whole to further validate their research. An analyst who employs a top down approach would look at how the economy as whole is performing and identify industries that will perform the best in the current and predicted economic climate. Once the industry is identified the analyst will try to identify the best performing company within that industry as a potential candidate for investment. Conversely, an analyst who employs a bottoms up approach would start their research with the company and expand it to the industry or sector and then finally to the economy as a whole to evaluate an investment opportunity.

DIVIDEND VALUATION MODELS

A fundamental analysts may use a dividend valuation model to determine a fair valuation for an equity security and to determine if an investment is warranted. The two dividend valuation models most often use are the dividend discount model and the dividend growth model.

The Dividend Discount Model: The dividend discount model takes the sum of all future dividends to be received and discounts them into a net present value. The model states that the market price of the stock should be equal to the net present value of all future cash flows. A simple way to estimate the value based on this method would be to take the annual dividend and divide it by the prevailing rate paid by other similar investments. If a utility stock is paying a $2 annual dividend and other similar utilities are yielding 5% the market price can be estimated to be $40. Found as follows:

$2 / .05 = $40

The dividend discount model may be used for issues that have both fixed and variable dividends over time.

The Dividend Growth Model: The Dividend Growth Model values the stock based on the net present value of the cash flow to be generated by a dividend that is expected to grow over time. It is unlikely that you will have to calculate the value of a stock based on the dividend growth model. It is important to know that the present value is significantly higher for an equity with a dividend that is predicted to grow. The higher the growth rate the higher the net present value. Because the dividend growth model calculates a higher net present value this model will predict a higher stock price than a dividend valuation model based on a constant dividend.

TECHNICAL ANALYSIS

A technical analyst uses the patterns created by the past price performance of the stock to predict the direction of the stock price in the future. A technical analyst is not concerned with the fundamentals of the company or even what business the company is in. They are only interpreting chart patterns and other technical factors relating to the price performance of the stock. Some of the chart patterns that a technical analyst will look to identify are:

- Support
- Resistance
- Trend lines
- Reversals
- Consolidations

Support: Support is created at the point to which the stock falls and attracts buyers. The new buyers that are brought into the market, because of the lower price, create demand for the stock and prevent it from falling any further.

Resistance: Resistance is created at the point to which the stock appreciates and attracts sellers. The new sellers that are brought into the market, because of the higher price, create supply for the stock and prevent it from rising any further.

Upward Trend Lines: An upward trend line is characterized by a series of higher highs and a series of higher lows. A chartist would draw a line connecting the series of higher lows to confirm the trend and the trend line should provide some support to the stock price.

Downward Trend Lines: A downward trend line is characterized by a series of lower highs and a series of lower lows. A chartist would draw a line connecting the series of lower highs to confirm the downward trend and the trend line should provide some resistance to the stock price.

Reversals: A reversal indicates a significant change in the price action of the stock. A bullish reversal indicates the end of a downward trend and the beginning of a new upward trend. A bearish reversal indicates the end of an upward trend and the beginning of a new downward trend. One of the most significant reversal patterns is the head-and-shoulders formation. A head-and-shoulders top is a bearish reversal of an uptrend, while a head-and-shoulders bottom is a bullish reversal of a downtrend.

Consolidation: A consolidation pattern is characterized by a horizontal movement in the stock price. Buyers and sellers are attracted to the market and are willing to trade the stock at almost the same prices.

The following illustrate the chart patterns just outlined:

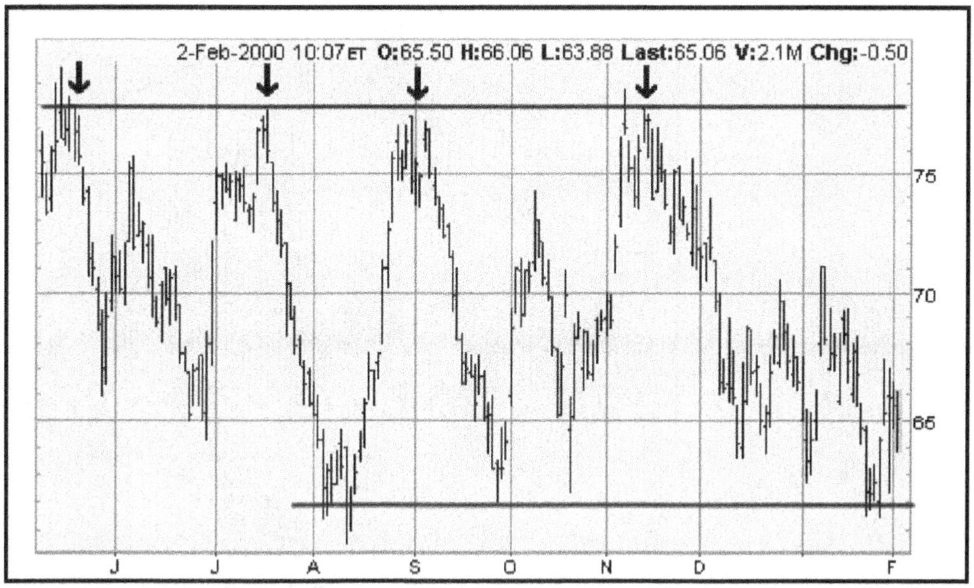

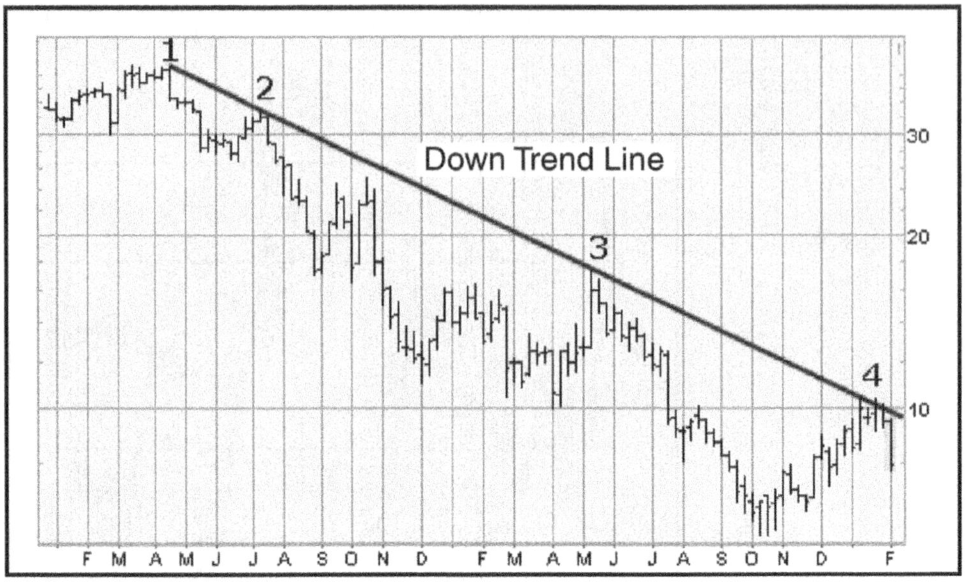
1
2
Down Trend Line
3
4
30
20
10
F M A M J J A S O N D F M A M J J A S O N D F

Head-and-Shoulders Reversal
Head
Right Shoulder
Left Shoulder
Neckline
1
2
Trendline
CNET - CNET
80
70
65
60
55
50
45
40
35
30
25
Jul Aug Sep Oct Nov Dec Feb Mar Apr May

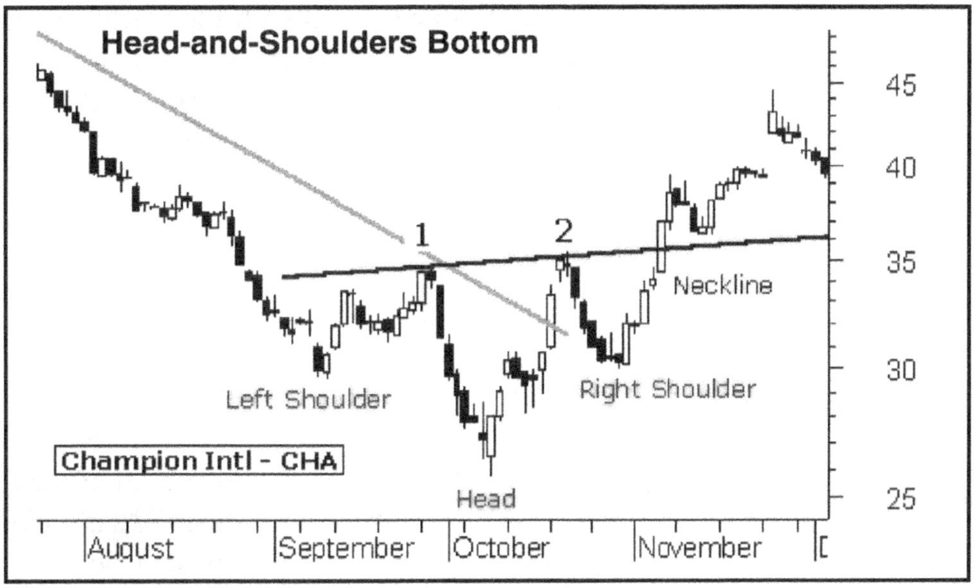

MARKET THEORIES AND INDICATORS

A technical analyst will look at various indicators to interpret the overall market's direction. These indicators include:

- Short interest
- Odd lot trading
- Advance decline line

Short Interest: Investors who have sold stock short are betting that the stock price falls. In order to close out their position, they must repurchase the stock. All investors who have sold stock short must eventually repurchase the stock. Because all of the short sellers are potential buyers for the stock, a high short interest is considered a bullish indicator.

Odd Lot Trading: The odd lot trading theory believes that smaller investors, who cannot afford to buy or sell one round lot of stock, will invariably buy and sell at the wrong time. A high level of odd lot purchases is indicative of a market top. A high level of odd lot sales is indicative of a market bottom.

TAKENOTE!

Both the short interest theory and the odd lot trading theory are contrarian indicators.

Advance Decline Line: The advance decline line indicates the breadth of the market. The market's breadth is a good indicator of the overall health of the market and can be used to confirm or reject a trend. The advance decline line will tell an investor how many stocks are trading higher in price and how many are trading lower in price.

A technical analyst will always look for volume confirmation of any trend. A trend is confirmed by high levels of volume in the stock or in the market as a whole.

EFFICIENT MARKET THEORY

The efficient market theory believes that all of the available information is priced into the market at any given time and it is impossible to beat the market by taking advantage of price or time inefficiencies. Proponents of the efficient market theory may follow the theory in the following ways:

Weak-form efficiency states that the future price of a security cannot be predicted by studying the past price performance of the security. This form of the theory believes that technical analysis cannot produce excess returns as all of the past prices and volume information relating to the security are widely known.

Semi-strong form efficiency states that the market price of a security adjusts too rapidly to newly available information to achieve an excess return by trading on that information. The information contained in the past price performance as well as information released in company quarterly, annual and other reports is widely known and is reflected in the price of the security.

Strong-form efficiency states that the current price of a security reflects all information known and unknown to the public and there is no opportunity to earn excess returns. Investors who subscribe to the strong form of the efficient market theory believe that even someone in possession of non public material information will not be able to earn excess returns by trading on that information.

TAKENOTE!

The random walk theory similarly states the prices of securities adjust too rapidly to all available information and that throwing a dart at a listing of stocks would produce the same returns as detailed analysis.

STATISTICAL ANALYSIS

Some analysts will employ statistical analysis or the study of mathematical data in security evaluation models. Analyst will plot the price points at which a security has traded under a standardized bell curve to determine the potential pricing outcomes for a security. The wider the distribution of the price points the wider the range. The range is the difference between the lowest price and highest price at which a security has traded over a given period. The wider the range the higher the standard deviation and therefore the higher the risk associated with the security and its potential return. Analysts will review the price points plotted underneath the bell curve distribution to determine various measures of central tendency. There are several measures that can be used to determine the midpoint of the range all distributions, these are the arithmetic mean, median and mode.

The arithmetic mean: the arithmetic mean is found by adding all of the price observations together and dividing the total by the number of price observation. The arithmetic mean can be thought of as the average price at which the security traded over the observation period.

The Median: the median is the exact middle of all price observations and is the price point on the bell curve that separates the higher prices from the lower prices. The median is found by listing all of the prices numerically from lowest to highest and picking the price in the exact middle. If there is an even number of price observations there will be no single median value therefore the median value will be the average of the two middle values.

The Mode: the mode is the price observation that appears most frequently on the price distribution curve. Simply put the mode is the price at which the security has most frequently traded. While the mode will have a significant impact on the mean and median as a result of the frequency of its occurrences it tends to be a price that is not like the price calculated by the mean and the median.

Statistical analysis may be applied to individual equities or to the returns generated by portfolios containing a number of securities. When comparing portfolios any portfolio with the highest mean relative to the median and mode contains investments that have significantly outperformed the other investments. Statistical analysis in finance is part of the broad school of quantitative analysis. Simply put quantitative analysis is based on the study of quantities (the number of occurrences and observations) analyst who employ quantitative analysis are known as "quants."

MARKET CAPITALIZATION

A company's market capitalization refers to the total value of all outstanding common shares. Market capitalization is divided into the following three categories:

- Large capitalization, companies with a market value greater than 5 billion dollars
- Middle capitalization, companies with a market value between 1-5 billion dollars
- Small capitalization, companies with a market value less than 1 billion dollars

MARKET INDEXES

Many market indexes have been developed to measure the performance of the overall stock market as well as the performance of sub sectors within the market. Investors may use these indexes as a way to measure the performance of the overall market and to measure the performance of a portfolio against a benchmark index. Market indexes are divided into two main types capitalization weighted and price weighted indexes. The two types are characterized as follows:

Capitalization weighted index: A market benchmark whose value is derived from the price action of the companies whose shares are included in the index. More weight is given to the price performance of the shares of the companies with the greatest market capitalization. Market capitalization is the total value of all the outstanding shares. The NASDAQ Composite, NASDAQ 100, NYSE Composite, Russell 2000, S & P 500 and S & P 100 and Wilshire 5000 are all capitalization weighted indexes.

Price weighted index: A market benchmark whose value is derived from the price action of the companies whose shares are included in the index. More weight is given to the price performance of the shares of the companies with higher stock prices. A change in the price of a $100 stock would have a greater impact on the value of the index than a change in the share price of a $10 stock. The Dow Jones Industrial, Transportation and Utility averages are all price weighted indexes.

CHAPTER 6

Pretest

FUNDAMENTAL AND TECHNICAL ANALYSIS

1. The financial officer of the XYZ must calculate the company's EPS. The company earned $2,000,000 after taxes and preferred dividends. The company has 3,000,000 shares issued stock, and 1,000,000 shares are treasury stock. What is the EPS?
   a. $1 per share
   b. 67 cents per share
   c. Unable to determine without more information
   d. 75 cents per share

2. What is the balance sheet equation?
   a. Liabilities + assets = net worth
   b. Liabilities – assets = net worth
   c. Assets + liabilities = net worth
   d. Assets – liabilities = net worth

3. XYZ has EPS of a $2 a quarterly dividend of $.70 and is quoted in the marketplace at 20. What is the current yield?
   a. 10%
   b. 14%
   c. 3.5%
   d. 7%

4. Capitalization refers to:
   a. A corporation's assets
   b. The company's net worth
   c. The total amount of money invested in a company
   d. The sources and makeup of the company's financial picture

5. An investor who is taking a fundamental approach to investing would look at all of the following except:
   a. P/E ratio
   b. Support levels
   c. EBIT
   d. Debt service

6. A software company's stock has declined dramatically over the past year and has a high sort interest. A technical analyst would consider this:
   a. Bullish
   b. Bearish
   c. An indication that the stock price will remain flat
   d. Of no value

7. The risk, which is inherent in any investment, is called:
   a. Credit risk
   b. Call risk
   c. Timing risk
   d. Systematic risk

CHAPTER 7

Economic Fundamentals

INTRODUCTION

Economics, put simply, is the study of shortages: supply versus demand. As the demand for a product or service rises, the price of those products or services will tend to rise. Alternatively, if the provider of those goods or services tries to flood the market with those goods or services, the price will tend to decline as the supply outpaces the demand. The supply and demand model works for all goods and services including stocks, bonds, real estate, and money. Series 65 candidates will see a fair number of questions on economics.

GROSS DOMESTIC PRODUCT

A country's gross domestic product (GDP) measures the overall health of a nation's economy. The GDP is defined as the value of all goods and services produced in a country including consumption, investments, government spending, and exports minus imports during a given year.

Economists chart the health of the economy by measuring the country's GDP and by monitoring supply and demand models, along with the nation's business cycle. A country's economy is always in flux. Periods of increasing output are always followed by periods of falling output. The business cycle has four distinct stages:

1. Expansion
2. Peak

3. Contraction
4. Trough

EXPANSION

During an expansionary phase, an economy will see an increase in overall business activity and output. Corporate sales, manufacturing output, wages, and savings will all increase while the economy is expanding or growing. An economy cannot continue to grow indefinitely and GDP will top out at the peak in the business cycle. An economic expansion is characterized by:

- Increasing GDP
- Rising consumer demand
- Rising stock market
- Rising production
- Rising real estate prices

PEAK

As the economy tops out, the GDP reaches its maximum output for this cycle as wages, manufacturing, and savings all peak.

CONTRACTION

During a contraction, GDP falls, along with productivity, wages, and savings. Unemployment begins to rise, the stock market begins to fall, and corporate profits decline as inventories rise.

TROUGH

The economy bottoms out in the trough as GDP hits its lowest level for the cycle. As GDP bottoms out, unemployment reaches its highest level, wages bottom out, and savings bottom out. The economy is now poised to enter a new expansionary phase and start the cycle all over again.

RECESSION

A recession is defined as a period of declining GDP, which lasts at least six months or two quarters. Recessions may vary in degree of severity and in duration. Extended recessions may last up to 18 months and may be accompanied by steep downturns in economic output. In the most severe recessions falling prices erode businesses' pricing power, margins, and profits as deflation takes hold. Recessions are generally triggered by an overall decrease in spending by businesses and consumers. As businesses and consumers pull back spending, overall demand falls. Businesses and consumers will often reduce spending as a cautionary measure in response to an economic event or shock, such as a financial crises, or the busting of a bubble in an inflated asset class, such as real estate or the stock market.

DEPRESSION

A depression is characterized by a decline in GDP, which lasts at least 18 months or six consecutive quarters. GDP often falls by 10% or more during a depression. A depression is the most severe type of recession and is accompanied by extremely high levels of unemployment and frozen credit markets. The steep fall in demand is more likely to lead to deflation during a depression.

ECONOMIC INDICATORS

There are various economic activities that one can look at to try to identify where the economy is in the business cycle. An individual can also use these economic indicators as a way to try and predict the direction of the economy in the future. The three types of economic indicators are:

1. Leading indicators
2. Coincident indicators
3. Lagging indicators

LEADING INDICATORS

Leading indicators are business conditions that change prior to a change in the overall economy. These indicators can be used as a gauge for the future direction of the economy. Leading indicators include:

- Building permits
- Stock market prices
- Money supply (M2)
- New orders for consumer goods
- Average weekly initial claims in unemployment
- Changes in raw material prices
- Changes in consumer or business borrowing
- Average work week for manufacturing
- Changes in inventories of durable goods

COINCIDENT INDICATORS

Changes in the economy cause an immediate change in the activity level of coincident indicators. As the business cycle changes, the level of activity in coincident indicators can confirm where the economy is. Coincident indicators include:

- GDP
- Industrial production
- Personal income
- Employment
- Average number of hours worked
- Manufacturing and trade sales
- Nonagricultural employment

LAGGING INDICATORS

Lagging indicators will only change after the state of the economy has changed direction. Lagging indicators can be used to confirm the new direction of the economy. Lagging indicators include:

- Average duration of unemployment
- Corporate profits

- Labor costs
- Consumer debt levels
- Commercial and industrial loans
- Business loans

SCHOOLS OF ECONOMIC THOUGHT

The study of economics is a social science with many different schools of thought. Economics has been referred to as the dismal science as it is largely focused on the study of shortages. Economists all generally believe that low inflation and low unemployment are signs of a healthy economy. However, the different schools of economic thought believe that economic prosperity can be restored or maintained through very different approaches.

CLASSICAL ECONOMICS

The classical economic theory also known as supply side economics believes that lower taxes, and less government regulation will stimulate growth and increase demand through higher employment. Less regulation of business creates lower barriers to entry for employers and allows employers to produce goods at lower prices and to create more jobs. As a result of the lower prices, lower taxes and higher employment, aggregate demand in the economy will increase positively impacting the nation's gross domestic product.

KEYNESIAN ECONOMICS

John Maynard Keynes first published his theories on economic in 1936 during the great deprecation. The Keynesian Economic model believes that a mixed economy based on private and public sector efforts would produce desired economic conditions. Keynesians believe that the decisions made in the private sector can lead to supply and demand imbalances at that an active policy response form the public sector in the form of government spending (fiscal policy) and adjustments to the money supply (monetary policy) is required.

THE MONETARISTS

Economists who subscribe to monetary economics believe that the supply of money in the economy can influence the direction of the economy and prices as a whole. During times of low demand and high unemployment the economy can be stimulated by increasing the money supply. As more money enters the system interest rates fall increasing demand. As more money enters the system the value of the currency tends to decline and during times of expansionary monetary policy inflation may increase. Milton Friedman the founder of the monetarist movement believed that the main focus of central banks should be on price stability.

ECONOMIC POLICY

The government has two tools that it can use to try to influence the direction of the economy. Monetary policy, which is controlled by the Federal Reserve Board, determines the nation's money supply, while fiscal policy is controlled by the president and Congress and determines government spending and taxation.

TOOLS OF THE FEDERAL RESERVE BOARD

The Federal Reserve Board will try to steer the economy through the business cycle by adjusting the level of money supply and interest rates. The Fed may:

- Change the reserve requirement for member banks
- Change the discount rate charged to member banks
- Set target rates for federal fund loans
- Buy and sell U.S. government securities through open-market operations
- Change the amount of money in circulation
- Use moral suasion

RESERVE REQUIREMENT

Member banks must keep a percentage of their depositors' assets in an account with the Federal Reserve. This is known as the reserve requirement. The reserve requirement is intended to ensure that all banks maintain a certain level of liquidity. Banks are in business to earn a profit by lending money. As the bank accepts accounts from depositors, it pays them interest on their money. The bank, in turn, takes the depositors' money and loans it out at higher rates, earning the difference. If the Fed wanted to stimulate the economy, it might reduce the reserve requirement for the banks, which would allow the banks to lend more. By making more money available to borrowers, interest rates will fall and, therefore, demand will increase, helping to stimulate the economy. If the Fed wanted to slow down the economy, it might increase the reserve requirement. The increased requirement would make less money available to borrowers. Interest rates would rise as a result and the demand for goods and services would slow down. Changing the reserve requirement is the least-used Fed tool.

CHANGING THE DISCOUNT RATE

The Federal Reserve Board may change the discount rate in an effort to guide the economy through the business cycle. Remember, the discount rate is the rate that the Fed charges member banks on loans. This rate is highly symbolic, but as the Fed changes the discount rate, all other interest rates change with it. If the Fed wanted to stimulate the economy, it would reduce the discount rate. As the discount rate falls, all other interest rates fall with it, making the cost of money lower. The lower interest rate should encourage borrowing and demand to help stimulate the economy. If the Fed wanted to slow the economy down, it would increase the discount rate. As the discount rate increases, all other rates go up with it, raising the cost of borrowing. As the cost of borrowing increases, demand and the economy slow down.

FEDERAL OPEN MARKET COMMITTEE

The Federal Open Market Committee (FOMC) is the Fed's most flexible tool. The FOMC will buy and sell U.S. government securities in the secondary market in order to control the money supply. If the Fed wants to stimulate the economy and reduce rates, it will buy government securities. When the Fed buys the securities, money is instantly sent into the banking system. As the money flows into the banks, more money is available to lend. Because there is more money available, interest rates will go down and borrowing and demand should increase to stimulate the economy. If the Fed wants to slow the economy down it will sell U.S. government securities. When the Fed sells the securities, money flows from the banks and into the Fed, thus reducing the money supply. Because there is less money available to be loaned out, interest rates will increase, slowing borrowing and demand. This will have a cooling effect on the economy.

MONEY SUPPLY

Prior to determining an appropriate economic policy, economists must have an idea of the amount of money that is in circulation, along with the amount of other types of assets that will provide access to cash. Economists gauge the money supply using three measures. They are:

- M1
- M2
- M3

M1

M1 is the largest and most liquid measure of the nation's money supply and it includes:

- Cash
- Demand deposits (Checking accounts)

M2

Includes all the measures in M1 plus:

- Money market instruments
- Time deposits of less than $100,000
- Negotiable CDs exceeding $100,000
- Overnight repurchase agreements

M3

Includes all of the measures in M1 and M2 plus

- Time deposits greater than $100,000
- Repurchase agreements with maturities greater than 1 day

DISINTERMEDIATION

Disintermediation occurs when people take their money out of low yielding accounts offered by financial intermediaries or banks and invest money in higher yielding investments.

MORAL SUASION

The Federal Reserve Board often will use moral suasion as a way to influence the economy. The Fed is very powerful and very closely watched. By simply implying or expressing their views on the economy, they can slightly influence the economy.

Monetarists believe that a well-managed money supply, with an increasing bias, will produce price stability and will promote the overall economic health of the economy. Milton Friedman is believed to be the founder of the monetarist movement.

FISCAL POLICY

Fiscal policy is controlled by the president and Congress and determines how they manage the budget and government expenditures to help steer the economy through the business cycle. Fiscal policy may change the levels of:

- Federal spending
- Federal taxation
- Creation or use of federal budget deficits or surpluses

Fiscal policy assumes that the government can influence the economy by adjusting its level of spending and taxation. If the government wanted to stimulate the economy, it may increase spending. The assumption here is that as the government spends more, it will increase aggregate demand and, therefore, productivity. Additionally, if the government wanted to stimulate the economy, it may reduce the level of taxation. As the government reduces taxes, it leaves a larger portion of earnings for the consumers and businesses to spend. This should also have a positive impact on aggregate demand. Alternatively, if the government wanted to slow down the economy, it may reduce spending to lower the level of aggregate demand or raise taxes to reduce demand by taking money out of the hands of the consumers. John Maynard Keynes believed that it was the duty of the government to be involved with controlling the direction of the economy and the nation's overall economic health.

As both the Federal Reserve Board and the government monitor the overall health of the U.S. economy, they look at various indicators some of which are:

- Consumer price index
- Inflation/deflation
- Real GDP

CONSUMER PRICE INDEX (CPI)

The consumer price index is made up of a basket of goods and services that consumers most often use in their daily lives. The consumer price index is used to measure the rate of change in overall prices. A CPI that is rising would indicate that prices are going up and that inflation is present. A falling CPI would indicate that prices are falling and deflation is present.

INFLATION/DEFLATION

Inflation is the persistent increase in prices, while deflation is the persistent decrease in prices. Both economic conditions can harm a county's economy. Inflation will eat away at the purchasing power of the dollar and results in higher prices for goods and services. Deflation will erode corporate profits as weak demand in the market place drives prices for goods and services lower.

REAL GDP

Real GDP is adjusted for the effects of inflation or deflation over time. GDP is measured in constant dollars so that the gain or loss of the dollar's purchasing power will not show as a change in the overall productivity of the economy.

Both monetary policy and fiscal policy have a major effect on the stock market as a whole.

The following are bullish for the stock market:

- Falling interest rates
- Increasing money supply
- Increase in government spending
- Falling taxes

The following are bearish for the stock market:

- Increasing taxes
- Increasing interest rates
- Falling government spending
- Falling money supply

INTERNATIONAL MONETARY CONSIDERATIONS

The world has become a global marketplace. Each country's economy is affected to some degree by the economies of other countries. Currency values relative to other currencies will impact a country's international trade and the balance of payments. The amount of another country's currency that may be received for a country's domestic currency is known as the exchange rate. The balance of payments measures the net inflow (surplus) or outflow (deficit) of money. The largest component of the balance of payments is the balance of trade. As the exchange rates fluctuate, one country's goods may become more expensive, while another county's goods become less expensive. A weak currency benefits exporters, while a strong currency benefits importers.

CHAPTER 7

Pretest

ECONOMIC FUNDAMENTALS

1. During an inflationary period, the price of which one of the following will fall the most?
   a. Preferred stock
   b. Treasury bills
   c. Treasury bonds
   d. Common stock

2. All of the following are bullish for the stock market, except:
   a. Falling taxes
   b. Increasing government spending
   c. Increasing money supply
   d. Increasing interest rates

3. Economic theories believe all of the following to be true, except:
   a. As supply rises, price tends to fall.
   b. As supply rises, prices tend to rise.
   c. A moderately increasing money supply promotes price stability.
   d. As demand rises, price tends to rise.

4. Which one of the following interest rates is controlled by the Federal Reserve Board?
   a. Prime rate
   b. Federal funds rate
   c. Broker call loan rate
   d. Discount rate

5. All of the following indicate a downturn in the business cycle, except:
   a. Rising inventories
   b. High consumer debt
   c. Falling inventories
   d. Falling stock prices

6. A bank with a shortfall meeting their reserve requirement could borrow money from another bank and pay the:
   a. Federal funds rate
   b. Broker call loan rate
   c. Prime rate
   d. Discount rate

7. The government has two tools it can use to try to influence the direction of the economy; they are:
   a. Monetary policy and fiscal policy
   b. Prime rate policy and fiscal policy
   c. Monetary policy and prime rate policy
   d. Fiscal policy and money market policy

8. Fiscal policy is controlled by:
   I. President
   II. FOMC
   III. Congress
   IV. FRB
   a. I and IV
   b. I and II
   c. II and IV
   d. I and III

9. The Federal Reserve Board sets all of the following except:
   a. Monetary policy
   b. Reserve requirement
   c. Governmental spending
   d. Discount rate

10. A decline in the GDP must last at least how long to be considered a recession?
    a. Two quarters
    b. One quarter
    c. Six quarters
    d. Four quarters

CHAPTER 8

Recommendations, Professional Conduct, and Taxation

INTRODUCTION

All recommendations to customers must be suitable based upon the customer's investment objectives, their financial profile, and their attitudes toward investing. Advisers usually make verbal recommendations to customers. The adviser will review the customer's investment objective with them and offer facts to support their basis for the recommendation, as well as an explanation as to how the recommendation will help the customer meet their objectives. Any predictions about the performance of an investment should be stated strictly as an opinion or belief, not as a fact. If the firm uses reports that cite past performance of the firm's previous recommendations, the report must contain:

- Prices and dates when the recommendations were made
- General market conditions
- Recommendations in all similar securities for 12 months
- Statement disclosing that the firm is a market maker (if applicable)
- Statement regarding whether the firm or its officers or directors own any of the securities being recommended, or options, or warrants for the same security
- If the firm managed or comanaged an underwriting of any of the issuers securities in the last three years
- Statement regarding the availability of supporting documentation for the recommendations

While making a recommendation, an adviser may not:

- Guarantee or promise a profit or promise no loss
- Make false, misleading, or fraudulent statements
- Make unfair comparisons to dissimilar products

PROFESSIONAL CONDUCT BY INVESTMENT ADVISERS

The fiduciary duty of an investment adviser goes beyond that of a broker dealer. The investment adviser is required to develop a client profile when opening the client's account and must update it regularly as the client's needs change. Investment advisers have a fiduciary duty to provide only suitable advice to clients. Violations of state and federal laws may result in fines, expulsion from the state or industry, or a jail term. Investment advisers are expected to adhere to all of the rules and regulations set forth in the Investment Advisers Act of 1940, as well as all state and federal laws.

THE UNIFORM PRUDENT INVESTORS ACT OF 1994

The Uniform Prudent Investors Act of 1994 (UPIA) sets the basic standards by which all investment professionals acting in a fiduciary capacity must abide. The UPIA updates the requirements and definitions of prudent standards in light of the application of modern portfolio theory and the advancement in the understanding of the behavior of capital markets. The UPIA laid out five fundamental changes in the approach to prudent investing for investment professionals acting in a fiduciary capacity. Those changes are:

1. The main consideration of a fiduciary is the management and trade off between risk and reward.
2. The standard of prudence for each investment will be viewed in relationship to the overall portfolio rather than as a stand alone investment.
3. The rules regarding diversification have become part or the definition of prudent investing.
4. The restrictions from investing in various types of investments have been removed and the trustee may invest in anything that is appropriate in light of the objectives of the trust and in line with other requirements of prudent investing.

5. The rules against delegating the duties of the trustee have been removed and the trustee may now delegate investment functions subject to safeguards.

FAIR DEALINGS WITH CLIENTS

All investment advisers are required to act in good faith in all of their dealings with customers and are required to uphold just and equitable trade practices. An investment adviser may not employ or engage in:

- Churning
- Manipulative and deceptive practices
- Unauthorized trading
- Fraudulent acts
- Blanket recommendations
- Misrepresentations
- Omitting material facts
- Making guarantees
- Selling dividends
- Recommending speculative securities without knowing the customer can afford the risk
- Short-term trading in mutual funds
- Switching fund families
- Charging fees in excess of fees disclosed in the advisory contract

CHURNING

Many advisers are compensated when the customer makes a transaction based on their recommendation. Churning is a practice of making transactions that are excessive in size or frequency with the intention to generate higher commissions for the adviser. When determining if an account has been churned, regulators will look at the frequency of the transactions, size of the transactions, and the amount of commission earned by the representative. Customer profitability is not an issue when determining if an account has been churned.

In addition to churning where the agent or firm executes too many transactions to increase revenue, a practice known as reverse churning is also a violation. Reverse churning is the practice of placing inactive accounts or accounts that do not trade frequently into fee based programs that charge an annual fee based on the assets in the account. This fee covers all advice and execution charges. Since these inactive accounts do not trade frequently it will cause the total fees charged to the account to increase and makes a fee based account unsuitable for inactive accounts and for accounts that simply buy and hold securities for a long period of time. These accounts will generally be charged an annual fee in the range of 1–2 percent of the total value of the assets in lieu of commissions when orders are executed.

MANIPULATIVE AND DECEPTIVE DEVISES

It is a violation for an adviser to engage in or employ any artifice or scheme that is designed to gain an unfair advantage over another party. Some examples of manipulative or deceptive devises are:

- Capping
- Pegging
- Front running
- Trading ahead
- Painting the tape/matched purchases/matches sales

Capping: A manipulative act designed to keep a stock price from rising or to keep the price down.

Pegging: A manipulative act designed to keep a stock price up or to keep the price from falling.

Front Running: The entering of an order for the account of an agent or firm, prior to the entering of a large customer's order. The firm or agent is using the customer's order to profit on the order they entered for their own account.

Trading Ahead: The entering of an order for a security, based on the prior knowledge of a soon-to-be-released research report.

Painting the Tape: A manipulative act by two or more parties designed to create false activity in the security without any beneficial change in ownership. The increased activity is used to attract new buyers.

CUSTOMER COMPLAINTS

All written complaints received from a customer or from an individual acting on behalf of the customer must be reported promptly to the principal of the firm. The firm must maintain a separate customer complaint folder, even if it has not received any written customer complaints. If the firm's file contains complaints, the file must state what action was taken by the firm, if any, and it must disclose the location of the file containing any correspondence relating to the complaint. When a written complaint is received by mail or email, the customer who has issued the complaint must be notified that the complaint has been received. If a customer files a complaint and subsequently withdraws the complaint, the firm is still requested to maintain the correspondence relating to the complaint in the firm's complaint file.

UNAUTHORIZED TRADING

An unauthorized transaction is one that is made for the benefit of a customer's account at a time when the customer has no knowledge of the trade and the adviser does not have discretionary power over the account.

FRAUDULENT ACTS

Fraud is defined as any act that is employed to obtain an unfair advantage over another party. Fraudulent acts include:

- False statements
- Deliberate omissions of material facts
- Concealment of material facts
- Manipulative and deceptive practices
- Forgery
- Material omission
- Lying

BLANKET RECOMMENDATIONS

It is inappropriate for an adviser to make blanket recommendations in any security, especially low-priced speculative securities. No matter what type of investment is involved, a blanket recommendation to a large group of people will always be wrong for some investors. Different investors have different objectives and the same recommendation will not be suitable for everyone.

EXAMPLE

Mr. Jones, an agent with XYZ brokers, has a large customer base that ranges from young investors who are just starting to save to institutions and retirees. Mr. Jones has been doing a significant amount of research on WSIA industries, a mining and materials company. Mr. Jones strongly believes that WSIA is significantly undervalued based on its assets and earning potential. Mr. Jones recommends WSIA to all his clients. In the next six months, the share price of WSIA increases significantly as new production dramatically increases sales just as Mr. Jones' research suggested. The clients then sell WSIA at Mr. Jones' suggestion and realize a significant profit.

ANALYSIS

Even though the clients who purchased WSIA based on Mr. Jones' recommendation made a significant profit, Mr. Jones has still committed a violation because he recommended it to all of his clients. Mr. Jones' clients have a wide variety of investment objectives and the risk or income potential associated with an investment in WSIA would not be suitable for every client. Even if an investment is profitable for the client, it does not mean it was suitable for the client. Blanket recommendations are never suitable.

> **TAKENOTE!**
>
> An investment adviser who has discretion over client accounts may in certain circumstances be found to have made unsuitable blanket recommendations if the adviser purchases a significant amount of an illiquid security for large number of client accounts. This action could also be deemed to be market manipulation.

SELLING DIVIDENDS

Selling dividends is a violation that occurs when an adviser uses a pending dividend payment as the sole basis of their recommendation to purchase the stock or mutual fund. Additionally, using the pending dividend as a means to create urgency on the part of the investor to purchase the stock is a prime example of this type of violation. If the investor was to purchase the shares just prior to the ex-dividend date simply to receive the dividend, the investor, in many cases, will end up worse off. The dividend in this case will actually be a return of the money that the investor used to purchase the stock and then the investor will have a tax liability when they receive the dividend.

MISREPRESENTATIONS

An adviser may not knowingly make any misrepresentations regarding:

- Client's account status
- Representative
- Firm

- Investment
- Fees to be charged

OMITTING MATERIAL FACTS

A representative may not omit any material fact either good or bad when recommending a security. A material fact is one that an investor would need to know in order to make a well-informed investment decision. The adviser may, however, omit an immaterial fact.

GUARANTEES

No representative, broker dealer, or investment adviser may make any guarantees of any kind. A profit may not be guaranteed and a promise of no loss may not be made.

RECOMMENDING MUTUAL FUNDS

An adviser recommending a mutual fund should ensure that the mutual fund's investment objective meets the customer's investment objective. If the mutual fund company or broker dealer distributes advertising or sales literature regarding the mutual fund, the following should be disclosed:

- Highest sales charge charged by the fund
- Fund's current yield based on dividends only
- Graph performance of the fund versus a broad-based index
- Performance of the fund for 10 years or the life of the fund, whichever is less
- Not imply that a mutual fund is safer than other investments
- Source of graphs and charts

Based on the fees and CDSC a mutual fund with a front end load may be more suitable for an investor with a shorter holding period if all other suitability requirements have been met by both funds.

PERIODIC PAYMENT PLANS

When recommending or advertising a periodic payment plan, the following must be disclosed:

- A statement that a profit is not guaranteed.
- A statement that investors are not protected from a loss.

- A statement that the plan involves continuous investments, regardless of market conditions.

DISCLOSURE OF CLIENT INFORMATION

Investment advisers may not disclose any information regarding clients to a third party, without the client's expressed consent or without a court order. If the client is an issuer of securities and the broker dealer is an underwriter, transfer agent, or paying agent for the issuer, then the broker dealer is precluded from using the information it obtains, regarding the issuer's security holders, for its own benefit.

BORROWING AND LENDING MONEY

Borrowing and lending of money between registered persons and customers is strictly regulated. If the broker dealer allows borrowing and lending between representatives and customers the firm must have policies in place the will allow for the loans to be made. Loans may be made between an agent or a customer if the customer is a bank or other lending institution, where there is a personal or outside business relationship and that relationship is the basis for the loan or between to agents registered with the same firm.

DEVELOPING THE CLIENT PROFILE

Recommendations to an advisory client must be suitable based on the client's investment objective and client profile. The adviser should obtain enough information about the customer to ensure that their recommendations are suitable, based on a review of the client's:

- Investment objectives
- Financial status
- Income
- Investment holdings
- Retirement needs
- College and other major expenses
- Tax bracket
- Attitude toward investing

The more you know about a client's financial position, the better you will be able help them meet their objectives. You should always ask questions like:

- How long have you been making these types of investments?
- Do you have any major expenses coming up?
- How long do you usually hold investments?
- How much risk do you normally take?
- What tax bracket are you in?
- How much money do you have invested in the market?
- Have you done any retirement planning?
- How old are you?
- Are you married?
- Do you have any children?
- How long have you been employed at your current job?

Advisers, who help people invest to meet a specific objective, must make sure that their recommendations meet that client's objective. Should a person have a primary and a secondary objective, an adviser must make sure that the recommendation meets the investor's primary objective first and the secondary objective second. When developing the client's profile, advisers should also calculate the client's:

- Assets
- Liabilities
- Net worth
- Monthly discretionary cash flow or income

TYPES OF ADVISORY CLIENTS

When an adviser meets with a potential new client, the adviser must determine the legal structure under which the client operates. Clients may hold investments in their own name, jointly with a spouse, for the benefit of a minor or for someone who has been deemed mentally incompetent as follows:

THIRD-PARTY AND FIDUCIARY ACCOUNTS

A fiduciary account is one that is managed by a third party for the benefit of the account holder. The party managing the account has responsibility for making all of the investment decisions and other decisions relating to the account. The individual with this responsibility must act as a prudent person would and may not speculate. This is known as the prudent man rule. Many states have an approved list of securities known as the legal list that may be purchased by fiduciaries. The authority to transact business for the account must be evidenced in writing by a power of attorney. The fiduciary may have full power of attorney, also known as full discretion, under which the fiduciary may purchase and sell securities as well as withdraw cash and securities from the account. Under a limited power of attorney, or limited discretion, the fiduciary may only buy and sell securities and may not withdraw assets. The fiduciary has been legally appointed to represent the account holder and may not use the assets in the account for his or her own benefit. The fiduciary may, however, be reimbursed for expenses incurred in connection with the management of the account.

Examples of fiduciaries include:

- Administrators
- Custodians
- Receivers
- Trustees
- Conservators
- Executors
- Guardians
- Sheriffs/marshals

When opening a third-party or fiduciary account, the registered representative is required to obtain documentation of the individual's appointment and authority to act on behalf of the account holder. Trust accounts require that the representative obtain a copy of the trust agreement. The trust agreement will state who has been appointed as the trustee and any limitations on the trust's operation. Most trusts may only open cash accounts and may not purchase securities on margin unless specifically authorized to do so in the agreement. When opening an account for a guardian, the representative must obtain a copy of the court order appointing the guardian. The court order must be dated within 60 days of the opening of the account. If the court order is more than 60 days old, the representative may not open the account until a new court order is obtained. Guardians are usually appointed in cases of mentally incompetent adults and orphaned children.

TAKENOTE!

In the case of a person who is deemed mentally incompetent, the registered representative will need a certificate of incumbency dated within 60 days of the account opening.

UNIFORM GIFTS TO MINORS ACT (UGMA)

Minors are not allowed to own securities in their own name because they are not of age to enter into legally binding contracts. The decision to purchase or sell a security creates a legally binding contract between two parties. The Uniform Gifts to Minors Act (UGMA) regulates how accounts are operated for the benefit of minors. All UGMA accounts must have:

- One custodian
- One minor
- UGMA and the state in the account title
- Assets registered to the child's name after he or she reaches the age of majority

All securities in a UGMA account will be registered in the custodian's name as the nominal owner for the benefit of the minor, who is the beneficial owner of the account. For example, the account should be titled: Mr. Jones as custodian for Billy Jones under New Jersey Uniform Gifts to Minors Act.

Only one custodian and one minor are allowed on each account. A husband and wife could not be joint custodians for their minor child. If there is more than one child, a separate account must be opened for each. The same person may serve as custodian on several accounts for several minors, and the minor may have more than one account established by different custodians. The donor of the security does not have to be the custodian for the account, and if neither of the parents are the custodian of the account, they have no authority over the account.

RESPONSIBILITIES OF THE CUSTODIAN

The custodian has a fiduciary duty to manage the account prudently for the benefit of the minor child within certain guidelines. Such as:

- No margin accounts
- No high-risk securities, such as penny stocks

- Custodian may not borrow from the account
- No commodities
- No speculative option strategies
- Custodian may not give discretion to a third party
- All distributions must be reinvested within a reasonable time
- Custodian may not let rights or warrants expire; they must be exercised or sold
- Custodian must provide support for all withdrawals from the account
- Withdrawals may only be made to reimburse the custodian for expenses incurred in connection with the operation of the account or for the benefit of the minor

CONTRIBUTIONS TO AN UGMA ACCOUNT

Gifts of cash and securities or other property may be given to the minor. There is no dollar limit as to the size of the gift that may be given. The limit on the size of the tax-free gift is $14,000 per year. An individual may give gifts valued at up to $14,000 to any number of people each year without incurring a tax liability. Once a gift has been given, it is irrevocable. Gifts to an UGMA account carry an indefeasible title and may not be taken back for any reason. The custodian may, however, use the assets for the minor's welfare and educational needs.

UGMA TAXATION

The minor is responsible for the taxes on the account. However, any unearned income that exceeds $1,500 per year will be taxed at the parents' marginal tax rate if the child is younger than 14 years. For gifts that exceed $14,000 per year, the tax liability is on the donor of the gift, not on the minor.

DEATH OF A MINOR OR CUSTODIAN

If the minor dies, the account becomes part of the minor's estate. It does not automatically go to the parents. If the custodian dies, a court or the donor may appoint a new custodian.

Additional types of advisory clients include the following entities:

- A sole proprietorship

- A C corporation
- An S corporation
- A partnership
- A limited partnership
- A family limited partnership
- A Limited Liability Company LLC
- A trust (discussed in detail later in this chapter)

Corporations are their own legal entities with perpetual life independent from their owners. How the corporation is taxed depends upon how the corporation is organized. C corporations are taxed at the corporate rate independent from the owners' tax rates. An S corporation allows the income to flow though to the owners and to be taxed as ordinary income. No more than 100 people can own an S corporation and the S corporation must be organized as a domestic corporation.

Partnerships are an association of two or more people who are either in business together or who hold assets in a partnership. The partnership agreement will detail each partner's ownership interest and authority to act on behalf of the partnership.

A limited partnership consists of at least one general partner and one or more limited partners. It is the duty of the general partner to manage the partnership in accordance with the partnerships objectives. The limited partners put up the investment capital required but may not exercise management or control over the partnership.

A family limited partnership is often used for estate planning. Parents may place significant assets into a family limited partnership as a way to transfer their ownership. Usually, the parents will act as the general partners and will transfer limited partnership interests to their children. As the interests are transferred to the children, the parents may become subject to gift taxes. However, the gift taxes usually will be lower than they would have suffered without the partnership.

A Limited Liability Company combines the limited liability of a C corporation with the benefit of the tax advantages of a partnership. The LLC will pass through of income without being taxed at the LLC level just like a partnership. The owners of the LLC are classified as members of the LLC not as shareholders and are not personally liable for the debts of the LLC.

INVESTMENT OBJECTIVES

All investors want to make or preserve money. There are, however, different ways to achieve these objectives. Some of the different investment objectives are:

- Income
- Growth
- Preservation of capital
- Tax benefits
- Liquidity
- Speculation

INCOME

Many investors are looking to have their investments generate additional income to help meet their monthly expenses. Some investments that will help to meet that objective are:

- Corporate bonds
- Municipal bonds
- Government bonds
- Preferred stocks
- Money market funds
- Bond funds

GROWTH

Investors who are seeking capital appreciation over time want their money to grow in value and are not seeking any current income. The only investments that will achieve this goal are:

- Common stock
- Common stock fund

PRESERVATION OF CAPITAL

People who have preservation of capital as an investment objective are very conservative investors and are more concerned with keeping the money they have saved. For these investors, high-quality debt will be an appropriate recommendation. Some choices are:

- Money market funds
- Government bonds
- Municipal bonds
- High-grade corporate bonds

TAX BENEFITS

For investors seeking tax advantages, the only two possible recommendations are:

- Municipal bonds
- Municipal bond funds

LIQUIDITY

Investors who need immediate access to their money need to own liquid investments that will not fluctuate wildly in value, in case they need to use the money. The following is a list from the most liquid to the least liquid:

- Money market fund
- Stocks/bonds/mutual funds
- Annuities
- CMOs
- Direct participation programs
- Real estate

SPECULATION

A customer investing in a speculative manner is willing to take a high degree of risk in order to earn a high rate of return. Some of the more speculative investments are:

- Penny stocks
- Small cap stocks
- Some growth stocks
- Junk bonds

CAPITAL ASSET PRICING MODEL (CAPM)

The capital asset pricing model (also known as CAPM) operates under the assumption that investors are risk averse. Investors who take on risk through the purchase of an investment must be compensated for that risk through a higher expected rate of return known as the risk premium. A security's risk is measured by its beta. Therefore, securities with higher betas must offer investors a higher expected return in order for the investor to be compensated for taking on the additional risk associated with that investment.

RISK VS. REWARD

Risk is the reciprocal of reward. An investor must be offered a higher rate of return for each unit of additional risk the investor is willing to assume. There are many types of risk involved with investing money. They are as follows:

- Capital risk
- Market risk
- Nonsystematic risk
- Legislative risk
- Timing risk
- Credit risk
- Reinvestment risk
- Call risk
- Liquidity risk

CAPITAL RISK

Capital risk is the risk that an investor may lose all or part of the capital they have invested. Investors who purchase securities are not assured of the return of their invested principal.

MARKET RISK

Market risk is also known as a systematic risk and it is the risk that is inherent in any investment in the markets. For example, you could own stock in the greatest company in the world and you could still lose money because the value of your stock is going down, simply because the market as a whole is going down.

NONSYSTEMATIC RISK

Nonsystematic risk is the risk that pertains to one company or industry. For example, the problems that the tobacco industry faced a few years ago would not have affected a computer company.

LEGISLATIVE RISK

Legislative risk is the risk that the government will do something that adversely affects your investment. For example, beer manufacturers probably did not fare too well when the government enacted prohibition.

TIMING RISK

Timing risk is simply the risk that an investor will buy and sell at the wrong time and will lose money as a result.

CREDIT RISK

Credit risk is the risk of default inherent in debt securities. An investor may lose all or part of their money because the issuer has defaulted and cannot pay the interest or principal payments owed to the investor.

REINVESTMENT RISK

When interest rates decline and higher yielding bonds have been called or have matured, investors will not be able receive the same return given the same amount of risk. This is reinvestment risk and the investor is forced to either accept the lower rate or must take more risk to obtain the same rate.

INTEREST RATE RISK

Interest rate risk is the risk that the price of bonds will fall as interest rates increase. As interest rate rise, the value of existing bonds fall and may subject the bondholder to a loss if they need to sell the bond.

CALL RISK

Call risk is the risk that, as interest rates decline, higher yielding bonds and preferred stocks will be called and investors will be forced to reinvest the proceeds at a lower rate of return or at a higher rate of risk to achieve the same return. Call risk only applies to preferred stocks and bonds with a call feature.

OPPORTUNITY RISK

Investors who hold long-term bonds until maturity must forgo the opportunities to invest that money in other potentially higher yielding investments.

LIQUIDITY RISK

Liquidity risk is the risk that an investor will not be able to liquidate their investment when they need to or that they will not be able to liquidate their investment without adversely affecting the price.

ALPHA

A stock's or portfolio's alpha is its projected independent rate of return or the difference between an investment's expected (benchmark) return and its actual return. Portfolio managers whose portfolios have positive alphas are adding value through their asset selection. The outperformance as measured by alpha indicates the portfolio manager is adding additional return for each unit of risk taken on in the portfolio.

BETA

A stock's beta is its projected rate of change relative to the market as a whole. If the market was up 10% for the year, a stock with a beta of 1.5 could reasonably be expected to be up 15%. A stock with a beta greater than one has a higher level of volatility than the market as a whole and is considered to be more risky than the overall market. A stock with a beta of less than one is less volatile than prices in the overall market and is considered to be less risky. An example of a low beta stock would be a utility stock. The price of utility stocks does not tend to move dramatically. A security's beta measures its nondiversifiable or systematic risk. For each incremental unit of risk an investor takes on, they must be compensated with additional expected returns. If the portfolio's actual return exceeds that of its expected return, the portfolio has generated excess returns. The Sharpe ratio can measure a portfolio's risk-adjusted return. If two portfolios both return 8%, but Portfolio A contains dramatically more risk than Portfolio B, then Portfolio B is a much better investment choice. The Sharpe ratio will tell an investor how well they are being compensated for the investment risk they are assuming. The Sharpe ratio takes the portfolio's return and subtracts the risk-free return offered on short-term Treasury bills (usually 90 days) to determine the level of return that the investor earned over the risk-free return. The risk premium then is divided by the portfolio's standard deviation. The Sharpe ratio appears as follows:

Sharpe ratio = (R – RFR)/SD

Series 65 candidates will have to be able to identify the Sharpe ratio, but most likely will not be required to calculate it. The degree to which a portfolio's performance is designed to mirror the return of a standard benchmark or index is measured by R-squared. If the portfolio has 100% of its assets tied to the index such as in an index fund, the portfolio will have an R-squared reading of 100 and the performance of the portfolio will mirror the performance of the index. The higher the R-squared reading for the portfolio, the higher the degree of correlation to the index. R-squared values range from 0 to 100 with the lower values having lower correlation to the index. A portfolio with a higher R-squared value will have a more accurate beta coefficient and as a result the volatility of the portfolio will be more predictable.

TAKENOTE!

Beta measures systematic risk in the price volatility of a security relative to the market as whole. Standard deviation measures both systematic and unsystematic risk in the volatility of the return of a security versus its expected return.

EXPECTED RETURN

Modern portfolio managers try to manage risk and evaluate investments by employing a variety of concepts under modern portfolio theory. Modern portfolio theory states that the expected rate of return for an investment is the sum of its weighted returns. An investment's weighted return is its possible return multiplied by the likelihood of that return being realized. The following table details the expected return for XYZ:

Opinion	Expected Return	Probability of Expected Return	Weighted Return
Outperform	20%	25%	5%
Market perform	10%	50%	5%
Underperform	5%	25%	1.25%
Expected return			11.25%

The following table details the expected return for ABC:

Opinion	Expected Return	Probability of Expected Return	Weighted Return
Outperform	40%	10%	4%
Market perform	20%	70%	14%
Underperform	(33.75%)	20%	(6.75%)
Expected return			11.25%

Notice that the expected rate of return for both XYZ and ABC is 11.25%. However, an investment in XYZ contains less risk than an investment in ABC because the distribution of potential returns is not as wide as the distribution of potential returns for ABC. An investor who is considering investing in either XYZ or ABC would consider the 11.25% expected return offered by XYZ to be more attractive than the same expected return offered by ABC. The distribution of an investment's varying expected returns is measured by the investment's standard deviation. The wider the distribution of an investment's expected returns, the greater its standard deviation. Investments with higher standard deviations contain more risk than investments with lower standard deviations. As an investment's results are plotted over time, there is a 95% chance that its actual return will be within two standard deviations of its expected return and a 67% chance that it will be within one standard deviation of its expected return. Portfolio managers will use computer simulations to examine the possibilities of various portfolio strategies. The Monte Carlo simulation is one such simulation used by portfolio managers.

TIME VALUE OF MONEY

As time progresses, inflation eats away at the value or the purchasing power of the dollar. That is to say that a dollar today is worth more than a dollar tomorrow.

Investors can determine the future value of a sum invested if they know the interest rate, the time horizon, and the compounding schedule. The future value of a sum invested today can be determined by using the following formula:

$$\mathbf{FV = PV\ (1 + R)^T}$$

FV = Future value
PV = Present value
R = Interest rate
T = Number of compounding periods for which the money will be invested

EXAMPLE

FV = ?
PV = $1,000
R = 5%
T = 5 years compounded annually

$$\mathbf{FV = \$1,000\ (1 + .05)^5}$$

$$\mathbf{FV = \$1,000\ (1.276)}$$

$$\mathbf{FV = \$1,276}$$

The future value of the investment will increase as the number of compounding periods increases. Let's look at what would happen to the same investment of $1,000 for five years at 5% if the interest was compounded semiannually. Everything would remain the same except T would be 10 and the interest rate for each semiannual period would be half the annual rate. In this example, we get:

$$\mathbf{FV = \$1,000\ (1 + .025)^{10}}$$

$$\mathbf{FV = \$1,000\ (1.28)}$$

$$\mathbf{FV = \$1,280}$$

More compounding periods increase the investor's total return.

An investor can also determine the present value a future payment by using the following formula:

$$\mathbf{PV = FV/(1 + R)^T}$$

An investor can also use the present value formula to determine how much they would have to invest today to have a given sum of money in the future. For example, let's say that an investor wants to have $10,000 saved for their child's college tuition five years from now. If the investor knows that they can receive 6% on their money, they can determine how much they must invest today. The present value of $10,000 five years from now at a 6% rate is found as follows:

$$PV = \frac{\$10,000}{(1 + .06)^5}$$

$$PV = \frac{\$10,000}{1.338}$$

$$PV = \$7,473$$

The investor would have to invest $7,473 today at a 6% rate to have $10,000 five years from now. Investors can also use the present value and future value to determine an investment's internal rate of return through a process call iteration. The internal rate of return or IRR takes into consideration the time value of money and all of the future cash flows generated by an investment. The IRR is the annualized effective compound rate of return. When evaluating an investment in a debt security the IRR is equal to the bond's yield to maturity. An investor would not use an IRR calculation to evaluate an investment in an equity security because dividends may be stopped or reduced and equity securities have no maturity date. The IRR is the discount rate that results in the future value and the present value being equal. The higher the IRR the more attractive the investment. Portfolio managers and business operators can use the IRR calculation to measure an investment's or project's IRR against their desired rate of return to determine if the investment meets their requirements. Series 65 candidates will not have to calculate an investment's internal rate of return.

WEIGHTED RETURNS

An investor who is evaluating the performance of a portfolio manager must take into consideration the impact that any contributions or withdrawals made by the investor will have on the overall performance of the account. In evaluating the performance of a manager who is overseeing an account where the investor will be making contributions and withdrawals, the investor should evaluate the performance by using the dollar weighted return method. The dollar weighted return method can be used to determine the IRR of the portfolio taking into consideration the cash flows in and out of the account. If the investor will not be making additional contributions to or making withdrawals from the account the investor may use the time weighted return method to determine the IRR of the portfolio.

ADDITIONAL WAYS TO MEASURE RETURNS

In addition to the weighted returns discussed above to provide additional and comparable return data investors may look at the total return, the holding period return and the annualized return.

Total Return: To determine the total return of an investment all dividend or interest cash flow must be taken into consideration. If the investment has increased in value, the sum of the cash flow is added to any capital appreciation. The addition of the cash flow will cause the total return to be higher. If the security has fallen in value the total of the cash flow may partially or totally offset the loss of value of the security in question.

Holding Period Return: The holding period for a security may be very long or very short depending on the investor. Some investors hold securities for years while others may only hold securities for a few days or less. The total return from any cash flow plus or minus any capital appreciation or depreciation realized during the time the investment was held equals the holding period return.

Annualized Return: Once the holding period return has been calculated it can then be used to determine the annualized rate of return. An investment's annualized rate of return will allow investors to compare the investment's return against the performance of relevant benchmarks. If a security was held for less than 1 year its results would have to be multiplied to determine an annualized rate of return. If the holding period was more than 1 year the results would have to be divided to determine the annualized rate of return. Examples of total return, holding period return and annualized return appear as follows:

EXAMPLE

SIA common stock appreciated 8% over an 18-month period and paid a 2 percent cash dividend over the 18 months

The total return in the this case would be 10 percent found by adding the to 2 percent in cash flow to the 8 percent appreciation

The holding period return would be 10 percent over the 18 months during which the investment was held.

The annualized return would be 6.66 percent found by dividing the 10 percent return by 1.5 as 18 months equals 1.5 years.

10 / 1.5 = 6.66

MODERN PORTFOLIO THEORY

As money management developed over the last century, analysts began to shift their focus from the returns available from individual investments to the returns available from an entire portfolio. This approach became known as the modern portfolio theory. The modern portfolio theory is based on the concept that investors are risk adverse. Through diversification of investments and asset classes, portfolios can be constructed with higher levels of expected return for each unit of risk assumed. Asset classes are divided into three main categories: stocks, bonds, and cash and cash equivalents. Through the modern portfolio theory, portfolio managers can construct portfolios based on various allocations over the three main asset classes whose return will be the greatest given each unit of risk. This level of optimal performance is known as the efficient frontier. Any portfolio whose returns are expected to be less than optimal are said to be operating behind the efficient frontier. Optimal portfolio performance will be achieved by constructing a portfolio whose securities prices move independently of one another or whose prices move inversely to one another.

Allocating a client's assets over various asset classes to achieve a given investment objective is known as strategic asset allocation. As the investment results of the different asset classes vary over time, the assets may have to be rebalanced. Asset rebalancing can be divided into two categories: systematic rebalancing and active rebalancing. Systematic rebalancing is designed to keep the original asset allocation model in place. For example, if a client's portfolio is designed to be 70%/25%/5% in stocks, bonds, and cash respectively, as the percentages shift, the portfolio manager would rebalance the assets to maintain the original percentages. Systematic rebalancing can be done at regular intervals such as quarterly or whenever the asset allocation shifts by a certain percentage, such as by 5% or more. Active rebalancing assumes that a portfolio manager can effectively shift the asset allocation to take advantage of shifts in the performance of the various asset classes. If an investor has the same original portfolio allocation (70%/25%/5%) and the portfolio manager thought that the bond market would outperform all other investments, they may use tactical rebalancing to rebalance as 40%/55%/5%. Alternatively, investors may elect to employ a buy-and-hold strategy and let the allocations go where they may. This buy-and-hold strategy would reduce transaction costs and tax consequences.

PREDICTING PORTFOLIO INCOME

Investors especially in retirement want to know how long their money will last given the fact they need to draw down on their savings to support their lifestyle. On the exam you may be required to estimate the amount of time it will take to exhaust the principal in an investment account given a certain interest rate and a fixed withdrawal. Since students do not receive financial calculators the number of years must be approximated by calculating the interest based on the declining balance and working the numbers out over time.

EXAMPLE

An investor who has saved $200,000 and is about to retire next year places the money in an account with a fixed interest rate of 4 percent. The investor wants to take out $20,000 at the beginning of each year starting at retirement. Given the principal, interest rate and withdrawal rate how long will the money last? The answer is approximately 14 years. At the end of 14 years the account will have slightly over $60 remaining.

Year	Withdrawal	Beginning Balance	Interest / Growth	Ending Balance
1	0	$200,000	$8,000	$208,000
2	$20,000	$188,000	$7,520	$195,520
3	$20,000	$175,250	$7,010	$182,260
4	$20,000	$162,260	$6,490	$168,750
5	$20,000	$148,750	$5,950	$154,700
6	$20,000	$134,700	$5,388	$140,088
7	$20,000	$120,088	$4,803	$124,891
8	$20,000	$104,891	$4,195	$109,086
9	$20,000	$89,086	$3,563	$92,649
10	$20,000	$72,649	$2,905	$75,554
11	$20,000	$55,554	$2,222	$57,776
12	$20,000	$37,776	$1,511	$39,287
13	$20,000	$19,287	$771	$20,058
14	$20,000	$58	$2.32	$60.32

PERPETUAL INCOME ACCOUNTS

An investor may wish to establish a fixed income for themselves, their spouse, a child or a grandchild with the objective of providing the income forever. An account may be established to provide perpetual income or income in perpetuity based on some simple calculations. If the investor knows the desired income level to be provided and that interest rate the account will generate, the lump sum needed to fund the account may be calculated. To determine the lump sum needed divide the annual income benefit by the annual interest rate.

EXAMPLE

If an investor wanted to generate a monthly income of $2,00 in perpetuity the annual income benefit would be $24,000. If the investor was placing the money in an account with a fixed rate of 6 percent the investor would have to place $400,000 in the account found as follows

$24,000 / .06 = $400,000

THE RULE OF 72

The Rule of 72 will tell an investor how many years it will take for the principal of an account to double in value. The rule of 72 assumes that the interest or earnings of the account are compounded. An investor who knows the interest rate that will be earned can simply divide 72 by that number to determine how long it will take the principal to double.

EXAMPLE

An investor who has $10,000 invested at an annual rate of 8% would like to know when the value of the account will reach $20,000. The answer is found by simply dividing 72 by the interest are of 8 percent as follows

72 / 8 = 9 years

The rule of 72 can also be used to calculate the rate of return on an investment given an initial value and a current value over time. If an investor placed $10,000 in to an account 12 years ago and the value of that account has grown to $40,000, the value has doubled twice. The compound rate of return can be found by dividing 72 by the amount of time it took for the account to double once. Since the account doubled twice in 12 years, it therefore doubled once in 6 years.

72 / 6 = 12%

TAX STRUCTURE

There are two types of taxes: progressive and regressive. A progressive tax levies a larger tax on higher income earners. Examples of progressive taxes are:

1. Income taxes
2. Estate taxes

Regressive taxes level the same tax rate on everyone, regardless of their income. As a result, a larger portion of the lower income earner's earnings will go toward the tax. Examples of regressive taxes are:

- Sales taxes
- Property taxes
- Gasoline taxes
- Excise taxes

INVESTMENT TAXATION

Investors must be aware of the impact that federal and state taxes will have on their investment results. A taxable event will occur in most cases when an investor:

- Sells a security at a profit
- Sells a security at a loss
- Receives interest or dividend income

CALCULATING GAINS AND LOSSES

When an investor sells their shares, in most cases, they will have a capital gain or loss. In order to determine if there is a gain or loss, the investor must first calculate their cost basis or cost base. An investor's cost base, in most cases, is equal to the price they paid for the shares, plus any commissions or fees paid in connection with the purchase. An investor's holding period begins the day after the purchase date and ends on the day of sale. Once an investor knows their cost base, calculating any gain or loss becomes easy. A capital gain is realized when the investor sells the shares at a price that is greater than their cost base.

EXAMPLE

An investor who purchased a stock at $10 per share three years ago and receives $14 per share when they sell the shares has a $4 capital gain that is found by subtracting the cost base from the sales proceeds: $14 – $10 = $4. If the investor had 1,000 shares, they would have a $4,000 capital gain.

An investor's cost base is always returned to them tax free. A capital loss is realized when the investor sells the shares at a price that is less than their cost base. If the investor in the previous example were to have sold the shares at $8 instead of $14, the investor would have a $2 capital loss or a total capital loss of $2,000 for the entire position.

Again this is found by subtracting the cost base from the sales proceeds: $8 – $10 = –$2.

Capital gains and losses are further classified as short-term or long-term capital gains or losses. Any gain or loss on an investment held for less than one year is classified as a short-term gain or loss. A short-term capital gain will be taxed as ordinary income. Long-term capital gains on assets held for more than one year will be taxed at a maximum rate of 15%. (This rule is subject to change.)

COST BASE OF MULTIPLE PURCHASES

Investors who have been accumulating shares through multiple purchases must determine their cost base at the time of sale through one of the following methods:

- First in, first out (FIFO)
- Share identification
- Average cost

FIRST IN, FIRST OUT (FIFO)

If the investor does not identify which shares are being sold at the time of sale, the IRS will assume that the first shares that were purchased are the first shares that are sold under the FIFO method. In many cases, this will result in the largest capital gain and as a result, the investor will have the largest tax liability.

SHARE IDENTIFICATION

At the time of the sale, an investor may specify which shares are being sold. By keeping a record of the purchase prices and the dates that the shares were purchased, the investor may elect to sell the shares that create the most favorable tax consequences.

AVERAGE COST

An investor may decide to sell shares based on their average cost. An investor must determine their average cost by using the following formula:

Average cost = total dollars invested/total shares purchased

Once an investor has elected to use the average cost method to calculate gains and losses, they may not change the method without IRS approval.

DEDUCTING CAPITAL LOSSES

An investor may use capital losses to offset capital gains dollar for dollar in the year in which they are realized. A net capital loss may be used to reduce the investor's taxable ordinary income by up to $3,000 in the year in which it is realized. Any net capital losses that exceed $3,000 may be carried forward into future years and may be deducted at a rate of $3,000 from ordinary income every year until the loss is used up. If the investor has a capital gain in subsequent years, the investor may use the entire amount of the net capital loss remaining to offset the gain up to the amount of the gain.

WASH SALES

An investor may not sell a security at a loss and, shortly after, repurchase the security (or a security that is substantially the same) to reestablish the position, if they intend to claim the loss for tax purposes and deduct the loss from their ordinary income. This is known as a wash sale and the IRS will disallow the loss. In order to claim the loss, the investor has to have held the securities for 30 days and must wait at least 30 days before repurchasing the same securities or securities that are substantially the same. The total number of days in the wash sale rule is 61.

✓	Holding period	30 days
✓	Sale date	1 day
✓	Waiting period	30 days
✓	Total	61 days

Securities that are substantially the same are call options, rights, warrants, and convertibles.

TAXATION OF INTEREST INCOME

Interest earned by investors may or may not be subject to taxes. The following table illustrates the tax consequences of various interest payment received by investors:

Resident	Investment	Taxation
New Jersey	Corporate bond	All taxes
New Jersey	CMO	All taxes
New Jersey	GNMA	All taxes
New Jersey	T-bond	Federal taxes only
New Jersey	New York muni bond	New Jersey taxes only
New Jersey	New Jersey muni bond	No taxes
New Jersey	Puerto Rico/Guam muni	No taxes

TAKENOTE!

An investor may deduct margin interest only to the extent of their investment income. An investor may not deduct margin expenses from municipal bonds.

INHERITED AND GIFTED SECURITIES

If an investor dies and leaves securities to another person, that person's cost base for those securities is the fair market value of the securities on the day the decedent died. The cost base of the original investor does not transfer to the person who inherited the securities. Any capital gain on the sale of inherited securities will be considered long term. If, during the course of an investor's life, they give securities to another person, the recipient will have two cost bases. Their cost base for determining a capital gain will be the giver's cost base; their cost base for determining a capital loss will be the giver's cost base or the fair market value of the securities on the day the gift was made, whichever is less.

DONATING SECURITIES TO CHARITY

An investor who donates securities to a charity will receive a tax deduction equal to the value of the securities. If the investor has an unrealized gain and has held the securities for more than 12 months, the investor will not owe any taxes on the appreciation. If the securities were held less than 12 months, the investor will be responsible for taxes on the appreciation. The recipient's cost base will be equal to the value of the securities on the day they received the gift.

TRUSTS

Trusts may be revocable or irrevocable. With a revocable trust, the individual who established the trust and contributes assets to the trust, known as the grantor or settlor, may, as the name suggests, revoke the trust and take the assets back. The income generated by a revocable trust is generally taxed as income to the grantor. If the trust is irrevocable, the grantor may not revoke the trust and take the assets back. With an irrevocable trust, the trust usually pays the taxes as its own entity or the beneficiaries of the trust are taxed on the income they receive. If the trust is established as a simple trust all income generated by the trust must be distributed to the beneficiaries in the year the income is earned. If the trust is established as a complex trust the trust may retain some or all of the income earned and the trust will pay taxes on the income that is not distributed to the beneficiaries. The grantor of an irrevocable trust is generally not taxed on the income generated by the trust unless the assets in the trust are held for the benefit of the grantor, the grantor's spouse, or if the grantor has an interest in the income of the trust of greater than 5 percent. While most trusts are established during a person's life time (known as an inter vivos trust) a trust may also be established to hold or to distribute assets after a person's death under the terms of their Will. Trusts that are established under the terms of a Will are known as Testamentary trusts. All assets placed into a Testamentary trust are subject to both estate taxes and probate. Trusts can be established to both protect assets from legal claims as well as for estate tax planning purposes. A bypass trust is one that is established to reduce the tax liability of an estate left to beneficiaries other than a spouse, such as to children. The bypass trust allows the grantor to take advantage of the life time estate tax exclusion and allows individuals with significant wealth to reduce the tax burden to their heirs. A generational skipping trust is a type of bypass trust that is established for the benefit of relatives more distant than one generation from the grantor such as grand children or great grandchildren. This type of bypass trust will allow assets to be passed on to grandchildren without first being passed to their parents and without potentially being taxed again upon their parents death. Assets left to grandchildren or unrelated persons more than 37.5 years younger than the grantor may be subject to a generation skipping transfer tax (GSTT).

EXAMPLE A grantor established generational skipping trust to provide income to his children during their lifetime and leaving the principal to the grandchildren upon the death of his children. Upon the death of the children the grandchildren would inherit the principal sometimes known as the corpus or body of the trust. At the time the grandchildren inherit the principal and the money would be subject to the generational skipping transfer tax. The trustee is responsible for paying the GSTT.

An additional benefit of the generational skipping trust is it will allow for the assets to appreciate over time without triggering additional tax liability. If a grantor funds the trust with assets in an amount under the estate tax exclusion limit and the assets in the trust appreciate over time past the estate tax exclusion limit after the grantor's death the assets will not be subject to estate taxes. A grantor retained annuity trust (GRAT) is yet one more way a trust can be established and used for estate planning. With this trust the grantor places assets into the trust with the intention of drawing an income from the trust as an annuity payment for a set number of years. Upon the grantor's death the remainder of the principal will be left to the beneficiaries. The IRS determines the value of the gift to be the estimated value of the remainder based on IRS discount models. If the account earns more than this rate the extra income will be added to the remaining principal left to the beneficiaries.

Trust taxation can be a complex matter. The income tax rate for net income received and retained by trusts can be subject to a very high rate of taxation and a relatively low level of net income. To avoid the high tax rate most trusts will be set up to distribute net income to the beneficiaries and the distribution will be taxable as income to the beneficiary. Should one of the beneficiaries to a trust die that person's interest in the trust will usually pass to his or her children known as their issue per stirpes

Trust and estates that retain net income must report that income to the IRS on form 1041.

> **TAKENOTE!**
>
> Capital gains on assets that are sold and reinvested as principal in the trust are not taxable to the trust and are not considered part of net income to the trust.

GIFT TAXES

When gifts are made to family members or others individuals, the donor does not receive any tax deduction. The donor's cost base will transfer to the recipient for tax purposes. Individuals may give gifts of up to $14,000 per person per year without incurring any tax liability. If a gift in excess of $14,000 is given to an individual, the donor owes the gift tax. Gifts to charity are always tax free, as is paying someone's educational expenses or medical expenses.

TAKENOTE!

A husband and wife may give up to $28,000 per year per person. The IRS considers half of the gift to be coming from each spouse. The annual gift limit is indexed for inflation since 1999.

ESTATE TAXES

Individuals (rule and amount subject to debate and change) may leave an estate of $5,000,000 without subjecting the beneficiaries to estate taxes. There is an unlimited marital deduction or unified credit that allows surviving spouses to inherit the entire estate tax free. An individual's gross estate includes all of the assets they owned at the time of death, including assets placed in any revocable trusts. Assets placed in an irrevocable trust are excluded from the individual's estate. Certain items will be added to the individual's gross estate including:

- Assets transferred within three years of death
- Annuity payouts payable to the estate or heirs
- Life insurance

The following are deducted from the value of the estate:

- Debts owed by the individual or estate
- Funeral expenses
- Charitable gifts made after death

Assets that are left to relatives more remote than children (for example, grandchildren) may be subject to a special tax if the amount left exceeds $1,000,000. This is known as generation skipping.

WITHHOLDING TAX

All broker dealers are required to withhold 31% of all sales proceeds, if the investor has not provided a social security number or a tax identification number. Thirty-one percent of all distributions from a mutual fund will also be withheld without a social security number or a tax identification number.

CORPORATE DIVIDEND EXCLUSION

Corporations that invest in the shares of other corporations will pay taxes only on 30% of the dividends it receives from those investments; 70% of the dividends are tax free to the corporation.

ALTERNATIVE MINIMUM TAX (AMT)

Certain items that receive beneficial tax treatment must be added back into the taxable income for some high-income earners. These items include:

- Interest on some industrial revenue bonds
- Some stock options
- Accelerated depreciation
- Personal property tax on investments that do not generate income
- Certain tax deductions passed through from DPPs

TAXES ON FOREIGN SECURITIES

U.S. investors who own securities issued in a foreign country will owe U.S. taxes on any gains or income realized. In the event that the foreign country withholds taxes from the investor, they may file for a credit with the IRS at tax time. Most foreign governments that withhold taxes will withhold 15%.

CHAPTER 8

Pretest

CUSTOMER RECOMMENDATIONS, PROFESSIONAL CONDUCT, AND TAXATION

1. Creating false activity in a security to attract a new purchaser is a fraudulent practice known as:
   - **a.** Trading ahead
   - **b.** Painting the tape
   - **c.** Active concealment
   - **d.** Front running

2. Which of the following could be subject to an investor's AMT?
   - **a.** A limited partnership
   - **b.** An open-end mutual fund
   - **c.** A convertible preferred stock owned by a wealthy investor
   - **d.** An industrial revenue bond

3. An investor has a conservative attitude toward investing and is seeking to invest $50,000 into an interest-bearing instrument that will provide current income and safety. You would most likely recommend:
   - **a.** Treasury bill
   - **b.** Ginnie Mae pass-through certificate
   - **c.** Treasury STRIP
   - **d.** Bankers' acceptance

4. A client has phoned in concerned about what will happen to his investment in a waste management company if the new EPA laws are enacted requiring disposal companies to reduce pollution. About what type of risk is he concerned?
   a. Call risk
   b. Environmental risk
   c. Investment risk
   d. Legislative risk

5. A customer has a large position in GJH, a thinly traded stock whose share price has remained flat for some time. The customer contacts the agent and wants to sell their entire position. The customer is most subject to:
   a. Liquidity risk
   b. Credit risk
   c. Conversion risk
   d. Execution risk

6. An investor who is most concerned with the changes in interest rates would least likely purchase which of the following?
   a. Long-term warrants
   b. Long-term corporate bonds
   c. Long-term equity
   d. Call options

7. An investor is looking for a risk-free investment. An agent should recommend which of the following for them?
   a. Series HH government savings bonds
   b. 90-day T-bill
   c. Convertible preferred stock
   d. Banker's acceptances

8. Which of the following is true?
   a. If the investor buys shares just prior to the ex date, he will have his investment money returned.
   b. After his money is returned, he will still be liable for taxes on the dividend amount.
   c. A registered representative may not use the pending dividend payment as the sole basis for recommending stock purchase.
   d. All of the above

9. A new investor is in the 15% tax bracket and is seeking some additional current income. Which of the following would you recommend?
   a. Growth fund
   b. Government bond fund
   c. Municipal bond fund
   d. Corporate bond fund

10. An investor gets advanced notice of a research report being issued and enters an order to purchase the security that is the subject of the research report. This is known as:
    a. Front running
    b. Trading ahead
    c. Insider trading
    d. Advance trading

11. An investor has a conservative attitude toward investing and is seeking to invest $100,000 into an instrument that will provide current income and the most protection from interest rate risk. You would most likely recommend:
    a. Ginnie Mae pass-through certificate
    b. Banker's acceptance
    c. Treasury STRIP
    d. A portfolio of Treasury bills

12. An investor, seeking some current income, would most likely invest in:
    a. Commercial paper
    b. Treasury bond
    c. Income bond
    d. Banker's acceptance

13. You have recommended a CMO to a sophisticated investor. Which of the following would they be most concerned with?
    a. Default risk
    b. Foreclosure risk
    c. Interest rate risk
    d. Prepayment risk

14. Mr. and Mrs. Jones, a couple in their early forties, enjoy watching their son play baseball on the weekends. He is planning to go to college 11 years from September and they are looking to start saving for their college cost expenses. What would you recommend?
    a. Educational IRA
    b. Growth fund
    c. Treasury STRIP
    d. Custodial account

15. All of the following are violations except:
    a. Recommending a security because of its future price appreciation
    b. Recommending a mutual fund based on a pending dividend to an investor seeking income
    c. Implying that FINRA has approved the firm
    d. Showing a client the past performance of a mutual fund for the last three years since its inception

16. An investor who may lose part or all of his investment is subject to:
    a. Capital risk
    b. Market risk
    c. Reinvestment risk
    d. Credit risk

17. A couple in their early thirties are seeking an investment for the $40,000 they have saved. They are planning on purchasing a new home in the next two years. You should most likely recommend:
    a. Preferred stock
    b. Common stock and common stock funds
    c. Money market funds
    d. Municipal bonds

CHAPTER 9

Securities Industry Rules and Regulations

INTRODUCTION

Federal and state securities laws, as well as industry regulations, have been enacted to ensure that all industry participants adhere to a high standard of just and equitable trade practices. In this chapter, we will review the rules and regulations that create the framework for securities industry regulation.

THE SECURITIES ACT OF 1933

The Securities Act of 1933 was the first major piece of securities industry regulation, which was brought about largely as a result of the stock market crash of 1929. Other laws also were enacted to help prevent another meltdown of the nation's financial system, such as the Securities Exchange Act of 1934, which will be discussed next.

The Securities Act of 1933 regulates the primary market. The primary market consists exclusively of transactions between issuers of securities and investors. In a primary market transaction, the issuer of the securities receives the proceeds from the sale of the securities. The Securities Act of 1933 requires nonexempt issuers, typically corporate issuers, to file a registration statement with the Securities Exchange Commission (SEC). The SEC will review the registration statement for a minimum of 20 days. During this time (known as the cooling-off period), no sales of securities may take place. If the SEC requires additional information regarding the offering, the SEC may issue a deficiency letter or a stop order that will extend the cooling-off period beyond the original 20 days. The cooling-off period will continue until the SEC has received all of the information it has requested. The registration statement—formally known as an S1—is the issuer's full-disclosure document for the registration of the securities with the SEC.

THE PROSPECTUS

While the SEC is reviewing the securities' registration statement, a registered representative is very limited as to what they may do with regard to the new issue. During the cooling-off period, the only thing a registered representative may do is obtain indications of interest from clients by providing them with a preliminary prospectus, also known as a red herring. The term red herring originated from the fact that all preliminary prospectuses must have a statement printed in red ink on the front cover stating: "These securities have not yet become registered with the SEC and therefore may not be sold." An indication of interest is an investor's or broker dealer's statement that they may be interested in purchasing the securities being offered. The preliminary prospectus contains most of the same information that will be contained in the final prospectus, except for the offering price and the proceeds to the issuer. All information contained in a preliminary prospectus is subject to change or revision.

THE FINAL PROSPECTUS

All purchasers of new issues must be given a final prospectus before any sales may be allowed. The final prospectus serves as the issuer's full-disclosure document for the purchaser of the securities. If the issuer has filed a prospectus with the SEC and the prospectus can be viewed on the SEC's web site, a prospectus will be deemed to have been provided to the investor through the access equals delivery rule. Once the issuer's registration statement becomes effective, the final prospectus must include:

- Type and description of the securities
- Price of the security
- Use of the proceeds
- Underwriter's discount

- Date of offering
- Type and description of underwriting
- Business history of issuer
- Biographical data for company officers and directors
- Information regarding large stockholders
- Company financial data
- Risks to purchaser
- Legal matters concerning the company
- SEC disclaimer

SEC DISCLAIMER

The SEC reviews the issuer's registration statement and the prospectus but does not guarantee the accuracy or adequacy of the information. The SEC disclaimer must appear on the cover of all prospectuses. It states: "These securities have not been approved or disapproved by the SEC nor have any representations been made about the accuracy or the adequacy of the information."

MISREPRESENTATIONS

Financial relief for misrepresentations made under the Securities Act of 1933 is available for purchasers of any security that is sold under a prospectus that is found to contain false or misleading statements. Purchasers of the security may be entitled to seek financial relief from any or all of the following:

- Issuer
- Underwriters
- Officers and directors
- All parties who signed the registration statement
- Accountants and attorneys who helped prepare the registration statement

THE SECURITIES EXCHANGE ACT OF 1934

The Securities Exchange Act of 1934 was the second major piece of legislation that resulted from the market crash of 1929. The Securities Exchange Act regulates the secondary market that consists of investor-to-investor transactions. All transactions between two investors that are executed on any of the exchanges or in the over-the-counter market are secondary market transactions. In a secondary market transaction, the selling security holder receives the money, not the issuing corporation. The Securities Exchange Act of 1934 also regulates all individuals and firms that conduct business in the securities industry. The Securities Exchange Act of 1934:

- Created the SEC
- Requires registration of broker dealers and agents
- Regulates the exchanges and FINRA
- Requires net capital for broker dealers
- Regulates short sales
- Regulates insider transactions
- Requires public companies to solicit proxies
- Requires segregation of customer and firm assets
- Authorized the Federal Reserve Board to regulate the extension of credit for securities purchases under Regulation T
- Regulates the handling of client accounts

THE SECURITIES EXCHANGE COMMISSION (SEC)

One of the biggest components of the Securities Exchange Act of 1934 was the creation of the SEC. The SEC is the ultimate securities industry authority and is a direct government body. Five commissioners are appointed to five-year terms by the president and each must be approved by the Senate. No more than three commissioners may be from any one political party. The SEC is not a self-regulatory organization (SRO) or a designated examining authority (DEA). A self-regulatory organization is one that regulates its own members such as the NYSE or FINRA. A designated examining authority is one that inspects a broker dealer's books and records and also can be the NYSE or FINRA. All broker dealers, exchanges, agents, and securities must register with the SEC. All exchanges are required to file a registration statement with the SEC that includes the articles of incorporation, bylaws, and constitution. All new rules and regulations adopted by the exchanges must be disclosed to the SEC as soon as they are enacted. Issuers of securities with more than 500 shareholders and with assets exceeding $5,000,000 must register with the

SEC, file quarterly and annual reports, and must solicit proxies from stockholders. A broker dealer who conducts business with the public must register with the SEC and maintain a certain level of financial solvency known as net capital. All broker dealers are required to forward a financial statement to all customers of the firm. Additionally, all employees of the broker dealer who are involved in securities sales, have access to cash and securities, or who supervise employees must be fingerprinted.

EXTENSION OF CREDIT

The Securities Act of 1934 gave the authority to the Federal Reserve Board (FRB) to regulate the extension of credit by broker dealers for the purchase of securities by their customers. The following is a list of the regulations of the different lenders and the regulation that gave the FRB the authority to govern their activities:

- Regulation T broker dealers
- Regulation U banks
- Regulation G all other financial institutions

PUBLIC UTILITIES HOLDING COMPANY ACT OF 1935

The Public Utilities Holding Company Act of 1935 regulates all companies that are in business to provide retail distribution of gas and electric power. Because the companies are regulated by this act, their securities are exempt from state registration requirements.

FINANCIAL INDUSTRY REGULATORY AUTHORITY (FINRA)

The Maloney Act of 1938 was an amendment to the Securities Exchange Act of 1934 that allowed the creation of the NASD. The NASD, now part of FINRA, is the self-regulatory organization for over-the-counter (OTC) market and its purpose is to regulate the broker dealers who conduct business in the OTC market. FINRA has four major bylaws. They are the:

1. Rules of fair practice
2. Uniform practice code

3. Code of procedure
4. Code of arbitration

THE TRUST INDENTURE ACT OF 1939

The Trust Indenture Act of 1939 requires that corporate bond issues in excess of $5,000,000 dollars that are to be repaid during a term in excess of one year issue a trust indenture for the issue. The trust indenture is a contract between the issuer and the trustee. The trustee acts on behalf of all of the bondholders and ensures that the issuer is in compliance with all of the promises and covenants made to the bondholders. The trustee is appointed by the corporation and is usually a bank or a trust company. The Trust Indenture Act of 1939 only applies to corporate issuers. Both federal and municipal issuers are exempt.

INVESTMENT ADVISERS ACT OF 1940

The Investment Advisers Act of 1940 regulates industry professionals who charge a fee for the advice they offer to clients. The Investment Advisers Act sets forth registration requirements for advisers as well as disclosure requirements relating to the adviser's:

- Methods of recommendations
- Types of securities recommended
- Professional background and qualifications
- Fees to be charged
- Method for computing and charging fees
- Types of clients

The Investment Advisers Act of 1940 prohibits an investment adviser from disclosing client information to a third party without the client's consent unless the adviser is required or compelled to disclose the information by law.

INVESTMENT COMPANY ACT OF 1940

The Investment Company Act of 1940 regulates companies that are in business to invest or reinvest money for the benefit of its investors. The Investment

Company Act sets forth registration requirements for the three types of investment companies. They are:

1. Management investment company
2. Unit investment trust (UIT)
3. Face amount company (FAC)

FINRA MEMBER COMMUNICATIONS WITH THE PUBLIC

FINRA member firms will seek to increase their business and exposure through the use of both retail and institutional communications. There are strict regulations in place in order to ensure all communications with the public adhere to industry guidelines. Some communications with the public are available to a general audience and include:

- Television/radio
- Publicly accessible websites
- Motion pictures
- Newspapers/magazine
- Telephone directory listings
- Signs/billboards
- Computer/internet postings
- Video tape displays
- Other public media
- Recorded telemarketing messages

Other types of communications are offered to a targeted audience. These communications include:

- Market reports
- Password protected websites
- Telemarketing scripts
- Form letters or emails (sent to more than 25 people)
- Circulars
- Research reports
- Printed materials for seminars

- Option worksheets
- Performance reports
- Prepared scripts for TV or radio
- Reprints of ads

FINRA RULE 2210 COMMUNICATIONS WITH THE PUBLIC

FINRA Rule 2210 replaces the advertising and sales literature rules previously used to regulate member communications with the public. FINRA Rule 2210 streamlines member communication rules and reduces the number of communication categories from six to three. The three categories of member communication are:

1. Retail communication
2. Institutional communications
3. Correspondence

RETAIL COMMUNICATION

Retail communication is defined as any written communication distributed or made available to 25 or more retail investors in a 30-day period. The communication may be distributed in hard copy or in electronic formats. The definition of a retail investor is any investor who does not meet the definition of an institutional investor. Retail communications now contain all components of advertising and sales literature. All retail communications must be approved by a registered principal prior to first use. The publication of a post in a chat room or other online forum will not require the prior approval of a principal so long as such post does not promote the business of the member firm and does not provide investment advice. Additionally, generic advertising will also be exempt from the prior approval requirements. All retail communication must be maintained by the member for three years. If the member firm is a new member firm, which has been in existence for less than 12 months based on the firm's approval date in the central registration depository or CRD, the member must file all retail communications with FINRA 10 days prior to its first use unless the communication has been previously filed and contains no material changes or has been filed by another member such as investment company or ETF sponsor. Member firms that have been established for more than 12 months may file retail communications with FINRA 10 days after the communication is first used. Investment companies, ETF sponsors and retail communications regarding variable annuities must be filed 10 days prior to first use. If the communication contains nonstandardized performance rankings. Should FINRA determine that a member firm is making false or misleading statements in its retail communications with the public, FINRA may require the member to file all of its retail communication with the public with the association 10 days prior to its first use.

INSTITUTIONAL COMMUNICATIONS

Intuitional communication is defined as any written communication distributed or made available exclusively to institutional investors. The communication may be distributed in hard copy or in electronic formats. Institutional communications do not have to be approved by a principal prior to first use so long as the member has established policies and procedures regarding the use of institutional communications and has trained its employees on the proper use of institutional communication. Institutional communication is also exempt from FINRA's filing requirement but like retail communications it must be maintained by a member for three years. If the member believes that the institutional communication or any part thereof may be seen by even a single retail investor the communication must be handled as all other retail communication and is subject to the approval and filing requirements as if it was retail communication. An institutional investor is a person or firm that trades securities for his or her own account or for the account of others. Institutional investors are generally limited to large financial companies. Because of their size and sophistication, fewer protective laws cover institutional investors. It is important to note that there is no minimum size for an institutional account. Institutional investors include:

- Broker dealers
- Investment advisers
- Investment companies
- Insurance companies
- Banks
- Trusts
- Savings and loans
- Government agencies

- Employment benefit plans with more than 100 participants
- Any non-natural person with more than $50,000,000 in assets

CORRESPONDENCE

Correspondence consists of electronic and written communications between the member and up to 25 retail investors in a 30 calendar day period. With the increase in acceptance of email as business communication, it would be impractical for a member to review all correspondence between the member and a customer. The member instead may set up procedures to review a sample of all correspondence, both electronic and hard copy. If the member reviews only a sample of the correspondence, the member must train their associated people on their firm's procedures relating to correspondence and must document the training and ensure the procedures are followed. Even though the member is not required to review all correspondence, the member must still retain all correspondence. The member should, where practical, review all incoming hard copy correspondence. Letters received by the firm could contain cash, checks, securities, or complaints.

CORPORATE WEBSITES

Neither an investment adviser nor a broker dealer be deemed to have a place of business in a state where it does not maintain an office simply by virtue of the fact that the publicly available website established by the firm or one of its agents is accessible from that state so long as the following conditions are met:

- The website clearly states that the firm may only conduct business in states where it is properly registered to do so.
- The website only provides general information about the firm and does not provide specific investment advice.
- The firm or its agent may not respond to Internet inquiries with the intent to solicit business without first meeting the registration requirements in the state of the prospective customer.

The content of any website must be reviewed and approved by a principal prior to its first use and must be filed with FINRA within 10 days of use. If the firm or its agent updates the website and the update materially changes the information contained on the website, the updates must be reapproved by a principal and refiled with FINRA. As changes are made to the website each version is subject to the filing requirements and the firm will often have various versions of the site archived to comply with the retention requirement. The website may use the FINRA logo so long as the use is only to demonstrate that the firm is a FINRA member and a hyperlink to the FINRA website is included in close proximity to the logo.

BLIND RECRUITING ADS

A blind recruiting ad is an ad placed by the member firm for the specific purpose of finding job applicants. Blind recruiting ads are the only form of advertising that does not require the member's name to appear in the ad. The ads may not distort the opportunities or salaries of the advertised position. All other ads are required to disclose the name of the member firm, as well as the relationship of the member to any other entities that appear in the ad.

GENERIC ADVERTISING

Generic advertising is generally designed to promote firm awareness and to advertise the products and services generally offered through the firm. Generic ads will generally include:

- Securities products offered, i.e., stocks, bonds, mutual funds
- Contact name, number, and address
- Types of accounts offered, i.e., individual, IRA, 401K

TOMBSTONE ADS

A tombstone ad is an announcement of a new security offering coming to market. Tombstone ads may be run while the securities are still in registration with the SEC and may only include:

- Description of securities
- Description of business

- Description of transaction
- Required disclaimers
- Time and place of any stockholders meetings regarding the sale of the securities

Tombstone ads must include:

- A statement that the securities registration has not yet become effective.
- A statement that responding to the ad does not obligate the prospect.
- A statement as to where a prospectus may be obtained.
- A statement that the ad does not constitute an offer to sell the securities and that an offer may only be made by the prospectus.

All advertising and sales literature is required to be approved by a principal of the firm prior to its first use. A general security principal (Series 24) may approve most advertising and sales literature. Any advertising or sales literature relating to options must be approved by a registered option principal or the compliance registered options principal. Research reports must be approved by a supervisory analyst.

TESTIMONIALS

From time to time, broker dealers will use testimonials made by people of national or local recognition in an effort to generate new business for the firm. If the individual giving the testimonial is quoting past performance relating to the firm's recommendations, it must be accompanied by a disclaimer that past performance is not indicative of future performance. If the individual giving the testimony was compensated in any way, the fact that the person received compensation must also be disclosed.

TAKENOTE!

An investment adviser may never use or refer to testimonials in any of its communications or advertising.

Should the individual's testimony imply that the person making the testimony is an expert, a statement regarding their qualifications as an expert must also be contained in the ad or sales literature. Research prepared by outside parties must disclose the name of the preparer.

TAKENOTE!

Investment advisers are prohibited from using testimonials or statement regarding a client's experience with the adviser as part of any advertisement or sales literature.

FREE SERVICES

If a member firm or investment adviser advertises free services to customers or to people who respond to an ad, the services must actually be free to everyone and with no strings attached.

MISLEADING COMMUNICATIONS

The following are some examples of misleading statements that are not allowed to appear in any communications with investors:

- Excessive hedge clauses
- Implying an endorsement by FINRA, NYSE, or SEC
- Printing the FINRA logo in type that is larger than the type of the member's name
- Implying the member has larger research facilities than they actually have
- Implying an individual has higher qualifications than they actually have

SECURITIES INVESTOR PROTECTION CORPORATION ACT OF 1970 (SIPC)

The Securities Investor Protection Corporation is a government-sponsored corporation that provides protection to customers in the event of a broker dealer's failure. All broker dealers who are registered with the SEC are required to be SIPC members. All broker dealers are required to pay annual dues to SIPC's insurance fund to cover losses due to broker dealer failure. If a broker dealer fails to pay their SIPC assessment, they may not transact business until it is paid.

NET CAPITAL REQUIREMENT

All broker dealers are required to maintain a certain level of net capital in order to ensure that they are financially solvent. A broker dealer's capital requirement is contingent upon the type of business that the broker dealer conducts. The larger and more complex the firm's business is, the greater the net capital requirement. Should a firm fall below its net capital requirement, it is deemed to be insolvent, and SIPC will petition in court to have a trustee appointed to liquidate the firm and protect the customers. The trustee must be a disinterested party and, once the trustee is appointed, the firm may not conduct business or try to conceal any assets.

CUSTOMER COVERAGE

SIPC protects customers of a brokerage firm in much the same way that the FDIC protects customers of banks. SIPC covers customer losses that result from broker dealer failure, not for market losses. SIPC covers customers for up to $500,000 per separate customer. Of the $500,000, up to $250,000 may be in cash. Most broker dealers carry additional private insurance to cover larger accounts, but SIPC is the industry-funded insurance and is required by all broker dealers. The following are examples of separate customers:

Customer	Securities Market Value	Cash	SIPC Coverage
Mr. Jones	$320,000	$75,000	All
Mr. & Mrs. Jones	$290,000	$90,000	All
Mrs. Jones	$397,000	$82,000	All

All of the accounts shown would be considered separate customers and SIPC would cover the entire value of all of the accounts. If an account has in excess of $250,000 in cash, the individual would not be covered for any amount exceeding $250,000 in cash and would become a general creditor for the rest. SIPC does not consider a margin account and cash account as separate customers and the customer would be covered for the maximum of $500,000. SIPC does not offer coverage for commodities contracts and all member firms must display the SIPC sign in the lobby of the firm.

FIDELITY BOND

All SIPC members are required to obtain a fidelity bond to protect customers in the event of employee dishonesty. Some things that a fidelity bond will insure against are check forgery and fraudulent trading. The minimum amount of the fidelity bond is $25,000; however, large firms are often required to carry a higher amount.

THE SECURITIES ACTS AMENDMENTS OF 1975

The Securities Acts Amendments of 1975 gave the authority to the MSRB to regulate the issuance and trading of municipal bonds. The MSRB has no enforcement division. Its rules are enforced by other regulators.

THE INSIDER TRADING AND SECURITIES FRAUD ENFORCEMENT ACT OF 1988

The Insider Trading and Securities Fraud Enforcement Act of 1988 established guidelines and controls for the use and dissemination of nonpublic material information. Nonpublic information is information that is not known by people outside of the company. Material information is information regarding a situation or development that will materially affect the company in the present or future. It is not only just for insiders to have this type of information, but it is required for them to do their jobs effectively. It is, however, unlawful for an insider to use this information to profit from a forthcoming move in the stock price. An insider is defined as any officer, director, 10% stockholder, or anyone who is in possession of nonpublic material information as well as the spouse of any such person. Additionally, it is unlawful for the insider to divulge any of this information to any outside party. Trading on inside information has always been a violation of the Securities Exchange Act of 1934, but the Insider Trading Act prescribed penalties for violators, which include:

- A fine of 300% of the amount of the gain or 300% of the amount of the loss avoided for the person who acts on the information
- A civil or criminal fine for the person who divulges the information
- Insider traders may be sued by the affected parties
- Criminal prosecutions: A fine of up to $1,000,000 and 20 years in prison

Information becomes public information once it has been disseminated over public media. The SEC will pay a reward of up to 10% to informants who turn in individuals who trade on inside information. In addition to the insiders already listed, the following are also considered insiders:

- Accountants
- Attorneys
- Investment bankers

FIREWALL

Broker dealers who act as underwriters and investment bankers for corporate clients must have access to information regarding the company in order to advise the company properly. The broker dealer must ensure that no inside information is passed between its investment banking department and its retail trading departments. The broker dealer is required to physically separate these divisions by a firewall. The broker dealer must maintain written supervisory procedures to adequately guard against the wrongful use or dissemination of inside information.

THE TELEPHONE CONSUMER PROTECTION ACT OF 1991

The Telephone Consumer Protection Act of 1991 regulates how telemarketing calls are made by businesses. Telemarketing calls that are designed to have consumers invest in or purchase goods, services, or property must adhere to the strict guidelines of the act. All firms must:

- Call only between the hours of 8 AM and 9 PM.
- Maintain a do-not-call list. Individuals placed on the do-not-call list may not be contacted by anyone at the firm for five years.
- Give the prospect the firm's name, address, and phone number when soliciting.
- Follow adequate policies and procedures to maintain a do-not-call list.
- Train representatives on calling policies and use of the do-not-call list.

- Ensure that any fax solicitations have the firm's name, address, and phone number.

EXEMPTION FROM THE TELEPHONE CONSUMER PROTECTION ACT OF 1991

The following are exempt from the Telephone Consumer Protection Act of 1991:

- Calls to existing customers
- Calls to a delinquent debtor
- Calls from a religious or nonprofit organization

Calls may be made prior to 8 AM or after 9 PM to places of business. The time regulation only relates to contacting noncustomers at home.

NATIONAL SECURITIES MARKET IMPROVEMENT ACT OF 1996

The National Securities Market Improvement Act of 1996, also known as the Coordination Act, eliminated the duplication of effort among state and federal regulators. Some of the key points of the act include:

- Federal law overrides state law
- Registration requirements for investment advisers
- Capital requirements
- Increased industry competition by eliminating collusive behavior

The National Securities Market Improvement Act of 1996 ensured that no action by any state or political subdivision could impose laws or requirements upon any broker dealer that differed from or are in addition to those of the Securities Exchange Act of 1934 relating to:

- Capital requirements
- Recordkeeping
- Financial reporting

- Margin
- Custody

THE UNIFORM SECURITIES ACT

In the early half of the twentieth century, state securities regulators developed their state's rules and regulations for transacting securities business within their state. The result was a nation of states with regulations that varied widely from state to state. The Uniform Securities Act (USA) laid out model legislation for all states in an effort to make each state's rules and regulations more uniform and easier to address. The USA (also known as the Act) sets minimum qualification standards for each state securities administrator. The state securities administrator is the top securities regulator within the state. The state securities administrator may be the attorney general of that state or may be an individual appointed specifically to that post. The USA also:

- Prohibits the state securities administrator from using the post for personal benefit or from disclosing information.
- Gives the state securities administrator authority to enforce the rules of the USA within that state.
- Gives the administrator the ability to set certain registration requirements for broker dealers, agents, and investment advisers.
- Administrators may set fee and testing requirements.
- Administrators may suspend or revoke the state registration of a broker dealer, agent, investment adviser, a security, or a security's exemption from registration.

The USA also sets civil and criminal penalties for violators.

The state-based laws set forth by the Uniform Securities Act are also known as Blue Sky laws.

CURRENCY TRANSACTIONS

All member firms must guard against money laundering. Every member must report any currency receipt of $10,000 or more from any one customer on a single day. The firm must fill out and submit a currency transaction report also known as Form 4789 to the Internal Revenue Service (IRS) within 15 days of the receipt of the currency. Multiple deposits that total $10,000 or more will also require the firm to file a currency transaction report (CTR). Additionally, the firm is required to maintain a record of all international wire transfers of $3,000 or greater.

THE PATRIOT ACT

The Patriot Act requires broker dealers to have written policies and procedures designed to detect suspicious activity. The firm must designate a principal to ensure compliance with the firm's policies and to train firm personnel. The firm is required to file a Suspicious Activity Report for any transaction of more than $5,000 that appears questionable. The firm must file the report within 30 days of identifying any suspicious activity Anti-money-laundering rules require that all firms implement a customer identification program to ensure that the firm knows the true identity of their customers. All customers who open an account with the firm, as well as individuals with trading authority, are subject to this rule. The firm must ensure that its customers do not appear on any list of known or suspected terrorists. A firm's anti-money-laundering program must be approved by senior management. All records relating to the SAR filing including a copy of the SAR report must be maintained by the firm for 5 years.

The money laundering process begins with the placement of the funds. This is when the money is deposited in an account with the broker dealer. The second step of the laundering process is known as layering. The layering process will consist of multiple deposits in amounts less than $10,000. The funds will often be drawn from different financial institutions; this is also known as structuring. The launderers will then purchase and sell securities in the account. The integration of the proceeds back into the banking system completes the process. At this point, the launderers may use the money to purchase goods and services and they appear to have come from legitimate sources. Firms must also identify the customers who open the account and must make sure that they are not conducting business with anyone on the OFAC list. This list is maintained by the Treasury Department Office of Foreign Assets Control. It consists of known and suspected terrorists, criminals, and members of pariah nations. Individuals and entities who appear on this list are known as Specially Designated Nationals and Blocked Persons Conducting business with anyone on this list is strictly prohibited. Registered representatives who aid the laundering of money are subject to prosecution and face up to 20 years in prison and a $500,000 fine per transaction. The representative does not even have to be involved in the scheme or even know about it to be prosecuted.

FinCEN is a bureau of the U.S. Department of the Treasury. FinCEN's mission is to safeguard the financial system and guard against money laundering and promote national security. FinCEN collects receives and maintains financial transactions data; and analyzes and disseminates that data for law enforcement purposes; and building global cooperation with counterpart organizations in other countries and with international bodies. FinCen will e-mail a list of individuals and entities to a designated principal every few weeks. The principal is required to check the list against the firm's customer list. If a match is found the firm must notify FinCen within 14 calendar days.

CHAPTER 9

Pretest

SECURITIES INDUSTRY RULES AND REGULATIONS

1. The Securities Exchange Act regulates which market?
   a. Third
   b. Fourth
   c. Primary
   d. Secondary

2. In the securities industry, which is highly regulated, what is the ultimate industry authority regulating conduct?
   a. NYSE
   b. SRO
   c. SEC
   d. FINRA

3. A testimonial by a compensated expert, citing the results they realized following a FINRA member's recommendations, must include which of the following?
   I. A statement detailing their credentials
   II. A statement that past performance is not a guarantee of future performance
   III. A statement that the individual is a compensated spokesperson
   IV. The name of the principal who approved the ad
   a. I, II, and III
   b. II and IV
   c. I and II
   d. I, II, III, and IV

4. The act that gave the NASD the authority to regulate the over-the-counter market is the:
   a. NASD Act of 1929
   b. Securities Act of 1933
   c. Securities Act of 1934
   d. Maloney Act of 1938

5. FINRA considers which of the following to retail communication?
   I. Video tape displays
   II. Listing in phone directories
   III. Circulars
   IV. Telemarketing scripts
   a. II and III
   b. I and II
   c. I, II, III, and IV
   d. I and III

6. A principal must do all of the following, except:
   a. Report violations of professional conduct by broker dealers to the SEC
   b. Supervise all of the actions of a firm and its employees
   c. Report violations of state and federal laws to the proper authorities
   d. Approve all transactions before they are executed to ensure suitability and to prevent violations

7. Your brokerage firm has placed an ad in the local newspaper advertising its new line of services being offered to investors. The firm must maintain the ad for how long?

   a. 24 months

   b. 36 months

   c. 12 months

   d. 18 months

8. According to Rule 135, as it relates to generic advertising, all of the following are true, except:

   a. It may contain information about the services a company offers.

   b. It may describe the nature of the investment company's business.

   c. It may contain information about exchange privileges.

   d. It may contain information about the performance of past recommendations.

9. During a new issue registration, false information is included in the prospectus to buyers. Which of the following may be held liable to investors?

   I. Officers of the issuer

   II. Accountants

   III. Syndicate members

   IV. People who signed the registration statement

   a. I and III

   b. I and II

   c. I, II, and III

   d. I, II, III, and IV

10. A syndicate has published a tombstone ad prior to the issue becoming effective. Which of the following must appear in the tombstone?

   I. A statement that the registration has not yet become effective

   II. The tombstone ad is not an offer to sell the securities

   III. Contact information

   IV. No commitment statement

   a. III and IV

   b. II and III

   c. I and II

   d. I, II, III, and IV

CHAPTER 10

Trading Securities

INTRODUCTION

Investors, who do not purchase their stocks and bonds directly from the issuer, must purchase them from another investor. Investor-to-investor transactions are known as secondary market transactions. In a secondary market transaction, the selling security owner receives the proceeds from the sale. Secondary market transactions may take place on an exchange or in the over-the-counter market known as Nasdaq. While both facilitate the trading of securities, they operate in a very different manner. We will begin by looking at the types of orders that an investor may enter and the reasons for entering the various types of orders. Series 65 candidates can expect to a number of questions on trading securities.

TYPES OF ORDERS

Investors can enter various types of orders to buy or sell securities. Some orders guarantee that the investor's order will be executed immediately. Other types of orders may state a specific price or condition under which the investor wants their order to be executed. All orders are considered day orders unless otherwise specified. All day orders will be canceled at the end of the trading day if they are not executed. An investor may also specify that their order remain active until canceled. This type of order is known as Good 'Til Cancel or GTC.

MARKET ORDERS

A market order will guarantee that the investor's order is executed as soon as the order is presented to the market. A market order to either buy or sell guarantees the execution but not the price at which the order will be executed. When a market order is presented for execution, the market for the security may be very different from the market that was displayed when the order was entered. As a result, the investor does not know the exact price at which their order will be executed.

BUY LIMIT ORDERS

A buy limit order sets the maximum price that the investor will pay for the security. The order may never be executed at a price higher than the investor's limit price. Although a buy limit order guarantees that the investor will not pay over a certain price, it does not guarantee them an execution. If the stock continues to trade higher away from the investor's limit price, the investor will not purchase the stock and may miss a chance to realize a profit.

SELL LIMIT ORDERS

A sell limit order sets the minimum price that the investor will accept for the security. The order may never be executed at a price lower than the investor's limit price. Although a sell limit order guarantees that the investor will not receive less than a certain price, it does not guarantee them an execution. If the stock continues to trade lower away from the investor's limit price, the investor will not sell the stock and may miss a chance to realize a profit or may realize a loss as a result.

FOCUSPOINT

It's important to remember that even if an investor sees stock trading at their limit price, it does not mean that their order was executed, because there could have been stock ahead of them at that limit price.

STOP ORDERS/STOP LOSS ORDERS

A stop order or stop loss order can be used by investors to limit or guard against a loss or to protect a profit. A stop order will be placed away from the market in case the stock starts to move against the investor. A stop order is not a live order; it has to be elected. A stop order is elected and becomes a live order when the stock trades at or through the stop price. The stop price is also known as the trigger price. Once the stock has traded at or though the stop price, the order becomes a market order to either buy or sell the stock depending on the type of order that was placed.

BUY STOP ORDERS

A buy stop order is placed above the market and is used to protect against a loss or to protect a profit on a short sale of stock. A buy stop order also could be used by a technical analyst to get long the stock after the stock breaks through resistance.

EXAMPLE

An investor has sold 100 shares of ABC short at $40 per share. ABC has declined to $30 per share. The investor is concerned that if ABC goes past $32 it may return to $40. To protect their profit, they enter an order to buy 100 ABC at 32 stop. If ABC trades at or through $32, the order will become a market order to buy 100 shares and the investor will cover their short at the next available price.

SELL STOP ORDERS

A sell stop order is placed below the market and is used to protect against a loss or to protect a profit on the purchase of a stock. A sell stop order also could be used by a technical analyst to get short the stock after the stock breaks through support.

EXAMPLE

An investor has purchased 100 shares of ABC at $30 per share. ABC has risen to $40 per share. The investor is concerned that if ABC falls past $38, it may return to $30. To protect their profit, they enter an order to sell 100 ABC at 38 stop. If ABC trades at or through $38, the order will become a market order to sell 100 shares and the investor will sell their short at the next available price.

Consider the same example if the order to sell 100 ABC at 38 stop was entered GTC. We could have a situation such as this:

ABC closes at 39.40. The following morning, ABC announces that they lost a major contract and ABC opens at 35.30. The opening print of 35.30 elected the order and the stock would be sold on the opening or as close to the opening as practical.

STOP LIMIT ORDERS

An investor would enter a stop limit order for the same reasons they would enter a stop order. The only difference is that once the order has been elected, the order becomes a limit order instead of a market order. The same risks that apply to traditional limit orders apply to stop limit orders. If the stock continues to trade away from the investor's limit, they could give back all of their profits or suffer large losses.

OTHER TYPES OF ORDERS

There are several other types of orders that an investor may enter. They are:

- All or none (AON)
- Immediate or cancel (IOC)
- Fill or kill (FOK)
- Not held (NH)
- Market on open/market on close

All or None Orders: These orders may be entered as day orders or GTC. As the name implies, all or none orders indicates that the investor wants to buy or sell all of the securities or none of them. All or none orders are not displayed in the market because the required special handling and the investor will not accept a partial execution.

Immediate or Cancel Orders: The investor wants to buy or sell whatever they can immediately and whatever is not filled is canceled.

Fill or Kill Orders: The investor wants the entire order executed immediately or the entire order canceled.

Not Held Orders: The investor gives discretion to the floor broker as to the time and price of execution. All retail not held orders given to a representative are considered day orders unless the order is received in writing from the customer and entered GTC.

Market on Open/Market on Close Orders: The investor wants their order executed on the opening or closing of the market or as reasonably close to the opening or closing as practical. If the order is not executed, it is canceled. Partial executions are allowed.

TAKENOTE!

The SEC has granted permission to the NYSE to stop using FOK and IOC orders.

THE EXCHANGES

The most recognized stock exchange in the world is the New York Stock Exchange or the NYSE. There are, however, many exchanges throughout the United States that all operate in a similar manner. Exchanges are dual-auction markets. They provide a central market place where buyers and sellers come together in one centralized location to compete with one another. Buyers compete with other buyers to be the highest price anyone is willing to pay for the security and sellers compete with other sellers to be the lowest price at which anyone is willing to sell a security. All transactions in an exchange-listed security that are executed on the exchange have to take place in front of the specialist or designated marker maker (DMM) for that security. The specialist/DMM is an exchange member who is responsible for maintaining a fair and orderly market for the stock in which they specialize. The specialist/DMM stands at the trading "post" where all the buyers and sellers must go to conduct business in the security. This is responsible for the crowd that you see on the news and financial reports when they show the floor of the exchange. All securities that trade on an exchange are known as listed securities.

PRIORITY OF EXCHANGE ORDERS

Orders that are routed to the trading post for execution are prioritized according to price and time. If the price of more than one order is the same, orders will be filled as follows:

- **Priority:** The order that was received first gets filled first.
- **Precedence:** If the time and price are the same, the larger order gets filled.
- **Parity:** If all conditions are the same, the orders are matched in the crowd and the shares are split among the orders.

THE ROLE OF THE SPECIALIST/DMM

The specialist is an independent exchange member who has been assigned a stock or group of stocks for which they are the designated market maker (DMM). They are responsible for:

- Maintaining a fair and orderly market for the securities
- Buying for their own account in the absence of public buy orders

- Selling from their own account in the absence of public sell orders
- Acting as an agent by executing public orders left with them

A large amount of capital is required in order to fulfill the requirements of a specialist/DMM. As a result, most specialists/DMMs are employees of specialist firms. Although the specialist is not required to participate in every transaction, every transaction for that security that is executed on the exchange must take place in front of the specialist. The specialist may act as either an agent or as a principal if they play a role in the transaction.

THE SPECIALIST/DMM ACTING AS A PRINCIPAL

In the absence of public orders the specialist/DMM is required to provide liquidity and price improvement for the stocks in which they are the designated market maker. Specialists/DMMs are required to trade against the market and may now trade for their own account at prices that would compete with public orders.

EXAMPLE

If the public market for XYZ is quoted as follows:

	Bid	Offer
10 × 10	20.45	20.55

There is a 20.45 bid for 1000 shares and 1000 shares offered at 20.55.

If a public sell order came in to sell the stock, the DMM could purchase the stock for their own account at 20.45 because they are on parity with the public. The DMM could also purchase the stock for their own account at 20.50 and would be improving the price that the seller would be receiving. This is known as price improvement. Alternatively, if a public buy order came in, the specialist/DMM could sell the stock from their own account at 20.55, because they are now allowed to compete with the public. They could also sell the stock to the customer at 20.50 because, once again, that would be providing price improvement for the order.

THE SPECIALIST/DMM ACTING AS AN AGENT

The specialist/DMM is also required to execute orders that have been left with them. Orders that have been left with the specialist/DMM for execution are said to be left or dropped on the specialist's/DMM's book. The specialist/DMM is required to maintain a book of public orders and to execute them when market conditions permit. The types of orders that may be left with the specialist are:

- Buy and sell limit orders
- Stop orders
- Stop limit orders
- Both day and GTC orders
- AON orders

The specialist/DMM will execute the orders if and when they are able to and will send a commission bill to the member who left the order with them for execution. This is known as a specialist bill and is usually only a cent or two per share. The specialist/DMM is also required to quote the best market for the security to any party that asks. The best or inside market is comprised of the highest bid and lowest offer. This is made up from bids and offers contained in the specialist's/DMM's book and in the trading crowd. The inside market is also the market that is displayed to broker dealers and agents on their quote system.

When quoting the inside market, the specialist/DMM will add all of the shares bid for at the highest price and all of the shares offered at the lowest price to determine the size of the market. There are certain types of orders that are not included when determining the inside market they are:

- Stop orders
- AON orders

A specialist/DMM may not accept the following types of orders:

- Market orders
- Immediately executable limit orders
- Not held orders
- Immediate or cancel orders
- Fill or kill orders

Market orders and immediately executable limit orders are filled as soon as they reach the crowd so there is nothing to leave with the specialist. In the case of a not held order, once a floor broker is given discretion as to time and price, they may not give it to another party.

A specialist's/DMM's book may look something like the following example:

Buy	XYZ	Sell
5 Goldman 10 JPM	20	
	20.05	
	20.10	1 Prudential 5 Fidelity
	20.15	2 Morgan
5 Merrill Stp	20.20	

The inside market for XYZ based on the specialist's/DMM's book would be:

	Bid	Ask
15 × 6	20.00	20.10

Buyers are bidding for 1,500 shares and sellers are offering 600 shares of XYZ.

> **TAKENOTE!**
>
> The buy stop entered over the market by Merrill is not contained in the quote, because the order has not been elected.

CROSSING STOCK

A floor broker from time to time may get an order from both a buyer and a seller in the same security. The floor broker may be allowed to pair off or cross the orders and execute both orders simultaneously. In order for the floor broker to cross the stock, the specialist/DMM must allow it and the floor broker must announce the orders in an effort to obtain price improvement for the orders. The floor broker must offer the stock for sale at a price above the current best bid and may purchase the stock using the buy order if no price improvement has been offered. This then will complete the cross and both orders will be filled.

DO NOT REDUCE (DNR)

GTC orders that are placed underneath the market and left with the specialist/DMM for execution will be reduced for the distribution of dividends. Orders that will be reduced are:

- Buy limits
- Sell stops

These orders are reduced because when a stock goes ex dividend, its price is adjusted down. To ensure that customer orders placed below the market are only executed as a result of market activity, the order will be adjusted down by the value of the dividend.

EXAMPLE

A customer has placed an order to buy 500 XYZ at 35 GTC. XYZ closed yesterday at 36.10. XYZ goes ex dividend for 20 cents and opens the next day at 35.90. The customer's order will now be an order to purchase 500 XYZ at 34.80 GTC.

If the customer had entered the order and specified that the order was not to be reduced for the distribution of ordinary dividends, it would have remained an order to purchase 500 shares at 35. The order in this case would have been entered as:

Buy 500 XYZ 35 GTC DNR

TAKENOTE!

Orders placed above the market such as sell limits and buy stops are not reduced for distributions.

ADJUSTMENTS FOR STOCK SPLITS

GTC orders that are left with the specialist must be adjusted for stock splits. Orders that are placed above and below the market will be adjusted so that the aggregate dollar value of the order remains the same.

EXAMPLE

A customer has placed a GTC order. Let's look at what happens to the order if the company declares a stock split:

Type of Split	Old Order	New Order
2:1	Buy 100 at 50	Buy 200 at 25
2:1	Sell 100 at 100	Sell 200 at 50
3:2	Buy 100 at 100	Buy 150 at 66.67
3:2	Sell 100 at 60	Sell 150 at 40

Notice that in all of the examples, the value of the customer's order remained the same. To calculate the adjustment to an open order for a forward stock split, multiply the number of shares by the fraction and the share price by the reciprocal of the fraction. Such as:

Buy 100 at 50 after a two-to-one stock split

$100 \times 2/1 = 200$

$50 \times 1/2 = 25$

The value of the order was $5,000 both before and after the order.

STOPPING STOCK

As a courtesy to a public customer, a specialist/DMM may guarantee an execution price while trying to find an improved or better price for the public customer. This is known as stopping stock if an order comes in to the crowd to purchase 500 ABC at the market when ABC is quoted as follows:

	Bid	Ask
15 × 20	40	40.20

If the specialist/DMM stopped the customer, they would guarantee that the customer would pay no more than 40.20 for the 500 shares. The specialist then would try to obtain a better price for the customer and would try to attract a seller by displaying a higher bid for that customer's order. ABC may now be quoted after the specialist/DMM stopped the stock as:

	Bid	Ask
5 × 20	40.10	40.20

In this case, the specialist/DMM is trying to buy the stock for the customer 10 cents cheaper than the current best offer. If, however, a buyer comes into the crowd and purchases the stock that is offered at 40.20, the specialist must sell the customer 500 shares from their own account no higher than 40.20.

COMMISSION HOUSE BROKER

A commission house broker is an employee of a member organization and will execute orders for the member's customers and for the member's own account.

TWO-DOLLAR BROKER

A two-dollar broker is an independent member who will execute orders for commission house brokers when they are too busy managing other orders.

REGISTERED TRADERS

A registered trader is an exchange member who trades for their own account and for their own profit and loss. Orders may not originate on the floor of the NYSE; however, registered traders are active on other exchanges such as the Amex (now part of NYSE). A supplemental liquidity provider/SLP is an off-the-floor market maker that directs orders to the floor of the NYSE for its own account. The SLP may compete with the DMM for order execution and must display a bid or offer at least 5% of the time. The SLP will receive a rebate from the NYSE when an order is executed against the SLP's quote that added liquidity to the market.

SUPER DISPLAY BOOK (SDBK)

Most customer orders will never be handled by a floor broker. Floor brokers usually only handle the large complex institutional orders. Customer orders will be electronically routed directly to the trading post for execution via the super display book system. The super display book bypasses the floor broker and sends the order right to the specialist/DMM for execution. If the order can be immediately executed, the system will send an electronic confirmation of the execution to the submitting broker dealer. All listed securities are eligible to be traded over the super display book system. All preopening orders that can be matched up are automatically paired off by the system and executed at the opening price. Any preopening orders that cannot be paired off are routed to the trading post for inclusion on the display book.

SHORT SALES

An investor who believes that a stock price has appreciated too far and is likely to decline may profit from this belief by selling the stock short. In a short sale, the customer borrows the security in order to complete delivery to the buying party. The investor sells the stock high hoping that they can buy it back cheaper and replace it. It is a perfectly legitimate investment strategy. The investor's first transaction is a sell and they exit the position by repurchasing the stock. The short sale of stock has unlimited risk because there is no limit to how high the stock price may go. The investor will lose money if the stock appreciates past their sales price.

REGULATION OF SHORT SALES/REGULATION SHO

The SEC continues to adopt new rules relating to the short sale of securities. Regulation SHO has been adopted to update prior short sale regulations and covers:

- Definitions and order marking
- Suspension of uptick and plus bid requirements
- Borrowing and delivery requirements for securities

Under Regulation SHO, the SEC has prohibited any SRO from adopting any price criteria as a requirement of executing a short sale.

RULE 200 DEFINITIONS AND ORDER MARKING

Rule 200 updates the definition of who is determined to be long a security. As new derivatives and trading systems and strategies have been introduced, amendments to the short sale rules under the Securities Exchange Act of 1934 needed to be updated. Most of the prior rules and definitions remain unchanged. The new updates under Rule 200 are:

- A person is considered long the security if they hold a security future contract and have been notified that they will receive the underlying security.

- A broker dealer must aggregate its net positions in securities unless it qualifies to allow each independent trading unit aggregate its positions independently.

A broker dealer may qualify to have its various trading departments determine their net long or short positions independently if:

- Traders are only assigned to one independent trading unit at any one time.
- Traders in each independent trading unit employ their own trading strategies and do not coordinate their trading with other independent trading units.
- The firm has documented each aggregation unit and the independent trading objectives of each unit.
- The firm supports the independent nature of each trading unit.
- At the time a sell order is entered, each independent aggregation unit determines its net position for the security.

The order marking requirements of Rule 200 require the broker dealer to mark all orders long, short, or short exempt. The definition of long and short include the definitions in the affirmative determination rule and have been expanded to include the following:

- An order may be marked long if the investor or broker dealer have possession of the security and can reasonably be expected to deliver the security by settlement date.
- An order must be marked short if the investor or broker dealer have possession of the security but cannot reasonably be expected to deliver the security by settlement date.
- An order does not need to be marked short exempt if the seller is only relying on a price test exemption under the tick test or bid test rule.

RULE 203 SECURITY BORROWING AND DELIVERY REQUIREMENTS

A broker dealer may not accept an order to sell short an equity security for the account of a customer or for its own account without having borrowed the security, having arranged to borrow the security, or without having a reasonable belief that the security can be borrowed. A broker dealer can rely on an easy-to-borrow list of securities as long as the list is less than 24 hours old. For sell orders that were marked long, the broker dealer must deliver the securities by settlement date and may not borrow the securities to complete delivery. However, a broker dealer may borrow securities to complete delivery under the following exceptions:

- To complete delivery to the buyer when a customer fails to deliver
- The security is being loaned to another broker dealer
- A fail to deliver resulting from a good-faith mistake and a buy in would create an undue hardship

A broker dealer must close out all customer fails to deliver within 35 days of the trade date. The broker dealer must borrow the securities or buy in the securities of a like kind and quantity.

A broker dealer is exempt from the locating requirements for short sales if:

- The broker dealer has accepted an order to sell short an equity security short from another broker dealer. The broker dealer entering the order is required to locate the securities unless the broker dealer accepting the order has a contractual obligation to comply.
- Transactions in securities futures.
- Transactions that are executed in accordance with bona fide market making.
- Transactions executed by a specialist, block positioner, or dealer.
- An order in which the customer has been determined to be long and will deliver the security when restrictions have been removed or expired. The seller must deliver the securities within 35 calendar days. If the broker dealer does not receive the securities, the broker dealer must buy in the customer or borrow the securities.

The firm must file a short interest report twice per month for short positions that have settled by the 15th and as of the last trading day of each month, using FINRA's Regulation Filing Application (RFA). All reports are required to be filed with the firm's designated examining authority (FINRA or NYSE) by the end of the second business day following the settlement date.

OVER THE COUNTER/NASDAQ

Securities that are not listed on any of the centralized exchanges trade over the counter or on the Nasdaq. Nasdaq stands for National Association of

Securities Dealers Automated Quotation System. It is the interdealer network of computers and phone lines that allows securities to be traded between broker dealers. Nasdaq is not an auction market but has been granted exchange status by the SEC. It is a negotiated market. One broker dealer negotiates a price directly with another broker dealer. None of the other interested parties for that particular security have any idea of what terms are being proposed. The broker dealers may communicate over their Nasdaq workstations or can speak directly to one another over the phone.

MARKET MAKERS

Because there are no specialists for the over-the-counter markets, bids and offers are displayed by broker dealers known as market makers. A market maker is a firm that is required to display a two-sided market. A two-sided market consists of a simultaneous bid and offer for the security quoted through the Nasdaq workstation. The market maker must be willing to buy the security and the bid price, which they have displayed, as well as be willing to sell the security at the offering price, which they have displayed. These are known as firm quotes. There is no centralized location for the Nasdaq market; it is simply a network of computers that connects broker dealers throughout the world. Market makers purchase the security at the bid price and sell the security at the offering price. Their profit is the difference between the bid and the offer known as the spread. Rule changes and new trading systems known as ECNs or electronic communication networks have narrowed the spreads on stocks significantly in recent years.

NASDAQ SUBSCRIPTION LEVELS

Broker dealers will subscribe to the Nasdaq workstation services that meet their firm's requirements. The levels of service are:

Level I: Nasdaq Level I subscription service only provides information relating to the inside market and provides quotes for registered representatives.

Level II: Nasdaq Level II subscription service is for broker dealers that are order-entry firms. Level II allows the broker dealer to see the inside market, as well as the quotes of all market makers and to execute orders over the Nasdaq workstation,

Level III: Nasdaq Level III is the highest level of service offered over the Nasdaq workstation. Level III contains all of the features of Level II and allows the firm to enter and update their own markets. Level III is only for approved market makers.

Nasdaq TotalView: Nasdaq TotalView quotation service allows professionals and nonprofessionals to view the entire Nasdaq book for securities traded over Nasdaq. TotalView displays the price and size quoted by all market makers, exchanges, and ECNs. TotalView also displays the total size of the market for the five best priced quotes as well as order imbalance information for all Nasdaq crossing sessions.

NASDAQ QUOTES

Most actively traded Nasdaq stocks are quoted by a large number of market makers. As market makers enter their quotes, some will be above or below the inside market. A market maker whose quote is above or below the inside market is said to be away from the market. As the market makers adjust their quotes, the market maker who is publishing the highest bid for the security has their bid displayed at the top of the list and their bid is published as the best bid to anyone with a Nasdaq Level I subscription. The market maker publishing the lowest offer will have their offer listed at the top of the list and published as the lowest offer to anyone with a Nasdaq Level I subscription. As a result, the best bid and offer from any two market makers will make up the inside market.

EXAMPLE

XYAD

Bid	**Ask**
15.00	**15.05**

MM 1	14.90	15.10
MM 2	15.00	15.20
MM 3	14.85	15.05
MM 4	14.95	15.15
MM 5	14.98	15.18

Note: Notice how the inside market for XYAD consists of the bid from market maker 2 and the offer from market maker 3. All of the other market makers are away from the market.

NOMINAL NASDAQ QUOTES

All quotes published over the Nasdaq workstation are firm quotes. A dealer who fails to honor their quotes has committed a violation known as backing away. Dealers who provide quotes over the phone that are clearly indicated as being subject or nominal cannot be held to trade at those prices. Nasdaq qualifiers are:

- "It looks like"
- "It's around"
- "Subject"
- "Nominal"
- "Work it out"
- "Last I saw"

A response of "it is" would indicate a firm quote. A firm quote is always good for at least one round lot or 100 shares.

NASDAQ EXECUTION SYSTEMS

Most Nasdaq trades are executed over the Nasdaq workstation using one of its automated execution systems. These systems allow dealers to execute orders without having to speak with one another on the phone.

NASDAQ MARKET CENTER EXECUTION SYSTEM (NMCES)

The Nasdaq Market Center Execution System also known as NMCES accepts market orders and immediately executable limit orders for both customer and firm accounts. Orders may be entered for up to 999,999 shares per order. The orders will immediately be routed to dealers on the inside market for automatic execution. Larger orders may be split up to meet the maximum order volume. However, a broker dealer may not split orders that would otherwise be able to be entered into the Nasdaq system in an effort to increase fees or rebates. This would be considered order shredding and is a violation. Orders executed through the Nasdaq execution system are automatically reported to ACT.

NASDAQ OPENING CROSS

The Nasdaq opening cross begins at 9:28 AM. At this time, the Nasdaq execution system automatically executes orders. Orders placed after 9:28 AM may not be canceled. Orders placed after 9:28 AM may be changed only if the change to the order makes the order more aggressive. A change that increases the size of the order or improves the price would make the order more aggressive. For a buy order, an improved price would be a higher limit price; for a sell order, an improved price would be a lower limit price. The opening cross creates the Nasdaq official opening price (NOOP). Like the opening cross, Nasdaq has developed the closing cross to determine the Nasdaq official closing price.

NON-NASDAQ OTCBB

The OTC bulletin board provides two-sided electronic quotes for OTC securities that cannot meet the listing standard of an exchange or Nasdaq. DPPs and ADRs will often be quoted on the OTCBB.

PINK SHEETS

Securities that do not qualify for listing on the Nasdaq, or that have been delisted from Nasdaq or one of the exchanges, may be quoted on the Pink Sheets. The Pink Sheets are now operated as an electronic marketplace. The Pink Sheets operate as the Pink OTC Market to facilitate trading for securities that are quoted on the Pink Sheets. All two-sided quotes displayed in the Pink OTC Market are firm quotes. The Pink Sheets also provides a list of phone numbers for market makers who display subject quotes. Stocks quoted on the Pink Sheets trading at under $5 per share are known as penny stocks. A firm that executes a customer's order for a Pink Sheet security is required to make a reasonable effort to obtain the best price for the customer. The firm is required to obtain quotes from at least three market makers for the security prior to executing the customer's order. If the security has less than three market makers, the firm is required to obtain a quote from all market makers.

THIRD MARKET

The third market consists of transactions in exchange-listed securities executed over the counter through the Nasdaq workstation. A broker dealer may wish to simply purchase or sell an exchange-listed security directly with another brokerage firm instead of executing the order on the floor of the exchange. These transactions are known as third-market transactions. All third-market transactions are reported through TRF to the consolidated tape for display.

FOURTH MARKET

A fourth-market transaction is a transaction between two large institutions without the use of a broker dealer. The computer network that facilitates these transactions is known as INSTINET. Large blocks of stock, both listed and unlisted, trade between large institutional investors in the fourth market. While many trades in the fourth market are executed through the INSTINET system, many large portfolio managers execute internal crosses that go unreported. Proprietary trading systems are not considered part of the fourth market because these systems are either registered as broker dealers or are operated by broker dealers.

BROKER VS. DEALER

The term broker dealer actually refers to the two capacities in which a firm may act when executing a transaction. When a firm is acting as a broker, it is acting as the customer's agent and is merely executing the customer's order for a fee known as a commission. The role of the broker is simply to find someone willing to buy the investor's securities if the customer is selling or to find someone willing to sell them the securities if they are buyers. The firm acts as a dealer when it participates in the transaction by taking the opposite side of the trade. For example, the firm may fill a customer's buy order by selling the securities to the customer from the firm's own account or the dealer may fill the customer's sell order by buying the securities for their own account. A brokerage firm is always acting as a dealer or in a principal capacity when it is making markets over the counter.

Broker	Dealer
Executes customer's orders	Participates in the trade as a principal
Charges a commission	Charges a markup or markdown
Must disclose the amount of the commission	Makes a market in the security Must disclose the fact that they are a market maker, but not the amount of the markup or markdown

FINRA 5% MARKUP POLICY

FINRA has set a guideline to ensure that the prices investors pay and receive for securities are reasonably related to the market for the securities. As a general rule, FINRA considers a charge of 5% to be reasonable. The 5% policy is a guideline, not a rule. Factors that go toward what is considered reasonable are the:

- Price of the security
- Value of the transaction
- Type of security
- Value of the member's services
- Execution expenses

When a customer is executing an order for a low price or low total dollar amount, a firm's minimum commission may be greater than 5% of the transaction.

EXAMPLE A customer wants to purchase 1,000 shares of XYZ at $1. If the firm's minimum commission is $100, that would be 10% of the trade—but in this case, it would be acceptable.

Stocks generally carry a higher degree of risk than bonds and, as a result, stocks justify a higher commission or profit to the dealer. Full-service firms may be able to justify a larger commission simply based on the value of the services they provide.

MARKUPS/MARKDOWNS WHEN ACTING AS A PRINCIPAL

A firm that executes customer orders on a principal basis is entitled to a profit on those transactions. If the firm is selling the security to the customer, they will charge the customer a markup. In the case of the firm buying the securities from the customer, they will charge the customer a markdown. The amount of the markup or markdown that a firm charges the customer is based on the inside market for the security.

EXAMPLE Let's assume that the brokerage firm is a market maker in ABCD. In the morning, the firm purchased shares of ABCD for its own account at 9.50. The stock has been trading higher all day and is now quoted as follows:

Bid	Ask
10.00	10.05

If a customer wants to purchase 100 shares ABCD from the dealer in this example, the customer's markup would be based on the current offering price of 10.05. As a result, the maximum amount the firm could charge the customer for the stock would be 10.552 per share or $1,055.20 for the entire order which would include a 5% markup. Notice that the markup to the customer did not take into consideration the firm's actual cost.

If a customer wanted to sell 100 shares of ABCD using the previous quote, the minimum proceeds to the customer would be 9.50 per share or $950 for entire order, which would include a 5% markdown.

To determine the maximum or minimum prices for a customer, use the following:

- 105% of the offer price for customers who are purchasing the security
- 95% of the bid price for customers who are selling the security

When determining the amount of the markup or markdown, the following are excluded:

- Firm's actual cost
- Firm's quote if they are a market maker in the security

RISKLESS PRINCIPAL TRANSACTIONS

If a brokerage firm receives a customer order to buy or sell a security and the firm does not have an inventory position in the security, the firm still may elect to execute the order on a principal basis. If the firm elects to execute the order on a principal basis, this is known as a riskless principal transaction. Because the dealer is only taking a position in the security to fill the customer's order, the dealer is not taking on any risk. As a result, the markup or markdown on riskless transactions will be based on the dealer's actual cost, not on the inside market. Let's look at an example:

EXAMPLE

Bid	Ask
10.00	10.05

A customer wants to purchase 100 shares ABCD from the dealer and the dealer executes the order on a principal basis by purchasing the shares for its own account at $10.02 only to immediately resell the stock to the customer.

The markup in this case must be based on the dealer's actual cost of $10.02 and the maximum the dealer could charge the customer would be $10.521 per share or $1,052.10 for the entire order.

PROCEEDS TRANSACTIONS

In a proceeds transaction, the customer sells a security and uses the proceeds from that sale to purchase another security on the same day. FINRA's 5% policy states that a firm may only charge the customer a combined commission or markup and markdown of 5% for both transactions, not 5% on each.

ARBITRAGE

Arbitrage is an investment strategy used to take advantage of market inefficiencies and to profit from the price discrepancies that result from those inefficiencies. There are three types of arbitrage. They are:

1. Market arbitrage
2. Security arbitrage
3. Risk arbitrage

Market Arbitrage: Securities that trade in more than one market will sometimes be quoted and trading at different prices. Market arbitrage consists of the simultaneous purchase and sale of the same security in two different markets to take advantage of the price discrepancy.

Security Arbitrage: Securities that give the holder the right to convert or exercise the security into the underlying stock may be purchased or sold to take advantage of price discrepancies between that security and the underlying common stock. Securities arbitrage consists of the purchase or sale of one security and the simultaneous purchase or sale of the underlying security.

Risk Arbitrage: Risk arbitrage tries to take advantage of the price discrepancies that come about as a result of a takeover. A risk arbitrageur will short the stock of the acquiring company and purchase the stock of the company being acquired.

CHAPTER 10

Pretest

TRADING SECURITIES

1. When making markets over the counter, the firm is acting in what capacity?
   a. Dealer
   b. Both
   c. Neither
   d. Broker

2. A bearish investor would establish a short position by entering what type of order?
   a. A buy stop
   b. A market order to buy
   c. AON
   d. A sell stop order

3. All of the following may trade on the floor of the NYSE except:
   a. Two-dollar broker
   b. Regular member
   c. Commission house broker
   d. Allied member

4. Your brokerage firm acts as a market maker for several high-volume stocks that are quoted on the Nasdaq. What is the firm's consideration for being a market maker?

   a. Commission

   b. Fees

   c. Spread

   d. 5%

5. All of the following are types of orders, except:

   I. All or none

   II. Fill or kill

   III. Mini/maxi

   IV. Best efforts

   a. I and II

   b. II and IV

   c. I and IV

   d. III and IV

6. INTC has been hitting a lot of resistance at $30. A technical analyst who wants to buy the stock would most likely place what type of order?

   a. Limit order to buy at $30

   b. Market order

   c. Buy stop at $31

   d. Buy limit at $29

7. Which of the following subjects the investor to unlimited risk?

   a. Selling stock short

   b. Converting a bond into the underlying common stock

   c. Purchase of a call

   d. Selling a naked put

8. The inside market is:
   I. Highest offer
   II. Lowest offer
   III. Highest bid
   IV. Lowest bid
   a. II and III
   b. I and II
   c. I and IV
   d. I and III

9. A bullish investor would enter which of the following orders?
   a. A sell limit thinking that the stock price will rise
   b. A sell stop below the market
   c. A buy stop above the market
   d. DNR GTC

10. ABC Technologies, a very volatile stock, closes at $180 per share. Your customer has placed an order to sell 500 ABC at 165 stop limit 160 GTC. After the close, the company announces bad earnings and the stock opens at 145. What happened to your customer's order?
    a. It has been canceled because the stock price is below the limit price.
    b. It has been elected and has become a limit order.
    c. It has been elected and executed.
    d. It has been canceled because the stock price is below the stop price.

CHAPTER 11

Options

INTRODUCTION

An option is a contract between two parties that determines the time and price at which a stock may be bought or sold. The two parties to the contract are the buyer and the seller. The buyer of the option pays money, known as the option's premium, to the seller. For this premium, the buyer obtains a right to buy or sell the stock depending on what type of option is involved in the transaction. The seller, because they received the premium from the buyer, now has an obligation to perform under that contract. Depending on the option involved, the seller may have an obligation to buy or sell the stock. Series 65 candidates can expect to see a number of questions on options. Most of these questions will be on equity options.

OPTION CLASSIFICATION

Options are classified as to their type, class, and series. There are two types of options:

1. Calls
2. Puts

CALL OPTIONS

A call option gives the buyer the right to buy or to "call" the stock from the option seller at a specific price for a certain period of time. The sale of a call option obligates the seller to deliver or sell that stock to the buyer at that specific price for a certain period of time.

PUT OPTIONS

A put option gives the buyer the right to sell or to "put" the stock to the seller at a specific price for a certain period of time. The sale of a put option obligates the seller to buy the stock from the buyer at that specific price for a certain period of time.

OPTION CLASSES

An option class consists of all options of the same type for the same underlying stock.

For example, all XYZ calls would be one class of options and all XYZ puts would be another class of option.

Class 1	Class 2
XYZ June 50 calls	XYZ June 50 puts
XYZ June 55 calls	XYZ June 55 puts
XYZ July 50 calls	XYZ July 50 puts
XYZ July 55 calls	XYZ July 55 puts
XYZ August 50 calls	XYZ August 50 puts

OPTION SERIES

An option series is the most specific classification of options and consists of only options of the same class with the same exercise price and expiration month. For example, all XYZ June 50 calls would be one series of options and all XYZ June 55 calls would be another series of options.

BULLISH VS. BEARISH

Option investors will seek to establish positions based on their market attitude. Option invests are either bullish or bearish.

BULLISH

Investors who believe that a stock price will increase over time are said to be bullish. Investors who buy calls are bullish on the underlying stock. That is, they believe that the stock price will rise and have paid for the right to purchase the stock at a specific price known as the exercise price or strike price. An investor who has sold puts is also considered to be bullish on the stock. The seller of a put has an obligation to buy the stock and, therefore, believes that the stock price will rise.

BEARISH

Investors who believe that a stock price will decline are said to be bearish. The seller of a call has an obligation to sell the stock to the purchaser at a specified price and believes that the stock price will fall and is therefore bearish. The buyer of a put wants the price to drop so that they may sell the stock at a higher price to the seller of the put contract. They are also considered to be bearish on the stock.

	Calls	Puts
Buyers	Bullish Have right to buy stock; want stock price to rise	Bearish Have right to sell stock; want stock price to fall
Sellers	Bearish Have obligation to sell stock; want stock price to fall	Bullish Have obligation to buy stock; want stock price to rise

Buyer vs. Seller

Buyer		Seller
Owner	**Known as**	Writer
Long	**Known as**	Short
Rights	**Has**	Obligations
Maximum speculative profit	**Objective**	Premium income
With an opening purchase	**Enters the contract**	With an opening sale
Exercise	**Wants the option to**	Expire

POSSIBLE OUTCOMES FOR AN OPTION

EXERCISED

If the option is exercised, the buyer has elected to exercise their rights to buy or sell the stock depending on the type of option involved. Exercising an option obligates the seller to perform under the contract.

SOLD

Most individual investors will elect to sell their rights to another investor rather than exercise their rights. The investor who buys the option from them will acquire all the rights of the original purchaser.

EXPIRE

If the option expires, the buyer has elected not to exercise their right and the seller of the option is relieved of their obligation to perform.

EXERCISE PRICE

The exercise price is the price at which an option buyer may buy or sell the underlying stock depending on the type of option involved in the transaction. The exercise price is also known as the strike price.

CHARACTERISTICS OF ALL OPTIONS

All standardized option contracts are issued and their performance is guaranteed by the Options Clearing Corporation (OCC). Standardized options trade on the exchanges such as the Chicago Board Options Exchange and the American Stock Exchange.

All option contracts are for one round lot of the underlying stock or 100 shares. To determine the amount that an investor either paid or received for the contract, take the premium and multiply it by 100. If an investor paid $4 for 1 KLM August 70 call, they paid $400 for the right to buy 100 shares of KLM at $70 per share until August. If another investor paid $2 for 1 JTJ May 50 put, they paid $200 for the right to sell 100 shares of JTJ at $50 until May.

MANAGING AN OPTION POSITION

In an option trade, both the buyer and seller establish the position with an opening transaction. The buyer has an opening purchase and the seller has an opening sale. To exit the option position, an investor must close out the position. The buyer of the option may exit their position through:

- A closing sale
- Exercising the option
- Allowing the option to expire

The seller of an option may exit or close out their position through:

- A closing purchase
- Having the option exercised or assigned to them
- Allowing the option to expire

Most individual investors do not exercise their options and will simply buy and sell options in much the same way as they would buy or sell other securities.

BUYING CALLS

An investor who purchases a call believes that the underlying stock price will rise and that they will be able to profit from the price appreciation by purchasing calls. An investor who purchases a call can control the underlying stock and profit from its appreciation while limiting their loss to the amount of the premium paid for the calls. Buying calls allows the investor to maximize their leverage and they may realize a more significant percentage return based on their investment. When looking to establish a position, the buyer must determine their:

- Maximum gain
- Maximum loss
- Breakeven

MAXIMUM GAIN LONG CALLS

When an investor has a long call position, their maximum gain is always unlimited. They profit from a rise in the stock price. Because there is no limit to how high a stock price may rise, their maximum gain is unlimited just as if they had purchased the stock.

MAXIMUM LOSS LONG CALLS

Whenever an investor is long or owns a stock, their maximum loss is always limited to the amount they invested. When an investor purchases a call option, the amount they pay for the option or their premium is always going to be their maximum loss.

DETERMINING THE BREAKEVEN FOR LONG CALLS

An investor who has purchased calls must determine where the stock price must be at expiration in order for the investor to break even on the transaction. An investor who has purchased calls has paid the premium to the seller in the hopes that the stock price will rise. The stock must appreciate by enough to cover the cost of the investor's option premium in order for them to break even at expiration. To determine an investor's break-even point on a long call, use the following formula:

Breakeven = strike price + premium

EXAMPLE An investor has established the following option position:

Long 1 XYZ May 30 call at 3

The investor's maximum gain, maximum loss, and breakeven will be:

Maximum gain: unlimited
Maximum loss $300 (amount of the premium paid)
Breakeven: $33 = 30 + 3 (strike price + premium)

If at expiration XYZ is at exactly $33 per share and the investor sells or exercises their option, they will break even excluding transactions costs.

SELLING CALLS

An investor who sells a call believes that the underlying stock price will fall and that they will be able to profit from a decline in the stock price by selling calls. An investor who sells a call is obligated to deliver the underlying stock if the buyer decides to exercise the option. When looking to establish a position, the seller must determine their:

- Maximum gain
- Maximum loss
- Breakeven

MAXIMUM GAIN SHORT CALLS

An investor who has sold uncovered or naked calls, maximum gain is always limited to the amount of the premium they received when they sold the calls.

MAXIMUM LOSS SHORT CALLS

An investor who has sold uncovered or naked calls does not own the underlying stock and, as a result, has unlimited risk and the potential for an unlimited loss. The seller of the calls is subject to a loss if the stock price increases. Because there is no limit to how high a stock price may rise, there is no limit to the amount of their loss.

DETERMINING THE BREAKEVEN FOR SHORT CALLS

An investor who has sold calls must determine where the stock price must be at expiration in order for the investor to break even on the transaction. An investor who has sold calls has received the premium from the buyer in the hopes that the stock price will fall. If the stock appreciates, the investor may begin to lose money. The stock price may appreciate by the amount of the option premium received and the investor still will break even at expiration. To determine an investor's break-even point on a short call, use the following formula:

Breakeven = strike price + premium

EXAMPLE

An investor has established the following option position:

Short 1 XYZ May 30 call at 3

The investor's maximum gain, maximum loss, and breakeven will be:

Maximum gain: $300 (amount of the premium received)
Maximum loss: Unlimited
Breakeven: $33 = 30 + 3 (strike price + premium)

If at expiration XYZ is at exactly $33 per share and the investor closes out the transaction with a closing purchase or has the option exercised against them, they will break even excluding transactions costs.

Notice the relationship between the buyer and the seller:

	Call Buyer	Call Seller
Maximum Gain	Unlimited	Premium received
Maximum Loss	Premium paid	Unlimited
Breakeven	Strike price + premium	Strike price + premium
Wants Option to	Exercise	Expire

Because an option is a two-party contract, the buyer's maximum gain is the seller's maximum loss and the buyer's maximum loss is the seller's maximum gain. Both the buyer and the seller will break even at the same point.

BUYING PUTS

An investor who purchases a put believes that the underlying stock price will fall and that they will be able to profit from a decline in the stock price by purchasing puts. An investor who purchases a put can control the underlying stock and profit from its price decline while limiting their loss to the amount of the premium paid for the puts. Buying puts allows the investor to maximize their leverage while limiting their losses and may realize a more significant percentage return based on their investment. When looking to establish a position, the buyer must determine their:

- Maximum gain
- Maximum loss
- Breakeven

MAXIMUM GAIN LONG PUTS

An investor who has purchased a put believes that the stock price will fall. There is, however, a limit to how far a stock price may decline. A stock price may never fall below zero. As a result, the investor who believes that the stock price will fall has a limited maximum gain. To determine the maximum gain for the buyer of a put, use the following formula:

Maximum gain = strike price – premium

MAXIMUM LOSS LONG PUTS

Whenever an investor is long or owns a stock, their maximum loss is always limited to the amount they invested. When an investor purchases a put option, the amount they pay for the option or their premium is always going to be their maximum loss.

DETERMINING THE BREAKEVEN FOR LONG PUTS

Whenever an investor has purchased a put, they believe that the stock price will decline. In order for the investor to break even on the transaction, the stock price must fall by enough to offset the amount of the premium paid for the option. At expiration, the investor will break even at the following point:

Breakeven = strike price – premium

EXAMPLE An investor has established the following option position:

Long 1 XYZ May 30 put at 4

The investor's maximum gain, maximum loss, and breakeven will be:

Maximum gain: $26 or $2,600 for the whole position
(strike price – premium)
Maximum loss: $400 (amount of the premium paid)
Breakeven = $26 = 30 – 4 (strike price – premium)

If XYZ is at exactly $26 per share at expiration and the investor sells or exercises their option, they will break even excluding transactions costs.

SELLING PUTS

An investor who sells a put believes that the underlying stock price will rise and that they will be able to profit from a rise in the stock price by selling puts. An investor who sells a put is obligated to purchase the underlying stock if the buyer decides to exercise the option. When looking to establish a position, the seller must determine their:

- Maximum gain
- Maximum loss
- Breakeven

MAXIMUM GAIN SHORT PUTS

For an investor who has sold uncovered or naked puts, maximum gain is always limited to the amount of the premium they received when they sold the puts.

MAXIMUM LOSS SHORT PUTS

An investor who has sold a put believes that the stock price will rise. There is, however, a limit to how far a stock price may decline. A stock price may never fall below zero. As a result, the investor who believes that the stock price will rise has a limited maximum loss. The worst thing that can happen for an investor who is short a put is that the stock goes to zero and they are forced to purchase it at the strike price from the owner of the put. To determine the maximum loss for the seller of a put, use the following formula:

Maximum loss = strike price – premium

DETERMINING THE BREAKEVEN FOR SHORT PUTS

Whenever an investor has sold a put, they believe that the stock price will rise. If the stock price begins to fall, the investor becomes subject to loss. In order for the investor to break even on the transaction, the stock price may fall by the amount of the premium they received for the option. At expiration, the investor will break even at the following point:

Breakeven = strike price – premium

EXAMPLE An investor has established the following option position:

Short 1 XYZ May 30 put at 4

The investor's maximum gain, maximum loss, and breakeven will be:

Maximum gain: $400 (amount of the premium received)
Maximum loss: $26 or $2,600 for the whole position (strike price – premium)
Breakeven = $26 = 30 – 4 (strike price – premium)

If XYZ is at exactly $26 per share at expiration and the investor closes out the position with a closing purchase or has the option exercised against them, they will break even, excluding transactions costs.

Notice the relationship between the buyer and the seller.

	Put Buyer	Put Seller
Maximum Gain	Strike price – premium	Premium received
Maximum Loss	Premium paid	Strike price – premium
Breakeven	Strike price – premium	Strike price – premium
Wants Option to	Exercise	Expire

Because an option is a two-party contract, the buyer's maximum gain is the seller's maximum loss and the buyer's maximum loss is the seller's maximum gain. Both the buyer and the seller will break even at the same point.

OPTION PREMIUMS

The price of an option is known as its premium. Factors that determine the value of an option and, as a result, its premium, are:

- Relationship of the underlying stock price to the option's strike price
- Amount of time to expiration
- Volatility of the underlying stock
- Supply and demand
- Interest rates

An option can be:

- In the money
- At the money
- Out of the money

These terms describe the relationship of the underlying stock to the option's strike price. These terms do not describe how profitable the position is.

IN-THE-MONEY OPTIONS

A call is in the money when the underlying stock price is greater than the call's strike price.

EXAMPLE An XYZ June 40 call is $2 in the money when XYZ is at $42 per share.

A put is in the money when the underlying stock price is lower than the put's strike price.

EXAMPLE An ABC October 70 put is $4 in the money when ABC is at $66 per share. It would only make sense to exercise an option if it was in the money.

AT-THE-MONEY OPTIONS

Both puts and calls are at the money when the underlying stock price equals the options exercise price.

EXAMPLE If FDR is trading at $60 per share, all of the FDR 60 calls and all of the FDR 60 puts will be at the money.

OUT-OF-THE-MONEY OPTIONS

A call is out of the money when the underlying stock price is lower than the option's strike price.

EXAMPLE An ABC November 25 call is out of the money when ABC is trading at $22 per share.

A put option is out of the money when the underlying stock price is above the option's strike price.

EXAMPLE A KDC December 50 put is out of the money when KDC is trading at $54 per share.

It would not make sense to exercise an out-of-the-money option.

	Calls	Puts
In the Money	Stock price > strike price	Stock price < strike price
At the Money	Stock price = strike price	Stock price = strike price
Out of the Money	Stock price < strike price	Stock price > strike price

INTRINSIC VALUE AND TIME VALUE

An option's total premium is comprised of intrinsic value and time value. An option's intrinsic value is equal to the amount the option is in the money. Time value is the amount by which an option's premium exceeds its intrinsic value. In effect, the time value is the price an investor pays for the opportunity to exercise the option. An option that is out of the money has no intrinsic value; therefore, the entire premium consists of time value.

EXAMPLE An XYZ June 40 call is trading at $2 when XYZ is trading at $37 per share. The June 40 call is out of the money and has no intrinsic value; therefore, the entire $2 premium consists of time value. If an XYZ June 40 put is trading at $3 when XYZ is at $44 dollars per share the entire $3 is time value.

If, in this example, the options were in the money and the premium exceeded the intrinsic value of the option, the remaining premium would be time value.

EXAMPLE An XYZ June 40 call is trading at $5 when XYZ is trading at $42 per share. The June 40 call is in the money and has $2 in intrinsic value; therefore, the rest of the premium consists of the time value of $3. If an XYZ June 40 put is trading at $4 when XYZ is at $39, the put is in the money by $1 and the rest of the premium or $3 is time value.

USING OPTIONS AS A HEDGE

Many investors will use options to hedge a position that they have established in the underlying stock. Options can be used to guard against a loss or to protect a profit the investor has in a position. Options in this case will operate like an insurance policy for the investor.

LONG STOCK LONG PUTS/MARRIED PUTS

An investor who is long stock and wishes to protect the position from downside risk will receive the most protection by purchasing a protective put. By purchasing the put, the investor has locked in or set a minimum sale price that they will receive in the event of the stock's decline for the life of the put. The minimum sale price in this case is equal to the strike price of the put. Long puts can be used with long stock to guard against a loss or to protect an unrealized profit. However, by purchasing the put, the investor has increased their break-even point by the amount of the premium they paid to purchase the put. When looking to establish a long stock long put position, the investor must determine their:

- Maximum gain
- Breakeven
- Maximum loss

MAXIMUM GAIN LONG STOCK LONG PUTS

An investor who is long stock and long puts has a maximum gain that is unlimited because they own the stock.

BREAKEVEN LONG STOCK LONG PUTS

To determine an investor's breakeven when they have established a long stock long put position, you must add the option premium to the cost of the stock.

Breakeven = stock price + premium

EXAMPLE An investor establishes the following position:

Long 100 XYZ at 55
Long 1 XYZ June 55 put at 3

The investor will break even if the stock goes to $58. The stock price has to appreciate by enough to offset the amount of the premium that the investor paid for the option. If, at expiration, the stock is at $58 per share and the put expires, the investor will have broken even, excluding transaction costs.

MAXIMUM LOSS LONG STOCK LONG PUTS

In order to determine an investor's maximum loss when they have established a long stock long put position, you must first determine the breakeven as just outlined. Once you have determined the breakeven, use the following formula:

Maximum loss = breakeven – strike price

Let's take another look at the previous example, only this time we will use it to determine the investor's maximum loss.

EXAMPLE An investor establishes the following position:

Long 100 XYZ at 55
Long 1 XYZ June 55 put at 3

We have already determined that the investor will break even if the stock goes to $58. To determine their maximum loss, subtract the put's strike price from the investor's breakeven as follows:

58 – 55 = 3

The investor's maximum loss is $3 per share or $300 for the entire position. Notice that the option's premium is the investor's maximum loss. When the purchase price of the stock and the strike price of the put are the same, the investor's maximum loss is equal to the premium paid for the option.

Let's take a look at another example where the investor's purchase price is different from the strike price of the put.

EXAMPLE An investor establishes the following position:

Long 100 XYZ at 58
Long 1 XYZ June 55 put at 2

In order to find the investor's maximum loss, we first need to determine their breakeven. This investor will break even if the stock goes to \$60, found by adding the stock price to the premium the investor paid for the put. To find their maximum loss, subtract the put's strike price from the breakeven.

60 – 55 = 5

The investor's maximum loss on this position is \$5 per share or \$500 for the entire position.

An investor who is long stock and long puts has limited their potential losses and has received the maximum possible protection while retaining all of the appreciation potential.

LONG STOCK SHORT CALLS/COVERED CALLS

An investor who is long stock can receive some partial downside protection and generate some additional income by selling calls against the stock they own. The investor will receive downside protection or will hedge their position by the amount of the premium received from the sale of the call. Although the investor will receive partial downside protection, they also will give up any appreciation potential above the call's strike price. An investor who is going to establish a covered call position must determine their:

- Breakeven
- Maximum gain
- Maximum loss

BREAKEVEN LONG STOCK SHORT CALLS

By selling the calls, the investor has lowered their breakeven on the stock by the amount of the premium received from the sale of the call. To determine the investor's breakeven in this case, the price to which the stock can fall, use the following formula:

Purchase price of the stock – premium received

EXAMPLE An investor establishes the following position:

Long 100 ABC at 65
Short 1 ABC June 65 call at 4

Using the formula we get:

65 – 4 = 61

The stock price in this case can fall to $61 and the investor will still break even.

MAXIMUM GAIN LONG STOCK SHORT CALLS

Because the investor has sold call options on the stock that they own, they have limited the amount of their gain. Any appreciation of the stock beyond the call's strike price belongs to the investor who purchased the call. To determine an investor's maximum gain on a long stock short call position, use the following formula:

Maximum gain = strike price – breakeven

Let's use the same example to determine the investor's maximum gain.

EXAMPLE An investor establishes the following position:

Long 100 ABC at 65
Short 1 ABC June 65 call at 4

Using this formula, we get:

65 – 61 = $4

The investor's maximum gain is $4 per share or $400 for the entire position. Notice that because the purchase price of the stock and the strike price of the call are the same, the investor's maximum gain is equal to the amount of the premium received on the sale of the call.

Let's look at an example in which the strike price and the purchase price for the stock are different.

EXAMPLE An investor establishes the following position:

Long 100 ABC at 65
Short 1 ABC June 70 call at 2

The investor will break even at $63 found by subtracting the premium received from the investor's purchase price for the stock. To determine their maximum gain, subtract the breakeven from the strike price and we get:

70 − 63 = 7

The investor's maximum gain is $7 per share or $700 for the entire position.

MAXIMUM LOSS LONG STOCK SHORT CALLS

An investor who has sold cover calls has only received partial downside protection in the amount of the premium received. As a result, the investor is still subject to a significant loss in the event of an extreme downside move in the stock price. To determine an investor's maximum loss when they are long stock and short calls, use the following formula:

Maximum loss = breakeven − 0

Said another way, an investor is subject to a loss equal to their break-even price per share. Using the same example, we get:

EXAMPLE An investor establishes the following position:

Long 100 ABC at 65
Short 1 ABC June 70 call at 2

The investor will break even at $63, found by subtracting the premium received from the investor's purchase price for the stock. To determine their maximum loss, we only need to look at the breakeven and we get a maximum loss of $63 per share or $6,300 for the entire position. The investor will realize their maximum loss if the stock goes to zero.

SHORT STOCK LONG CALLS

An investor who sells stock short believes that they can profit from a fall in the stock price by selling it high and repurchasing it cheaper. An investor who has sold stock short is subject to an unlimited loss if the stock price should begin to rise. Once again there is no limit to how high a stock price may rise. An investor who has sold stock short would receive the most protection by purchasing a call. A long call could be used to guard against a loss or to protect a profit on a short stock position. By purchasing the call, the investor has set the maximum price that they will have to pay to repurchase the stock for the life of the option. Before establishing a short stock long call position, the investor will have to determine their:

- Breakeven
- Maximum gain
- Maximum loss

DETERMINING THE BREAKEVEN SHORT STOCK LONG CALLS

An investor who has sold stock short will profit from a fall in the stock price. When an investor has purchased a call to protect their position, the stock price must fall by enough to offset the premium the investor paid for the call. To determine the breakeven for a short stock long call position, use the following formula:

Breakeven = stock price – premium

EXAMPLE An investor establishes the following position:

Short 100 ABC at 60
Long 1 ABC October 60 call at 2

Using the formula, we get:

60 – 2 = 58

The stock would have to fall to $58 by expiration in order for the investor to break even.

MAXIMUM GAIN SHORT STOCK LONG CALLS

The maximum gain on the short sale of stock is always limited because a stock cannot fall below zero. When an investor has a short stock long call position, their maximum gain is found by using the following formula:

Maximum gain = breakeven – 0

Said another way, the investor's maximum gain per share would be equal to their break-even price per share. Using the same example, we get:

EXAMPLE An investor establishes the following position:

Short 100 ABC at 60
Long 1 ABC October 60 call at 2

Using this formula, we get:

58 – 0 = 58

If the stock fell to $0 by expiration, the investor would realize their maximum gain of $58 per share or $5,800 for the entire position.

MAXIMUM LOSS SHORT STOCK LONG CALL

An investor who has sold stock short and has purchased a call to protect their position is only subject to a loss up to the strike price of the call. In order to determine the investor's maximum loss, use the following formula:

Maximum loss = strike price – breakeven

Using the same example, we get the following:

EXAMPLE An investor establishes the following position:

Short 100 ABC at 60
Long 1 ABC October 60 call at 2

60 – 58 = 2

The investor is subject to a loss of $2 per share or $200 for the entire position. Notice that the price at which the investor sold the stock short at and the strike price of the call are the same. As a result, the investor has set a maximum repurchase price equal to the price at which they sold the stock short. The investor's maximum loss when the sale price and strike price are the same is the amount of the premium that the investor paid for the call.

Let's take a look at a position where the sale price of the stock and strike price of the option are different.

EXAMPLE An investor establishes the following position:

Short 100 ABC at 56
Long 1 ABC October 60 call at 2

This investor will break even at $54 per share. To determine their maximum loss, subtract the breakeven from the strike price of the option.

60 − 54 = 6

The investor is subject to a loss of $6 per share or $600 for the entire position.

SHORT STOCK SHORT PUTS

An investor who has sold stock short can receive some protection and generate premium income by selling puts against their short stock position. Selling puts against a short stock position will only partially hedge the unlimited upside risk associated with any short sale of stock. Additionally, the investor, in exchange for the premium received for the sale of the put, has further limited their maximum gain. Before entering a short stock short put position, an investor must determine their:

- Breakeven
- Maximum gain
- Maximum loss

BREAKEVEN SHORT STOCK SHORT PUTS

An investor who has sold stock short and sold puts against their position is subject to a loss if the stock price begins to rise. To determine how high a stock price could rise after establishing a short stock short put position and still allow the investor to break even, use the following formula:

Breakeven = stock price + premium

EXAMPLE

An investor establishes the following position:

Short 100 ABC at 55
Short 1 ABC November 55 put at 4

Using the formula, we get:

55 + 4 = 59

In this case, the stock could rise to $59 by expiration and still allow the investor to breakeven excluding transaction costs.

MAXIMUM GAIN SHORT STOCK SHORT PUTS

An investor who has established a short stock short put position has limited the amount of their gain even further by selling puts, because the investor will be required to purchase the shares at the put's strike price if the stock declines.

To determine the investor's maximum gain, use the following formula:

Maximum gain = breakeven − strike price

EXAMPLE

An investor establishes the following position:

Short 100 ABC at 55
Short 1 ABC November 55 put at 4

The investor will break even at 59 found by adding the stock price of 55 and the option premium of 4 together.

Using this formula, we get:

59 − 55 = 4

The investor's maximum gain in this case is $4 per share or $400 for the entire position. The investor received a total of $59 per share by establishing the position. If the stock fell to zero, they still would be required to repurchase the shares at 55 under the terms of the put contract. Notice that the sales price and the put's exercise price are the same and the amount of the investor's maximum gain is equal to the amount of the premium received.

Let's look at a position where the sale price of the stock and the strike price of the put are different.

EXAMPLE

An investor establishes the following position:

Short 100 XYZ at 60
Short 1 XYZ November 55 put at 4

The investor will break even at 64; $64 dollars per share were the total proceeds received by the investor for establishing the position. To determine their maximum gain using the pervious formula, we get:

64 − 55 = 9

The investor's maximum gain is $9 per share or $900 for the total position.

MAXIMUM LOSS SHORT STOCK SHORT PUTS

An investor who has sold puts against their short stock position has only limited their loss by the amount of the premium received from the sale of the put. As a result, the investor's loss in a short stock short put position is still unlimited.

Underlying Position	Most Protection	Some Protection and Income
Long stock	Long puts	Short calls
Short stock	Long calls	Short puts

TESTPOINT

It's important to note that anytime an investor wants the most protection, they are going to buy the hedge. If the investor wants some protection and income, they will sell the hedge.

LONG STRADDLES

A long straddle is the simultaneous purchase of a call and a put on the same stock with the same strike price and expiration month. An option investor would purchase a straddle when he or she expects the stock price to be extremely volatile and to make a significant move in either direction. An investor who owns a straddle is neither bullish nor bearish. Such investors are not concerned with whether the stock moves up or down in price, so long as it moves significantly. An investor may purchase a straddle just prior to a company announcing earnings, with the belief that if the company beats its earnings estimate the stock price will appreciate dramatically. Or, if the company's earnings fall short of expectations, the stock price will decline dramatically.

SHORT STRADDLES

A short straddle is the simultaneous sale of a call and a put on the same stock with the same strike price and expiration month. Options investors would sell a straddle when they expect the stock price to trade within a narrow range or to become less volatile and not to make a significant move in either direction. An investor who is short a straddle is neither bullish nor bearish. Such investors are not concerned with whether the stock moves up or down in price, so long as it does not move significantly. An investor may sell a straddle just after a period of high volatility, with the belief that the stock will now move sideways for a period of time.

FUTURES AND FORWARDS

Futures, like options, are a two-party contract. Many future contracts are an agreement for the delivery of a specific amount of a commodity at a specific place and time. Futures began to trade for commodities such as wheat and gold and over the years have expanded to include financial futures such as on Treasury securities and, most recently, single stock futures. The specific terms and conditions of the contracts are standardized and set by the exchanges on which they trade. The contract amount, delivery date, and type of settlement vary between the different futures contracts. Most investors will use futures as a hedge or to speculate on the value of the underlying commodity or instrument. Forwards are privately negotiated contracts for the purchase and sale of a commodity or financial instrument. Forwards often are used in the currency markets by corporations and banks doing business internationally. If a corporation knows that it needs to make a payment for a purchase in foreign currency three months from now, the corporation can arrange to purchase the currency from a bank the day before the payment is due. The big draw back with forwards is that there is no secondary market for the contracts.

CORRELATION

Prices of two investments that move together are said to be correlated. The value of a call would move in the same direction as the price of the underlying stock. If the price of the stock rises, the value of the call will rise. If the value of the stock falls, the value of the call will also fall. If the prices of two investments move together at the same rate, the investments are said to be perfectly correlated. If the prices of two investments move in opposite directions, the investments are said to be negatively correlated. Examples of investments that are negatively correlated would be common stock and a put on the common stock. As the price of the stock increases, the value of the put decreases. Alternatively, if the price of the stock falls, the price of the put will rise. If the price of two investments move independently of one another, the investments are said to be uncorrelated. For example, the change in the price of oil futures often will have nothing to do with a change in the price of Treasury bonds or the change in the price of shares of IBM. As such, the investments would be considered to be uncorrelated.

CHAPTER 11

Pretest

OPTIONS

1. You sold 10 IBM May 95 puts at 5.70. Your maximum gain is:
   a. $570
   b. $5,700
   c. Unlimited
   d. $95,000

2. Your customer sells 10 IBM Nov 95 puts to open at 3.15. Their maximum gain is:
   a. Unlimited
   b. $95,000
   c. $3,150
   d. $91,850

3. You are long 10,000 shares of XYZ at 42 and are concerned about a market decline and you would like to take in some additional income. You should:
   a. Sell 10 XYZ Oct 45 puts
   b. Sell 100 XYZ Oct 45 calls
   c. Sell 100 XYZ Oct 45 puts
   d. Sell 10 XYZ Oct 45 calls

4. Which of the following are true about an option?
   - **I.** It is a contract between two parties that determines the time and place at which a security may be bought or sold.
   - **II.** The two parties are known as the buyer and the seller. The money paid by the buyer of the option is known as the option's premium.
   - **III.** The buyer has bought the right to buy or sell the security depending on the type of option.
   - **IV.** The seller has an obligation to perform under the contract, possibly to buy or sell the stock depending on the option involved.

   a. I, III, and IV
   b. I, II, III, and IV
   c. I, II, and III
   d. II, III, and IV

5. Which of the following are bearish?
   - **I.** Call seller
   - **II.** Put seller
   - **III.** Call buyer
   - **IV.** Put buyer

   a. II and III
   b. II and IV
   c. I and IV
   d. I and II

6. An investor buys 10 XYZ Nov 75 calls at 4.10 on Monday, May 11. The trade will settle on:

   a. Thursday, May 14
   b. Tuesday, May 12
   c. Monday, May 11
   d. Monday, May 18

7. Which of the following issues standardized options?

   a. Exchanges
   b. OCC
   c. Company
   d. Nasdaq

8. An investor buys 10 XYZ May 70 calls at 3.10 when XYZ is at 68. At expiration, the stock is at 77 and the investor closes out the position at its intrinsic value. What is the profit or loss?

   a. $7,000 profit
   b. $7,000 loss
   c. $3,100 loss
   d. $3,900 profit

9. The OCC is:

   a. Options Clearing Corporation
   b. Options Counseling Committee
   c. Options and Claims Corporation
   d. Options Clearing Committee

CHAPTER 12

Definition of Terms

INTRODUCTION

In order to successfully complete the Series 65 exam, it is important to have an in-depth understanding of the terms used within the securities industry—specifically within the framework of the Uniform Securities Act. The terms used by the USA (also known as the Act) may have broader meanings than we are accustomed to in everyday usage.

SECURITY

A security is anything that can be exchanged for value that involves a risk to the holder. A security also represents an investment in an entity managed by a third party. The Howey test was used by the Supreme Court to determine a security and states that a security must meet the following four characteristics. It must:

1. Be an investment of money
2. Involve a common enterprise
3. Give the investor an expectation of a profit
4. Entail the management of a third party

The following are examples of securities:

- Stocks
- Bonds
- Notes
- Debentures
- Evidence of indebtedness
- Transferable shares
- Warrants, rights, or options for securities
- Mutual fund shares
- Exchange traded funds and notes ETFs/ETNs

Most times when you see the term certificate, you have a security that is a:

- Certificate of interest in profit sharing or a partnership agreement
- Preorganization certificate
- Collateral trust certificate
- Voting trust certificate
- Certificate of interest in oil or a gas mining title
- Certificate of deposit for a security such as an American depositary receipt (ADR) or an American depositary share (ADS)

The term variable will also identify a security, as in:

- Variable annuity
- Variable life insurance
- Variable contract

The phrase interest in is another key to identifying a security on the Series 65 exam. All of the following are securities:

Interest in:

- Farmland and animals
- Whiskey warehouse receipts
- Commodity options (not futures)
- Insurance company separate accounts

- Real estate condominiums or cooperatives
- Merchandise marketing programs, franchises, or schemes
- Multilevel distributorships such as Amway

The term option is also a good way to identify a security, such as:

- Stock option
- Index option
- Futures option
- Commodity futures option

The following are not considered securities:

- Real estate
- Retirement plans such as IRAs and 401Ks
- Bank accounts
- Collectibles
- Precious metals
- Fixed annuities/fixed contracts
- Whole and term life policies
- Antiques
- Futures contracts (commodities)
- Trade confirmations
- Prospectuses

The term future as it appears alone is an indication that a security is not involved. If the question is asking about a commodity future option, however, then a security is involved. Also the term fixed is a good indication that a security is not involved. If a person commits a fraudulent act in the sale of an investment that is not deemed to be a security, that person has not violated securities laws but has committed a fraudulent act in violation of other state and federal laws.

PERSON

The term person as it is used in the USA refers to any entity who may enter into a legally binding contract. Any entity who can enter into a legally binding contract may transact business in the securities markets. Agreeing to buy or sell a security represents a legally binding contract. For the Series 65 exam, a person is any of the following:

- Natural person
- Corporation
- Trust
- Government organization
- Partnership
- Joint stock company
- Sole proprietor
- Association
- Unincorporated organization

A nonperson is an individual or entity who may not enter into a legally binding contract and therefore may not transact business in the securities market. A nonperson is:

- A minor
- Someone deemed to be legally incompetent
- A deceased individual

BROKER DEALER

A broker dealer is a person or a firm who maintains a place of business and affects transactions in the securities markets for its own account or for the account of others. A broker dealer must be registered in the home state as well as in the states of its individual clients. A broker dealer is not a(n):

- Agent
- Bank
- Savings and loan
- Person with no place of business in the state, who deals exclusively with financial institutions or issuers

- Person with no place of business in the state who conducts business with existing clients who do not reside in the state and are in state for less than 30 days

AGENT

An agent or registered representative may only be an individual (natural person) who represents the issuer or a broker dealer in the purchase and sale or the attempted purchase and sale of securities with the public. Agents are required to register in their home state, their state of employment, and the state of residence of their customers. An agent is not required to register if:

- They represent the issuer or a broker dealer in an underwriting transaction.
- They represent a bank or a savings and loan in the issuance of securities.

Agents who represent exempt issuers are not required to register. Examples of exempt issuers are:

- U.S. government
- State and municipal governments
- Canadian federal and municipal governments
- Commercial paper with maturities of less than 270 days, sold in denominations exceeding $50,000
- Investment contracts associated with employee pension plans, profit sharing, stock purchase, or savings plans
- Foreign national governments recognized by the United States

ISSUER

An issuer is any person who issues or simply proposes to issue a security. Issuers include:

- Corporations
- U.S. government and agencies
- State and local governments

In an issuer or primary transaction, the issuer receives the proceeds from the sale.

NONISSUER

A nonissuer is anyone who does not issue or propose to issue a security. All secondary market transactions that take place on an exchange or in the over-the-counter (OTC) market are nonissuer transactions, and the selling security holder receives the proceeds from the sale.

INVESTMENT ADVISER

An investment adviser is any person who is actively involved in and receives a fee for any of the following:

- Issuing research reports or analysis
- Publishing a market letter based on market events
- Advising clients as to the advisability of the purchase or sale of a security
- Providing investment advisory services as a complement to their services and claiming to provide such services for a fee
- Presenting themselves as investment advisers, also known as the Shingle Rule
- Act as a pension consultant

PENSION CONSULTANTS

A pension consultant is anyone who advises employees on how to fund their employee benefit plan. A person also would be considered to be a pension consultant if they advise the employees on the selection of asset managers or investment advisers for the plan. An investment adviser is not:

- A bank or savings and loan
- A broker dealer
- An agent
- A lawyer, accountant, teacher, engineer (LATE) whose services are incidental to their business and who do not receive a specific fee for such services
- Any person exempted by the administrator
- Publishers of newspapers and magazines

FORM ADV

An investment adviser will begin its formal registration process by filling out Form ADV. The ADV form will provide detailed information regarding the investment adviser and it is comprised of four parts: Part 1A, Part 1B, Part 2A, and Part 2B.

ADV Part 1A includes general information about the investment adviser, including:

- Principal office address
- Type of organization such as corporation or partnership
- How the adviser will conduct business
- If the firm engages in other activities such as that of a broker dealer
- Biographical data on the officers, directors, or partners
- Disciplinary history of the officers, directors, partners, and the firm
- Location of books and records if other than principal office
- If the adviser has custody of customer assets
- If the adviser has discretionary authority over customer assets

ADV Part 1B is filed with the state securities administrator for advisers registered at the state level. Advisers who are federally registered do not file ADV Part 1B.

Form ADV Part 2A will disclose information relating to clients. ADV Part 2A will state:

- How and when fees are charged
- Types of securities the adviser does business in
- How recommendations are made
- Type of clients the adviser has
- Qualifications of officers and directors

Form ADV Part 2B provides information relating to individuals who:

- Provide investment advice and who have direct contact with advisory clients
- Have discretion over client assets regardless of whether the individual has contact with clients

INVESTMENT ADVISER REPRESENTATIVE

An investment adviser representative is a natural person who is under the control of the investment adviser and includes:

- Officers and directors
- Partners
- Solicitors
- Supervisors

Clerical employees are not considered investment advisory representatives and are not required to register.

SOLICITOR

A solicitor is any person who, for compensation, actively seeks new business for an investment adviser. A solicitor can also include professionals who refer clients to the investment adviser for a fee. All solicitors must be registered as investment adviser representatives.

ACCESS PERSON

An access person is anyone employed by the investment adviser who has access to nonpublic information relating to activity and holding in client accounts or in the investment adviser's portfolio account. A person will also be deemed to be an access person if that individual makes recommendations to clients or has access to recommendations prior to the release of such recommendations. All of the firms officers and directors are deemed to be access persons at advisory firms where the primary business is providing investment advice. All access persons must report their personal transactions to the firm's chief compliance officer or duly designated compliance officer. The firm must maintain a list of all individuals who were deemed to be access persons in the last five years.

INSTITUTIONAL INVESTOR

An institutional investor is a person or firm who trades securities for his or her own account or for the account of others. Institutional investors are generally limited to large financial companies. Because of their size and sophistication, fewer protective laws cover institutional investors. It is important to note that there is no minimum size for an institutional account. Institutional investors include:

- Broker dealers
- Investment advisers
- Investment companies
- Insurance companies
- Banks
- Trusts
- Savings and loans
- Government agencies
- Employment benefit plans with more than $1,000,000 in assets

ACCREDITED INVESTOR

An accredited investor is an individual who meets one or more of the following criteria:

- Has a net worth of $1,000,000 excluding the primary residence;

  or

- Earns $200,000 per year or more for the last two years and has the expectation of earning the same in the current year;

  or

- Is part of a couple earning $300,000 per year or more

QUALIFIED PURCHASER

A qualified purchaser must meet strict minimum financial requirements. Securities sold to qualified purchasers are not required to register in the state where the qualified purchaser resides. A qualified purchaser is a(n):

- Individual with at least $5,000,000 in investments
- Family-owned business with at least $5,000,000 in investments
- Trust sponsored by qualified purchasers

PRIVATE INVESTMENT COMPANY

A private investment company is an unregistered investment company or hedge fund that raises funds through the sale of securities to qualified purchasers for any business purposes.

OFFER/OFFER TO SELL/OFFER TO BUY

An offer is any attempt to solicit the purchase or sale of a security for value. An offer is considered to have been made in the state where the offer originated, as well as in the state where it is received or directed. An offer will not be considered to have been made if it was received through a television or radio broadcast originating outside the state. Additionally, an offer will not be considered to have been made if received by a newspaper or magazine published out of the state or by a magazine published in state that has two-thirds of its paid circulation outside of the state.

The state securities administrator does not have jurisdiction over offers that are deemed to be made exclusively outside of the administrator's state.

SALE/SELL

To sell a security, its ownership must be conveyed for value. A sale is considered to have been made at the time of the contract (trade). A sale of a security that has warrants or a right attached is also considered a sale of the attached security. A sale of any security that is convertible or exercisable into another security is considered to include a sale of the security for which the security is convertible or exercisable. A gift of assessable stock is also considered a sale. Assessable stock is stock that may require the holder to make additional payments as a term of ownership. A sale does not include a dividend or the pledge of a security for a collateral loan.

GUARANTEE/GUARANTEED

The term guarantee means that another party other than the issuer of the security has guaranteed the payment of principal, interest, or dividends. Only three parties may guarantee something. They are:

1. U.S. government
2. Insurance company
3. Parent company—they may guarantee obligations of a subsidiary

CONTUMACY

Contumacy is the willful display of contempt for the administrator's order. An act of contumacy may result in the agent's or firm's registration being revoked or other disciplinary action.

The administrator may petition the court to have a person who has displayed contumacy for their order to be found in contempt of court. A finding of contempt of court may result in the court ordering a jail term.

FEDERALLY COVERED EXEMPTION

A **federally covered exemption** provides for a full exemption from state registration for federally covered investment advisers and federally covered securities.

A **federally covered investment adviser** is one who meets the requirements for assets under management and is registered with the Securities Exchange Commission (SEC).

A **federally covered security** is any of the following:

- A security listed on a centralized U.S. stock exchange or on the Nasdaq
- An investment company security issued under the Investment Company Act of 1940
- Securities sold to qualified purchasers

POWER OF ATTORNEY

A power of attorney once given to an individual allows that person to make decisions on behalf of the grantor with the same force and effect as if the grantor themselves had entered into the agreement. Most powers of attorney in the investment world are limited powers of attorney that allow an investment professional to purchase and sell securities without speaking to a client first. A full power of attorney will allow the individual to withdrawal cash and securities from an account. A standard power of attorney will terminate upon the death or incapacitation of the grantor. A durable power of attorney will remain in full force during the incapacitation of the grantor and will only terminate upon the grantor's death. Discretion may not be exercised by until the power of attorney has been received and approved.

NEGOTIABLE CERTIFICATE OF DEPOSIT

A negotiable CD is one that may be sold by the holder prior to the maturity date of the certificate. With a standard certificate of deposit issued by a bank if the holder needed to access the funds prior to the maturity date the owner would pay a penalty for early termination. A negotiable or jumbo CD is issued by a bank for a time deposit in excess of $100,000 with many jumbo CDs being in excess of $1,000,000. The CDs pay periodic interest and will trade in the money market with accrued interest. FDIC insurance only covers the first $250,000 of the principal amount should the bank fail.

CHAPTER 12

Pretest

DEFINITION OF TERMS

1. Which of the following is not considered a person under the Uniform Securities Act (USA)?
   - **a.** A joint stock company
   - **b.** A trust
   - **c.** A 17-year-old honor student
   - **d.** A government agency

2. All of the following are considered a sale of a security except a:
   - **a.** Gift of assessable stock
   - **b.** Contract to convey ownership for value
   - **c.** Pledge of securities as collateral for a margin loan
   - **d.** Bonus of securities

3. The minimum financial requirement for an individual to be considered a qualified purchaser is:
   - **a.** $1,000,000
   - **b.** $2,500,000
   - **c.** $5,000,000 individually or $10,000,000 jointly with a spouse
   - **d.** $5,000,000 individually or jointly with a spouse

4. As it pertains to the USA, which of the following are considered institutional investors?
   I. A bank
   II. An insurance company
   III. An employee benefit plan with $800,000 in assets
   IV. A trust

   a. I and II
   b. I and IV
   c. I, II, and IV
   d. I, II, III, and IV

5. All of the following are considered securities except:
   a. Whiskey warehouse receipts
   b. Trust indenture
   c. Commodity future option
   d. Interest in a marketing scheme

6. An individual gives 1,500 shares of assessable stock to their child. Under the USA, this is:
   a. Subject to approval of the state securities administrator
   b. Considered an offer of securities
   c. Irrevocable
   d. Considered a sale of securities

7. Which of the following is considered an investment adviser?
   a. The publisher of a market report with a $495 subscription fee based on market events
   b. A publisher of a financial newspaper
   c. An accountant
   d. A person paid a commission for executing a securities transaction

8. Which of the following is considered a qualified purchaser?
   a. An individual with $1,000,000 in investments held jointly with a spouse and with annual income of $375,000
   b. A publicly held company with at least $5,000,000 in net assets
   c. A pension plan with $2,000,000 in assets
   d. A family-owned business with at least $5,000,000 in assets

9. XYZ common stock trades on the Boston Stock Exchange. XYZ common stock is an example of a(n):
   a. Blue-chip security
   b. Federally covered security
   c. Exempt security
   d. Security of an exempt issuer

10. A security is represented by an interest in:
    I. Farmland or animals
    II. A cooperative
    III. Marketing scheme
    IV. Multilevel distributorship

    a. None of the choices listed
    b. I and II
    c. I, II, and III
    d. I, II, III, and IV

11. Under the USA, an investment adviser is:
    I. XYZ Advisers, Inc.
    II. Mr. Jones, the owner of XYZ Advisers, Inc.
    III. The publisher of a market-based letter charging $800 per year
    IV. A partner for XYZ who solicits new clients for XYZ advisers

    a. I only
    b. I and III
    c. I, II, and IV
    d. I, II, III, and IV

12. When using the Howey test to determine if an investment is a security, all of the following are used except:
    a. Third-party management
    b. Investment of money
    c. A common enterprise
    d. The promise of a profit

13. A broker is a(n):
    a. Registered representative
    b. Duly licensed agent
    c. Issuer of collateralized securities
    d. Person who executes transactions for the accounts of others

14. An offer of securities is considered to have been made in which of the following circumstances?
    a. A sales presentation for a fixed annuity
    b. Delivering a market report
    c. Mailing a form letter
    d. Delivering a prospectus

15. The Uniform Securities Act defines an issuer as a:
    a. Broker dealer
    b. Bank
    c. Corporation proposing the sale of common shares
    d. Savings and loan

16. An individual in which of the following situations is considered an agent?
    a. An individual represents a bank as the issuer of securities
    b. An individual represents a corporate issuer in the sale of large denomination commercial paper
    c. An individual who represents a Canadian province
    d. An individual who represents an out-of-state broker dealer selling securities to residents

17. A broker dealer is not:

    I. A firm with no office in the state that transacts business only with existing customers who do not reside within the state

    II. A firm with no office in the state that transacts business only with broker dealers in state

    III. A firm with an office in state that only transacts business with other broker dealers

    IV. A firm with no office in the state that only transacts business with wealthy clients in state

    a. I and II

    b. II and IV

    c. I, II, and IV

    d. I, II, III, and IV

18. A federally covered security is all of the following except a:

    a. Security issued by an investment company

    b. Security issued by a UIT

    c. Security only sold to qualified purchasers

    d. Security listed on Nasdaq OTCBB

19. A guarantee may be issued by:

    I. An insurance company

    II. The U.S. government

    III. A parent company

    IV. An investment adviser

    a. I and IV

    b. I and III

    c. I, II, and III

    d. I, II, III, and IV

20. An offer to sell has been made when:

    a. Stock has been pledged as collateral for a loan at the bank

    b. A gift of securities to a charity results in tax credit for the donor

    c. A representative calls a client and recommends a security

    d. An account is transferred to the surviving party under joint tenants with rights of survivorship

CHAPTER 13

Registration of Broker Dealers, Investment Advisers, and Agents

INTRODUCTION

In this chapter, we will examine the state registration process for broker dealers, investment advisers, and agents. An important part of this chapter will be to know when registration is required and when an exemption is offered to the subject in question.

REGISTRATION OF BROKER DEALERS AND AGENTS

Prior to conducting business in any state, a broker dealer must be properly registered or exempt from registration in that state. The first test when deciding if the broker dealer must register is determining if the firm has an office in the state. If the firm maintains an office within the state, it must register with that state. An agent must register in their state of residence even if their firm is located in another state.

EXAMPLE An agent who lives in New Jersey and who commutes to their office in New York must register in both New Jersey and New York.

Agents also must register in the states where they sell securities or offer to sell securities as well as where they advertise. If the firm does not have an office in the state, they may or may not be required to register depending on with whom they do business. If a broker dealer does not have an office in the state and engages in securities transactions with the general public, then they must register. If a broker dealer with no office in the state conducts business exclusively with any of the following, they are not required to register in that state:

- Other broker dealers
- Issuers of securities
- Investment companies
- Insurance companies
- Banks
- Savings and loans
- Trust companies
- Pension plans with more than 100 participants
- Other financial institutions
- Institutional buyers
- Existing customers with less than 30 days' temporary residency in the state (on vacation or business trips)

A broker dealer will not be deemed to have a place of business in a state where it does not maintain an office simply by virtue of the fact that the firm's website is accessible from that state as long as the following conditions are met:

- The firm's website clearly states that the firm may only conduct business in states where it is properly registered to do so.
- The firm's website only provides general information about the firm and does not provide specific investment advice.
- The firm may not respond to Internet inquiries with the intent to solicit business without first meeting the registration requirements in the state of the prospective customer.

AGENT REGISTRATION

It is unlawful for a broker dealer to employ any agent who is not properly registered under the Uniform Securities Act (USA). When determining if an agent must register, first look for whom the agent works. If the agent works for a broker dealer, the agent must register. The only exception is for officers and directors of a broker dealer who have no involvement with customers, securities transactions, or supervision. If the agent works for an exempt issuer, the agent is exempt from registration no matter what security is involved. Exempt issuers are:

- U.S. and municipal governments
- Canadian federal and municipal governments
- Foreign federal governments recognized by the United States
- Banks, savings and loans, and trust companies

An agent is also exempt from registering if they represent an issuer in the sale of an exempt security such as:

- Bankers' acceptances or time drafts with less than 270 days to maturity sold in denominations of $50,000 or more
- Investment contracts relating to employee savings, stock purchases, pension plans, or other benefit plans as long as no commission is received for such sales

REGISTERING BROKER DEALERS

A broker dealer wishing to become registered in a state must first file an application with the state securities administrator. The broker dealer must also pay all filing fees and sign consent to service of process. By signing the consent to service of process, the broker dealer appoints the administrator as their attorney in fact and allows the administrator to receive legal papers for the applicant. Any legal papers received by the administrator will have the same force and effect as if they were served on the broker dealer. All applications must also include:

- Type of organization (corporation, partnership)
- Address of business
- Description of business to be conducted
- Backgrounds and qualifications of officers and directors
- Disclosure of any legal actions
- Financial condition

The firm's registration will become effective at noon 30 days after the initial application has been received or at noon 30 days after the administrator has received the last piece of required information. Registering a broker dealer in a state automatically requires that any officers and directors who act in a sales capacity register as agents in that state.

FINANCIAL REQUIREMENTS

A broker dealer must be able to meet the minimum capital requirements set forth by the state securities administrator. If the broker dealer is unable to meet this capital requirement, they must post a surety bond to ensure their solvency. Broker dealers that meet the Securities Exchange Commission's (SEC) minimum net capital requirements are exempt from USA's capital and surety bond requirements. The administrator may also require that an officer or agent of the broker dealer take an exam that may be oral, written, or both.

BROKER DEALERS ON THE PREMISES OF OTHER FINANCIAL INSTITUTIONS

As the financial services business continues to bring together investments services with other more traditional banking services, it is more common to see brokerage services offered at retail bank locations. Broker dealers who offer investment services at bank branches must follow certain guidelines. The setting in which the broker dealer conducts its business should be separate from where the retail banking business is being conducted, if practical. Broker dealers must disclose to the customer—at or before the time that the customer opens the account—that their deposits are not guaranteed by the FDIC or the financial institution and are subject to the loss of principal. These same disclosures must also appear in all advertising and sales literature issued by the broker dealer operating on the location of other financial institutions. The host financial institution must sign an agreement stating that FINRA and the SEC are allowed to have access to any location where the member conducts its business. The member is required to promptly notify the financial institution if it terminates an associated person for cause.

REGISTERING AGENTS

Most states require that agents successfully complete the Series 65 exam before they may conduct business within their state. In addition to successfully passing the Series 65 exam, an agent also must:

- Abide by and understand state securities laws and regulations
- Recognize that the state may require additional certification regarding the state's securities laws

- Understand that they may not conduct business until they are properly registered

TESTFOCUS!

- An agent does not become registered in a state simply by passing the Series 63, 65, or 66 exam. An agent becomes registered only when the state securities administrator notifies them that they have become registered.
- An agent may not be registered in any state without being employed by a broker dealer or issuer and no broker dealer or issuer shall employ an agent that is not duly registered.

CHANGES IN AN AGENT'S EMPLOYMENT

When an agent changes firms, the agent, former employer, and new employer all must notify the state securities administrator. This is done in most cases quite easily through the central registration depository (CRD) system for all firm and agent information. An agent's termination becomes effective 30 days after notifying the state unless the administrator is in the process of suspending or revoking the agent's registration. The administrator may still revoke an agent's registration for up to one year after their registration has been terminated.

MERGERS AND ACQUISITIONS OF FIRMS

If a broker dealer is acquiring another broker dealer, the successor firm must file an application for registration within the state. The successor firm's registration will become effective upon completion of the transaction. The registration fees for the successor firm will be waived.

RENEWING REGISTRATIONS

All state registrations expire on December 31 and all broker dealers, investment advisers, and agents are required to file renewal application and pay a renewal fee.

CANADIAN FIRMS AND AGENTS

A Canadian firm or agent may engage in securities transactions with financial institutions and existing customers without registering under the USA as long as they do not maintain an office within the state. A Canadian broker dealer or agent who is a member in good standing with a Canadian securities regulator is allowed to register through a simplified registration process. The state registration will become effective 30 days after the application has been received with the consent to service process. The Canadian broker dealer must advise the state of any disciplinary action.

INVESTMENT ADVISER REGISTRATION

It is unlawful for an investment adviser to conduct securities business without being properly registered or exempt from registration. State registration exemptions are provided for investment advisers who:

- Are federally registered
- Manage portfolios for investment companies
- Manage portfolios in excess of $110,000,000
- Have no office in the state and conduct business exclusively with financial institutions
- Have no office in the state and offer advice to five clients or less in any 12-month period. This is known as the de minimis exemption.

If an investment adviser with no office in the state advertises to the public the ability to meet and offer investment advisory services with clients in a hotel or other temporary location, the investment advisor is required to register with the state.

An investment adviser will not be deemed to have a place of business in a state where it does not maintain an office simply by virtue of the fact that the firm's website is accessible from that state as long as the following conditions are met:

- The firm's website clearly states that the firm may only conduct business in states where it is properly registered to do so.
- The firm's website only provides general information about the firm and does not provide specific investment advice.

- The firm may not respond to Internet inquiries with the intent to solicit business without first meeting the registration requirements in the state of the prospective customer.

NATIONAL SECURITIES MARKET IMPROVEMENT ACT OF 1996/COORDINATION ACT

The National Securities Markets Improvement Act of 1996 eliminated regulatory duplication of effort and established registration requirements for investment advisers. A federally covered investment adviser must register with the SEC and is any investment adviser who:

- Manages at least $110,000,000
- Manages investment company portfolios
- Is not registered under state laws

All federally registered investment advisers must pay state filing fees and notify the administrator in the states in which they conduct business. The state securities administrator may not audit a federally covered investment adviser unless that adviser's principal offices are located in that administrator's state. An investment adviser is required to register with the state if they manage less than $100,000,000. Once the investment advise reaches $100,000,000 in assets under management (AUM), the adviser becomes eligible for federal registration. An investment adviser who manages between $100,000,000 and $110,000,000 may choose to register either with the state or with the SEC. If the investment adviser thinks that their asset base will exceed $110,000,000, they should register with the SEC. An investment adviser who manages $110,000,000 or more must register with the SEC. If a federally covered investment adviser's AUM falls below $90,000,000, the adviser must withdraw its federal registration by filling Form ADV-W and is required to registered with the appropriate states within 180 days. Like most regulations, there are rare exceptions to the rule of when an investment adviser may register with the SEC. The Dodd Frank Wall Street Reform Act of 2010 increased the AUM for federal registration to its current levels and defined three categories of investment advisers as follows:

1. Small adviser: advisers with less than $25,000,000 AUM
2. Mid-size advisers: advisers with $25,000,000 to $100,000,000 AUM
3. Large advisers: advisers with more than $100,000,000 AUM

Pension consultants must have at least $200,000,000 AUM to be eligible to become federally registered.

INVESTMENT ADVISER REPRESENTATIVE

All investment adviser representatives who maintain an office within the state must register within the state. An investment adviser representative is an individual who:

- Gives advice on the value of the securities
- Gives advice on the advisability of buying or selling securities
- Solicits new advisory clients
- Is an officer, director, or partner of the investment adviser

An investment adviser may not employ any representative who is not properly registered. Clerical and administrative employees are not considered representatives and do not need to register. An investment adviser representative who has no place of business in the state and who offers to meet a client in a hotel or other place of convenience is not considered to have an office in the state as long as the representative does not advertise the office and only offers the ability to meet directly to clients.

TESTFOCUS!

An investment adviser representative who represents a federally covered investment adviser must register with the state where they work as well as where they have clients even though their firm is not required to register.

INVESTMENT ADVISER REGISTRATION

An investment advisory firm that is required to register with the state must file the following with the state securities administrator before they become registered:

- Application Form ADV
- Filing fees
- Audited balance sheet within 90 days of year end

CAPITAL REQUIREMENTS

An investment adviser must maintain a minimal level of financial solvency. For advisers with custody of customer's cash and securities, the investment adviser must maintain a minimum net capital of $35,000. If the adviser is unable to meet this requirement, they may post a surety bond. Deposits of cash and securities will alleviate the surety bond requirement. An adviser is considered to have custody if they have their customers' cash and securities held at their firm or if they have full discretion over their customers' accounts. Full discretion allows the adviser to withdraw cash and securities from the customer's account without consulting the customer. Advisers who have only limited discretionary authority over customers' accounts need to maintain a minimum of $10,000 in net capital. An adviser with limited discretionary authority may only buy and sell securities for the customer's benefit without consulting the customer. They may not withdraw or deposit cash or securities without the customer's consent. If a state-registered investment adviser meets the capital requirements in its home state, then that will be deemed to have met the capital requirements in any other state in which the adviser wishes to register even if the other states have higher next capital or bonding requirements. Should a state-registered adviser's net capital fall below the minimum requirement, the adviser must notify the state administrator of the adviser's net worth by the close of the next business day. The adviser then must file a financial disclosure report with the administrator by the end of the next business day. Investment adviser representatives are not required to maintain a minimum level of liquidity.

EXAMS

The state securities administrator may require investment adviser representatives as well as the officers and directors of the firm to take an exam, which may be oral, written, or both. All registration becomes effective at noon 30 days after the application has been filed. The administrator may require that an announcement of the investment adviser's intended registration be published in the newspaper.

Requirement	Broker Dealer	Investment Adviser	Agents
Net capital	Yes	Yes	No
Surety bond	Yes	Yes	Yes
Exams	Yes	Yes	Yes
Fees	Yes	Yes	Yes

ADVERTISING AND SALES LITERATURE

All advertising and sales literature for an investment adviser must be filed with the state securities administrator. The administrator may require prior approval of:

- Form letters
- Prospectuses
- Pamphlets

Investment advisers must keep the following records for a minimum of five years unless the state securities administrator requires a different period of time:

- Advertising and sales literature
- Account statements
- Order tickets/order memorandum

All investment advisers must keep accurate records relating to the following:

- Cash receipts and disbursements
- Income and expense ledgers
- Order tickets, including customer's name
- Adviser's name, including executing broker and discretionary information
- Ledgers and confirmations for all customers for whom the adviser has custody
- Financial statements and trial balance
- All written recommendations to customers
- Copies of advertisements, circulars, and articles sent to more than 10 people
- Copies of calculations sent to more than 10 people

All books and records must be kept for five years readily accessible and for two years at the adviser's office. Records may be kept on a computer or microfiche as long as the data may be viewed and printed.

BROCHURE DELIVERY

An investment adviser is required to provide all prospective clients with a brochure or with Form ADV Part II at least 48 hours prior to the signing of the contract or at least at the time of the signing of the contract, if the client is given a five-day grace period to withdraw without penalty. The brochure or Form ADV Part II will state:

- How and when fees are charged
- Types of securities the adviser does business in
- How recommendations are made
- Type of clients the adviser has
- Qualifications of officers and directors

THE ROLE OF THE INVESTMENT ADVISER

An investment adviser charges a fee for his or her services for advising clients as to the value of securities or for making recommendations as to which securities should be purchased or sold. Unlike a broker dealer, the investment adviser has a contractual relationship with his or her clients and must always adhere to the highest standards of professional conduct.

ADDITIONAL COMPENSATION FOR AN INVESTMENT ADVISER

In addition to the fees charged by an investment adviser, an investment adviser may also:

- Receive commissions for executing a customer's transaction through certain broker dealers
- Act as a principal in a customer's transaction

These sources of additional revenue must be disclosed to the client in writing prior to the investment adviser executing such transactions.

AGENCY CROSS TRANSACTIONS

An agency cross transaction is one in which the investment adviser represents both the purchasing and selling security holder either as an investment adviser or as a broker dealer. If the investment adviser is going to execute an agency cross transaction, they must get the advisory client's authorization in writing. The authorization may be pulled at any time verbally and the adviser may not have solicited both sides of the trade. The investment adviser still maintains a duty to obtain the best execution for both clients and may not execute the cross at a price that favors one client over the other. The adviser must send notice to its clients annually detailing the number of all agency cross transactions completed by the adviser.

DISCLOSURES BY AN INVESTMENT ADVISER

An investment adviser must update its form ADV annually within 90 days of its fiscal year end. Additionally, the investment advisor must provide each client with an updated brochure annually within 120 of the advisors fiscal year end. The brochure must be provided free of charge and must provide a summary of material changes to the advisory firm.

- Conflicts of interest
- Sources of recommendations
- Location of customer's funds for advisers with custody
- Any legal actions taken against the adviser
- Material facts
- Soft-dollar arrangements

If the change to the investment advisor's business is material, it must be disclosed promptly. Of critical importance is to know what changes to the investment advisory firm are deemed material and when those changes must be disclosed. Most investment advisory firms other than small sole proprietorships are organized either as a corporation or as a partnership. A material change to the ownership or control of the adviser is considered to be material and must be disclosed promptly. If the adviser is a corporation and one of the firm's major stockholders sells, pledges, or assigns their block of controlling voting shares, this would be seen as both material and as an assignment of the contract and must be disclosed promptly. If the nature of the transfer is deemed to be an assignment, the client would also have to give their consent to continue the relationship. However, if an officer of the corporation leaves, no disclosure is required. If the advisory firm is organized as a partnership and a major partner dies or departs from the partnership, this would be considered material and as an assignment. Therefore, the material change must be disclosed promptly and the client must give their consent to continue the advisory relationship. However, if the partnership adds or removes minority partners, these events would not be deemed material.

An investment adviser may not:

- Borrow from a customer.
- Commingle customer's funds with the adviser's funds.
- Accept an order from a party not named on the account of the customer.
- Churn customer accounts.
- Make unsuitable recommendations.
- Charge unreasonable fees.

An investment adviser with custody of customer's funds must:

- Segregate all customer funds and securities.
- Give the customer a written notice of the location of the funds.
- Establish a separate bank account for the customer's funds.
- Provide quarterly statements showing all transactions and account status.
- Go through an annual surprise audit.

TAKENOTE!

The state securities administrator may or may not allow advisers to have custody of clients' funds. If custody is allowed, the adviser must notify the state that they have custody and adhere to all requirements relating to custody of client funds.

INVESTMENT ADVISER CONTRACTS

All investment adviser contracts must be in writing and must contain disclosures of:

- Length
- Services to be provided
- Fees to be charged and how they are assessed
- Amount of any prepaid fees to be returned upon cancellation of the contract
- Statement prohibiting the investment adviser from assigning the contract without the customer's consent
- Notification of any changes in the adviser's management
- Limits on the adviser's discretionary authority over the customer's account, if any

> **TAKENOTE!**
>
> If an investment adviser uses an outside solicitor (such as an accounting firm) to refer business, the client must get both the advisory's brochure and the solicitor disclosure document or solicitor's brochure.

ADDITIONAL ROLES OF INVESTMENT ADVISERS

As the business services offered by various professionals have expanded, so has the definition of who must register as an investment adviser. Sports and entertainment representatives now often advise their clients on how or with whom to invest their earnings. As a result, the representative is considered an investment adviser, even if investment advice is only a small part of the services they perform. Individuals who advise pension funds on the merits of portfolio managers or who act as pension consultants also must register as investment advisers.

PRIVATE INVESTMENT COMPANIES/HEDGE FUNDS

A private investment company/3C7 funds may charge performance-based compensation to clients, provided that the clients have a minimum of $1,000,000 of assets under the adviser's management or have a net worth of

$2,000,000. Corporations with $25 million in assets and individuals with at least $5 million in investments also may participate.

FULCRUM FEES

Advisers, who manage accounts for investment companies or accounts with a value greater than $1 million (if those accounts are not for trusts or retirement plans), may charge fulcrum fees. A fulcrum fee provides the adviser with additional compensation for outperforming a broad-based index such as the S&P 500 and less compensation for underperforming the index. The amount of the additional compensation received for outperforming the index must be equal to the amount of compensation that would be lost for underperformance. The index used as the basis to determine the adviser's performance must contain similar securities and risks.

WRAP ACCOUNTS

A wrap account is an account that charges one fee for both the advice received as well as the cost of the transaction. All clients who open wrap accounts must be given the wrap account brochure that will provide all of the information that is found on Form ADV Part II.

SOFT DOLLARS

Brokerage firms will oftentimes provide investment advisers with services to assist the investment adviser in their business that go beyond execution and research. These services are provided in exchange for commission business and are known as soft dollars. The services received should normally be research related. However, there are instances when the services received are used for other purposes. Investment advisers must ensure that the services received are for the benefit of the client and need to pay careful attention to the disclosure requirements relating to soft dollars.

If an adviser receives soft dollar compensation from broker dealer to whom the adviser directs customer transactions (known as directed transactions) the adviser must disclose any arrangement to clients. The fees charged to execute the transactions should by fair and reasonable in line with what Is available in the marketplace and in line with the value of the services offered to the adviser and its clients. The execution fees are not required to be the lowest and simply using a broker dealer whose services are more expensive will not constitute a break of the adviser's fiduciary duty. If the advisor directs transactions to a broker dealer in exchange services that benefit the adviser the adviser must disclosure all facts relating the arrangement and receive the client's written consent to enter into the arrangement even if such arrangement does not increase the costs to the client. Client consent for soft dollar compensation may be obtained on a separate authorization or as part of the adviser's form ADV disclosure. The disclosure on form ADV must include a list of the products and services provided to the adviser, the process the adviser uses to allocate customer order execution, and if the fees being paid are higher than they otherwise would be.

The SEC has divided soft dollar consideration into the following categories:

- Goods/services
- Accounting fees
- Association membership fees
- Commission rebates
- Computer hardware
- Computer software
- Conferences/seminars
- Consulting services
- Courier/postage/express mail
- Custodial fees
- Electronic databases
- Employee salary/benefits
- Execution assistance
- Industry publications
- Internet television
- Legal fees
- Management fees
- Miscellaneous expenses
- Office equipment/supplies
- Online quotation and news services
- Portfolio management software
- Rent

- Research/analysis reports
- Telephone expenses
- Travel expenses
- Tuition/training costs
- Utilities expenses

TAKENOTE!

Not all of these items are for the research benefit of clients.

CHAPTER 13

Pretest

REGISTRATION OF BROKER DEALERS, INVESTMENT ADVISERS, AND AGENTS

1. An individual representing which of the following is always required to register?
   - **a.** Government
   - **b.** Nonexempt issuers
   - **c.** Issuers in the sale of commercial paper
   - **d.** A broker dealer

2. A broker dealer is exempt from the surety bond requirement if the broker dealer:
   - **a.** Does not maintain an office in the state
   - **b.** Deals only with existing customers
   - **c.** Meets the SEC's net capital requirement
   - **d.** Has customer funds segregated from their own funds

3. An investment adviser may conduct business with how many people and still qualify for the de minimis exemption?
   - **a.** Fewer than 12 in six months
   - **b.** Fewer than 10 in 12 months
   - **c.** Fewer than five in 12 months
   - **d.** Fewer than eight in 12 months

4. A small New Jersey broker dealer with five partners who all manage client portfolios registers as a broker dealer in Connecticut. Which of the following is true?
   a. Only the partners with clients in Connecticut must register as agents in the state.
   b. Only one of the partners is required to register as a supervisor for all of the firm's activities in Connecticut.
   c. There is no requirement for the partners of a broker dealer to register in a state where the firm has no office.
   d. All of the partners must register.

5. All of the following would be considered soft-dollar compensation except:
   a. Profit-and-loss accounting software
   b. High-speed Internet services
   c. Commissions paid by the adviser
   d. Custodial fees

6. You work for a newly formed investment adviser that has just received $107,000,000 to manage. The firm should register:
   a. With the SEC only
   b. With the state only
   c. With either the SEC or the state depending on the prospects for receiving additional funds
   d. The adviser does not have to register if it has no office in the state.

7. All of the following must be disclosed to a new investment advisory client except:
   a. Type of clients
   b. Basis for recommendations
   c. Advisory fees
   d. Investment adviser representative's compensation

8. An agent is exempt from registration if they represent:
   I. A municipality
   II. A Canadian corporation
   III. A trust company
   IV. The government of Brazil
   a. I and IV
   b. I and II
   c. I, III, and IV
   d. I, II, III, and IV

9. Which of the following must register as an investment adviser?
   a. Publisher of financial newspapers
   b. Company representative who is paid a salary for explaining the employer's benefit plan to employees
   c. An individual who represents a broker dealer
   d. An individual who solely advises as to the value of securities

10. Which of the following must notify the state securities administrator when an agent changes firms?
    a. The old broker dealer
    b. The agent
    c. The new broker dealer
    d. All of the above

11. Which of the following is true regarding a broker dealer?
    a. A broker dealer may not also be registered as an investment adviser.
    b. A broker dealer may not be an individual.
    c. A broker dealer may also be registered as an investment adviser and may be a corporation or an individual.
    d. A broker dealer may only execute orders for its customers on an agency basis.

12. An investment adviser with $75,000,000 under management and registered with the state must typically keep records readily accessible:
    - a. Two years
    - b. Three years
    - c. Five years
    - d. 10 years

13. A simplified registration is available for which of the following?
    - a. A broker dealer in good standing with a securities regulator in Great Britain
    - b. A broker dealer in a neighboring state
    - c. A broker dealer in good standing with a Canadian regulator
    - d. A broker dealer in good standing with FINRA/NYSE

14. An investment adviser who provides advisory services to individual investors may receive:
    - I. A fee based on the customer's assets
    - II. Commissions for executing transactions with certain broker dealers
    - III. A percentage of the profits in the account
    - IV. A profit on principal transactions

    - a. I and II
    - b. I and III
    - c. I, II, and IV
    - d. I, II, III, and IV

15. A broker dealer has been declared insolvent. Which of the following is true regarding the agent's registrations?
    - a. The administrator holds all agents' registrations until the agent becomes employed by another firm.
    - b. All agents' registrations are suspended.
    - c. All agents' registrations are revoked.
    - d. All agents' registrations are canceled.

16. An investment adviser without custody of funds is subject to all of the following except:

a. Filing fees

b. Surprise audits

c. $35,000 surety bond

d. Net capital requirements

17. An investment adviser with no office in the state has given advice to nine individuals in the last 17 months. Which of the following is true?

a. Because the investment adviser has no office in the state and has given advice to fewer than 10 people, they are not required to register.

b. An investment adviser is always required to register prior to offering any advice to individuals.

c. The investment adviser must be registered in this situation even though they have no office in the state.

d. The investment adviser still qualifies for the de minimis exemption in this case.

18. Your client has just opened up a wrap account. Which of the following is true?

a. They will be charged one fee for advice and execution.

b. They must be given Form PART II.

c. They must be accredited investors.

d. They must deposit at least $150,000 to open the account.

19. All registrations of firms, agents, and advisers:

a. Expire on December 31

b. Expire after 24 months

c. Expire after 12 months

d. Are good for the life of the agent or firm

CHAPTER 14

Securities Registration, Exempt Securities, and Exempt Transactions

INTRODUCTION

This chapter covers some of the more difficult topics regarding securities registration and may mean the difference between successfully completing the exam and having to retake it at a later time. All securities that are sold to state residence must either be:

- Properly registered;

  or
- Exempt from registration;

  or
- Sold through an exemption transaction.

EXEMPT SECURITIES

Exempt securities are exempt from the registration requirements of the Securities Act of 1933. Exempt securities are not exempt from the antifraud provisions of the USA. Exempt securities are:

- Issued by exempt issuers, such as governments
- Short-term debt instruments with less than 270 days to maturity

SECURITIES REGISTRATION

Nonexempt securities become federally registered by submitting a registration statement to the Securities Exchange Commission (SEC). Nonexempt securities also must register in the states in which the securities will be sold. The three methods of registering securities in a state are:

1. Coordination
2. Notice filing
3. Qualification

It is important to understand how the three types of securities registration differ and under what circumstances the different registration methods are used.

REGISTRATION OF IPOs THROUGH COORDINATION

When a company first sells stock to the public during an initial public offering (IPO), the company must file a registration statement with the SEC. The company also must file documents with the state securities administrator in the states where the issue will be sold. Most IPOs will register with the state securities administrator at the same time that they registering with the SEC. This process of simultaneous registration is known as coordination. The following must be submitted to the administrator:

- Copies of the prospectus
- Any amendments to the prospectus
- Amount of the securities to be offered within the state
- List of other states where the securities will be offered
- Consent to service of process
- Other information as required by the state securities administrator, including the corporate bylaws, articles of incorporation, specimen of the security, and indenture of any kind

If an amendment has been made to the federal registration, it must also be made to the state registration. A security's state registration will become effective at the time the federal registration takes effect as long as no stop order has been issued and the documents have been on file with the state for the minimum number of days (usually 10 to 20 days). It is important to note that a state registration may not become effective prior to the security's federal registration becoming effective.

REGISTRATION THROUGH NOTICE FILING

The National Securities Market Improvement Act of 1996 withdrew the states' authority to require the registration of investment companies registered under the Investment Company Act of 1940. The states preserved the right to require investment companies to file a notice and pay a fee. When the issuer of a security notice files with the state securities administrator, the following must be submitted:

- Issuer's name and address
- Type of organization
- Description of the securities to be offered
- Copy of the prospectus
- Copy of documents filed with the SEC
- Consent to service of process
- State fee

Even though the state securities administrator no longer maintains jurisdiction over the registration process of the securities, the administrator still maintains broad investigative powers over any suspected fraudulent sales practices relating to the securities. The administrator may investigate the firms and agents who offer the securities for sale to investors within their state. Notice filing may also be used by other federally covered and federally registered securities who meet the minimum requirements. The administrator may require that an issuer of a federally covered security trading on an exchange to file all information on file with the SEC and to submit a consent to service of process prior to offering any securities to state residence. A security that is federally registered and trading on the OTC bulletin board or on the pink sheets may be federally registered but may not meet the minimum criteria to notice file.

REGISTRATION OF NONESTABLISHED ISSUERS/ REGISTRATION THROUGH QUALIFICATION

Securities of issuers who do not meet the requirements for registering through notice filing and that are not an IPO must register through qualification.

Securities of issuers that will be sold only in one state through an intrastate offering will also be registered through qualification. Registration through qualification is the most complex method of registration. The issuer must file a statement containing all of the information required by the state securities administrator. It may include:

- Name and address of the issuer
- Type of organization
- Nature of the issuer's business
- Description of industry
- Description of issuer's assets
- Biographical information on officers and directors including name, address, compensation, and number of shares owned
- Type of securities to be offered
- Price of securities
- Underwriter's discount
- Issuer's capitalization and long-term debt
- Audited balance sheet dated within four months of filing
- Income statements for three years prior to date of balance sheet
- Amount and use of proceeds
- Copy of prospectus or offering circular
- Copy of advertising and sales literature
- Specimen of security to be offered
- Any other information requested by the administrator
- Consent to service of process

A securities registration under qualification becomes effective when the administrator so orders.

The following apply to all types of securities registration:

- Registration is effective for up to one year from the effective date or until all securities have been sold, whichever is longer.
- State securities administrators set filing fees.
- The registration statement may be amended after its effective date to increase the size of the offering as long as the price and underwriter's compensation remains unchanged.

- The administrator may not require the issuer to file reports more often than quarterly.
- The administrator may require the issuer to report on the progress of the sale of the securities.
- The person who files the registration statement with the state may be the issuer, a broker dealer, or a large stockholder selling shares as part of the offering.

The following apply to registration though coordination and qualification:

- State securities administrators may require that the proceeds from the offering be held in escrow until a certain amount has been sold.
- The administrator may require that the securities be sold on a specific subscription form.

EXEMPT SECURITIES/FEDERALLY COVERED EXEMPTION

The National Securities Market Improvement Act of 1996 provided federally covered exemptions for securities that have met the stringent listing requirements of any U.S. stock exchange including the Nasdaq stock exchange. An issuer whose common stock is listed on a centralized U.S. stock exchange such as the NYSE or on the Nasdaq stock exchange is provided an exemption for all of its securities, regardless of their type. An exemption from state registration is also provided to:

- Securities that are sold exclusively to qualified purchasers
- Investment company securities
- Securities and transactions exempt from federal registration
- Debt securities with maturities of less than 270 days and sold in denominations of $50,000 or more
- Exempt issuers
- Employee benefit plans
- Option contracts, both puts and calls on stocks and indexes
- Equipment trust securities issued by a federally covered or exempt issuer

Certain securities are exempt from state registration and sales literature requirements because the issuer is exempt. Examples of exempt issuers are:

- U.S. government
- State and municipal governments
- Foreign national governments
- Canadian federal and municipal governments
- Insurance companies
- Banks and trusts
- Credit unions and savings and loans
- Common carriers (railroad, trucking, and airlines) who are subject to the Interstate Commerce Commission (the term "consolidated" is a key word)
- Religious and charitable organizations
- Public utility securities
- Securities issued by a cooperative

EXEMPT TRANSACTIONS

Sometimes a security that would otherwise have to register is exempt from state registration because of the type of transaction that is involved. The way in which the securities are sold removes the securities from the jurisdiction of the administrator. The following are all exempt transactions:

PRIVATE PLACEMENTS/REGULATION D OFFERINGS

A private placement is a sale of securities that is made to a group of accredited investors and the securities are not offered to the general public. Accredited investors include institutional investors and individuals who:

- Earn at least $200,000 per year if single;

  or

- Earn at least $300,000 jointly with a spouse;

  or

- Have a net worth of at least $1,000,000 excluding the primary residence

Sales to nonaccredited investors are limited to 10 in any 12-month period. No commission may be paid to representatives who sell a private placement to a nonaccredited investor. All investors in private placements must hold the securities fully paid for at least six months.

TRANSACTIONS WITH FINANCIAL INSTITUTIONS

All transactions with financial institutions are exempt. The Uniform Securities Act was designed to protect the individual investor, not the sophisticated financial institution. Financial institutions include:

- Banks
- Insurance companies
- Investment companies
- Broker dealers
- Pension plans with at least $1,000,000 in assets

TRANSACTIONS WITH FIDUCIARIES

All transactions with fiduciaries are exempt from registration with the administrator. Transactions with any of the following are considered transactions with fiduciaries and are exempt:

- Trustees
- Executors
- Guardians
- Sheriffs/marshals
- Administrators
- Receivers

TRANSACTIONS WITH UNDERWRITERS

All transactions with underwriters of securities are exempt from state registration. For example, if XYZ Corporation is selling 10,000,000 shares of its common stock to its investment bank under a firm commitment underwriting agreement, the transaction is an exempt transaction.

UNSOLICITED ORDERS

All orders that are executed through a broker dealer at the sole request of the customer are considered unsolicited orders and are exempt from registration. The administrator may require proof that the order was unsolicited and may require that the customer sign an acknowledgement to that fact.

TRANSACTIONS IN MORTGAGE-BACKED SECURITIES

Because of the high quality of the collateral, transactions in mortgage-backed securities are exempt so long as the entire mortgage or deed of trust is sold as a unit in the transaction.

PLEDGES

Should a person pledge securities as collateral for a loan, the pledge does not constitute a sale. Additionally, should the borrower default on the loan, the person who now has ownership of the securities by way of default may sell those securities without being required to register the securities to recoup their losses.

OFFERS TO EXISTING SECURITIES HOLDERS

Transactions with existing holders of:

- Convertible securities
- Nontransferable warrants
- Transferable warrants exercisable within 90 days

These transactions with existing securities holders are all exempt provided no commission was paid directly or indirectly for soliciting the security holder.

PREORGANIZATION CERTIFICATES

Certain regulations may require that a corporation receive a minimum level of capital in order to be formed. A preorganization certificate is an agreement to purchase securities prior to the formation of a corporation. The offer or sale of the certificate is exempt if no commission was received for soliciting the sale. The number of subscribers may not exceed 10, and the subscriber may not make any payments.

ISOLATED NONISSUER TRANSACTIONS

An agent or a broker dealer may occasionally recommend a security to a client that is not registered in the client's state of residence as long as it is an isolated event. An isolated transaction means one or very few are performed per year per broker dealer. The number of transactions that qualifies as isolated transactions varies from state to state. An isolated nonissuer transaction may also include a transaction between two individuals without the use of a broker dealer. In this type of transaction, the owner of the securities may sell the securities to another interested party directly.

NONISSUER TRANSACTIONS

A nonissuer transaction is a transaction of publicly traded securities and is exempt if the issuer meets the following requirements:

- The issuer has securities registered under Section 12 of the Securities Exchange Act of 1934 and has been reporting for at least 180 days;

  or

- The issuer has securities registered under the Investment Company Act of 1940;

  or

- The issuer has filed the information required by the Securities Exchange Act of 1934 with the administrator for at least 180 days prior to the transaction.

CHAPTER 14

Pretest

SECURITIES REGISTRATION, EXEMPT SECURITIES, AND EXEMPT TRANSACTIONS

1. A broker dealer sells a nonexempt unregistered security to an investment company. Which of the following is true?
   a. This is a prohibited practice.
   b. The broker dealer must offer rescission.
   c. This is an exempt transaction.
   d. This is a nonexempt transaction.

2. An exemption that applies to a security with information available through a nationally recognized publisher of financial information is known as a(n):
   a. Blue-chip exemption
   b. Manual exemption
   c. Issuer exemption
   d. Security exemption

3. A registered representative may sell a nonexempt unregistered security in which of the following:
   a. An IPO
   b. A private placement
   c. In a wash sale
   d. During arbitrage transactions only

4. Which of the following is an exempt transaction?
   a. A transaction involving $100,000 worth of Treasury bonds
   b. A transaction involving commercial paper
   c. A transaction involving an unsolicited order
   d. A transaction involving a common stock listed on the NYSE

5. Commercial paper must be issued in which of the following to be considered an exempt security?
   I. Denominations of less than $50,000
   II. Denominations of more than $50,000
   III. Have a maturity of less than 270 days
   IV. Be issued by a bank

   a. I, III, and IV
   b. II and III
   c. II, III, and IV
   d. II and III

6. A large broker dealer has recommended a nonexempt unregistered security to three individual investors in the last 12 months. According to the USA, this is:
   a. A violation and the broker dealer must offer rescission to the customers involved
   b. A violation of both state and federal laws and the broker dealer may be fined, sanctioned, or both
   c. Examples of isolated nonissuer transactions and the transactions are exempt
   d. Examples of unsolicited orders for government or municipal securities and the securities are exempt from registration

7. All of the following are federally covered securities except:
   a. Stock listed on the NYSE
   b. Shares of an investment company
   c. Common stock that has been duly registered within the state through filing
   d. A common stock listed on the Nasdaq OTCBB

8. Under the USA, transactions with all of the following are exempt except:
   a. Beneficial owners
   b. Trustees
   c. Administrators
   d. Underwriters

9. All of the following are exempt from state registration except:
   a. Common stock of Houston Power and Light Co.
   b. Common stock of XYZ Consolidated
   c. Warrants of ALG Company. ALG's common stock is listed on the American Stock Exchange.
   d. XYZ common stock listed on Vancouver Stock Exchange

10. A securities state registration becomes effective under coordination:
    a. After 10 days
    b. After 30 days
    c. After 25 days
    d. After 20 days

11. A broker dealer distributing a private placement may sell the offering to how many nonaccredited investors?
    a. No more than 35 in 12 months
    b. No more than 10 in 12 months
    c. No more than 15 in 12 months
    d. No more than 10 in six months

12. Which of the following becomes effective the same time as the SEC registration?
    a. Qualification
    b. Coordination
    c. Application
    d. Notification

13. Which of the following is not an exempt transaction?
    a. A transaction involving $4,200 worth of securities executed at the customer's request
    b. Sales of unregistered securities to an investment company
    c. Recommendation to an individual investor to purchase 500 shares of XYZ: XYZ is listed on the NYSE
    d. An issuer sells 5,000,000 shares of common stock to its underwriter

14. All of the following are ways to register a security within a state except:
    a. Application
    b. Notification
    c. Qualification
    d. Coordination

15. A federally covered security is:
    a. Exempt from both SEC and state registration
    b. Only issued by exempt issuers
    c. Not required to register with the state securities administrator
    d. Has a maximum maturity of 270 days

CHAPTER 15

State Securities Administrator: The Uniform Securities Act

INTRODUCTION

The state securities administrator has the authority to enforce all of the provisions of the Uniform Securities Act (USA) within their state. The state securities administrator may deny, revoke, or suspend the registration of a security, an agent, or a firm. The administrator may also revoke an exemption from registration, subpoena and investigate any registrant, and amend rules as required. The administrator's rules and orders have the same authority as any part of the USA but the administrator's rules and orders do not become part of the USA. The USA requires the administrator to publish all rules and orders.

ACTIONS BY THE STATE SECURITIES ADMINISTRATOR

A state securities administrator may take action to bar, suspend, censure, or restrict the activities of a registrant if the administrator finds it in the public interest, and the applicant or registrant does one or more of the following:

- Fails to pay filing fees
- Is insolvent

- Fails to supervise employees
- Willfully violates the securities or banking laws of another country or has had a foreign regulator deny, revoke, or suspend its registration within the last five years
- Violates federal securities or commodities laws
- Has been convicted of any felony within the last 10 years
- Has been convicted of a securities-related misdemeanor
- Willfully violates any provision of the USA
- Files an incomplete, false, or misleading application for registration
- Has been temporarily or permanently enjoined from the securities business by a court of law
- Has been subject to an order by a state securities administrator denying, revoking, or suspending its registration
- Is deemed unqualified due to a lack of experience, training, or knowledge
- Engages in unethical or dishonest business practices

The administrator deeming it is in the public interest is not enough to take action. The applicant must have been involved in one or more of the activities just listed. If the administrator is going to take action against the applicant, it must notify them promptly in writing of their intention and must provide a hearing for the applicant within 15 days of receiving the request for a hearing. An administrator may deny an applicant's registration based on lack of knowledge, training, or experience but a lack of experience may not be the sole basis for the denial of a registration.

CANCELATION OF A REGISTRATION

The administrator may cancel the registration of a broker dealer, investment adviser, or an agent if the registrant or applicant no longer exists, has ceased doing business, or cannot be located. If, for example, the administrator sends a notice to a registrant and the notice is returned to the administrator as undeliverable with no known forwarding address, the administrator would have reasonable grounds for canceling the registrations. Additionally, an individual's registration may be canceled if they have been deemed mentally incompetent by a court of law. The cancelation of a registration by the administrator is not a disciplinary or punitive action, it is more clerical in nature.

WITHDRAWAL OF A REGISTRATION

A broker dealer, investment adviser, or an agent may request that their registration with the state be withdrawn. The withdrawal will become effective 30 days after the administrator receives the request if no revocation or suspension proceedings are in process. The administrator has up to one year after the withdrawal of an applicant's registration to take action against the applicant to suspend or revoke their registration.

ACTIONS AGAINST AN ISSUER OF SECURITIES

The administrator may deny, revoke, or suspend the registration of a security if it deems it is in the public interest and:

- Any officer or director has been convicted of a securities crime.
- The registration statement is false, misleading, or incomplete.
- The security is subject to a court injunction.
- Promoter's fees or offering expenses are excessive or unreasonable.
- The offering is fraudulent.

The administrator also may revoke a security's exemption from registration if it is in the public interest and the exemption was based on a false, misleading, fraudulent, or unethical practice or statement. An administrator may, without prior notice, revoke the exempt status of a securities transaction.

RULE CHANGES

An administrator may change or amend rules as he or she deems necessary. All rules enacted by the administrator will have the same force and effect as rules enacted under the USA. An administrator's order may be appealed to the court system within 60 days. A rule enacted by the administrator applies to all registrants in the administrator's state.

ADMINISTRATIVE ORDERS

If the state securities administrator issues an order, that order will be enforced against a specific registrant or activity. For example, if a broker dealer was engaging in sales practices that violated the USA, the administrator may issue an order suspending that broker dealer's registration with the state for 60 days.

An administrator may enter an order against a registered firm agent or security without holding a hearing. This is known as a summary order. A summary order may be issues in any of the following circumstances

- To deny or revoke the exemption from registration of a security or transaction
- To postpone or suspend the registration of an agent during an investigation of a potential violation or registration issue pending a final decision
- To postpone or suspend the registration of a security during an investigation of a potential violation or registration issue pending a final decision

If the administrator enters an order on a summary basis the administrator must send notice to all parties against whom the order was entered. The notice must provide the details of the order as well as the reasons for entering the order. The parties must also be notified that a hearing will be granted within 15 days of receipt of a written request. Once an order becomes final the administrator must provide a detail of all facts that lead to the order and the legal basis for the order. No order entered by the administrator may become final without prior written notice and the opportunity for a hearing. The administrator's order may be appealed to the court system within 60 days. The appeal will not act as a stay of the order unless a court issues a stay.

TAKENOTE!

If the administrator suspends the registration of a firm all of the individual who are registered with the firm will have their registrations placed in suspense status. After the term of suspension has been completed all registrations will be reactivated. If the firm's registration had been revoked all individuals whose registrations were not revoked would be required to find a new firm to become associated with.

INTERPRETIVE OPINIONS

A person who is actively engaged in the securities business may from time to time seek the opinion of the state securities administrator to ensure that the business that they are conducting is in line with the rules of the USA as amended within the state. In response to the request, the administrator may issue an opinion regarding the activity, issue a no-action letter, or may elect not to issue an opinion. If the administrator issues an interpretive opinion, the administrator may change a fee for the interpretation of its rules.

ADMINISTRATIVE RECORDS

The state securities administrator will maintain all records relating to the business of the state securities administrator and will make the records available upon request. The administrator will provide certified copies if specifically requested. The administrator may charge a reasonable fee for the production and delivery of the records. The records to be maintained include:

- All applications for broker dealer registration
- All applications for investment adviser registration
- All applications for agent registration for broker dealers and investment advisers
- All applications for registrations of securities and registration statements
- All orders, actions, and interpretive opinions entered
- All written claims for exemptions from registration

The records may be maintained electronically, on microfilm, or on any other device the administrator may elect.

INVESTIGATIONS

A state securities administrator may investigate a broker dealer, a state investment adviser, or an agent in any state if they feel that a violation has taken or may take place. The administrator may also subpoena people, books, and records in any state and may administer oaths to compel people to testify. Anyone who displays contempt for the administrator's order is guilty of contumacy and may be found in contempt of court if the administrator asks the court to enforce its orders.

TAKENOTE!

While the Administrator may investigate and take action in all of the above situations, the administrator does not have jurisdiction over activities that take place exclusively outside of the administrator's state.

CIVIL AND CRIMINAL PENALTIES

A state securities administrator may issue a cease-and-desist order without a prior hearing or notice. The administrator may appoint a receiver to oversee the assets of violators and may require them to make restitution. The administrator does not have the power to arrest anyone and must refer the case to the attorney general or other office empowered to make arrests. Anyone who is found to have knowingly and willfully criminally violated the laws of the Uniform Securities Act is subject to a $5,000 fine and/or three years in prison. People who criminally violate the Investment Advisers Act of 1940 are subject to a $10,000 fine and/or five years in prison. The statute of limitations for an administrator taking action is five years.

An investor who sues for a violation of the Uniform Securities Act is entitled to receive:

- The value that they paid for the securities minus any income received during the holding period (for example, dividends)
- Interest on their money for the holding period
- Court costs
- Civil actions may be taken against:
- An agent
- A firm
- The agent's supervisor

If an investment adviser violates the provisions of the USA, clients may sue to recover:

- Advisory fees
- Losses
- Interest on the money
- Attorney fees and court costs, minus any income received as a result of the advice

JURISDICTION OF THE STATE SECURITIES ADMINISTRATOR

While the USA sets forth model legislation for state securities laws, it is the responsibility of the state securities administrator to administer the laws within their state.

The powers granted to the administrator under the Uniform Securities Act include the ability to:

- Cancel, deny, suspend, or revoke a registration of an agent, firm or security
- Cancel, deny, suspend, or revoke an exemption from registration of an agent, firm or security
- Conduct investigations
- Issue subpoenas
- Issue cease and desist orders
- Seek injunctions
- Amend, make, and rescind rules and orders

ADMINISTRATOR'S JURISDICTION OVER SECURITIES TRANSACTIONS

The state securities administrator has jurisdiction over securities transactions that:

- Originated within their state
- Are directed into their state
- Are accepted in their state

If a client draws a check on an out-of-state bank or if they have the securities sent to another state, that does not give the securities administrator in those states jurisdiction.

The offer and acceptance of a security constitutes a transaction or the sale of a security. It is the actual conveyance of the ownership of the security for value.

TESTFOCUS!

Mr. Jones, a resident of Texas, receives a call from his investment representative, Bob, in New York. Bob recommends that Mr. Jones purchase 500 shares of XYZ based on his company's research and in line with Mr. Jones' investment objectives. Mr. Jones accepts the recommendation and purchases the 500 shares at the market.

In this case, the securities administrators from both Texas and New York have jurisdiction over the transaction. The state securities administrator from Texas can review the transaction because the sale was directed and accepted in Texas. Additionally, the state securities administrator from New York may review the transaction because the transaction originated from the representative's office within the state.

If, in this case, Mr. Jones tells his representative that he'll think about it, then calls his representative in New York the next day from his summer home in California and purchases XYZ, the transaction would be subject to the jurisdiction of three state securities administrators:

1. The administrator from New York—because that is where the sale originated.
2. The administrator from Texas—because that is where the sale was directed.
3. The administrator from California—because that is where the sale was accepted.

The state securities administrator also has jurisdiction over offers of securities that:

- Originated within their state
- Are directed into their state

An offer is considered to have been made in the state in which it originated as well as the state to which it is directed.

If, in our example, Bob, the representative in New York, directs the offer of XYZ to Mr. Jones in Texas and Mr. Jones elects not to purchase the stock, the offer would be subject to the jurisdiction of the securities administrators in both New York and Texas. The state securities administrator in New York would have jurisdiction because that is where the representative was sitting when he made the offer. The administrator in Texas would have jurisdiction because that is where the offer was directed.

An offer or sale of a security that may be converted or exchanged into another security also constitutes an offer or sale of the security into which the original security may be converted.

The state securities administrator may:

- Investigate securities-related business within their borders
- Issue subpoenas for people, books, and records from any state

- Compel witnesses to testify
- Issue cease-and-desist orders and seek injunctions
- Deny, suspend, or revoke registrations, licenses, and exemptions
- Adopt and amend rules

The administrator may investigate complaints and alleged violations both in and out of their home state. The investigation may be conducted publicly or in private. During the course of the investigation, the administrator may subpoena people, books, and records from any state and may compel witnesses to testify under oath or to give a written sworn statement.

An individual brought before the administrator may not invoke their Fifth Amendment right against self-incrimination. The administrator may force them to testify about the matter being investigated. However, a person who is forced to testify may not be prosecuted based on the testimony that they were compelled to offer; a witness in this situation is given partial immunity.

If the administrator finds that a person has engaged in or is about to engage in any activity that would violate the USA, the administrator may issue a cease-and-desist order. A cease-and-desist order may be issued without a hearing. The administrator has the power to prevent violations before they take place. However, only a court of law has the authority to force compliance with the order and to prescribe penalties for violating the order.

RIGHT OF RESCISSION

If the seller of a security determines that they have made a sale of securities that violates any provision of the USA, they may offer the affected parties rescission. All offers of recession must be in writing and include an agreement to repurchase the securities at the original purchase price and must include interest for the time period that the money was invested.

If the buyer does not accept the offer of rescission within 30 days, the seller has no further liability with regard to the sale of those securities and the buyer forfeits their right to sue.

An investor's acknowledgement that a sale is in violation of the USA is never valid.

EXAMPLE A customer with an investment objective of speculation convinces their representative to sell them an interest in a private placement that will pay the representative a commission and is in violation of the USA. The investor is a nonaccredited investor and signs a letter stating that they recognize that the investment is in violation of the USA and will not sue or otherwise hold the representative or their firm responsible for any losses.

This acknowledgement by the client is neither valid nor enforceable and in no way protects the representative or the firm.

STATUTE OF LIMITATIONS

If a buyer of a security finds that the sale of the security violates any of the provisions of the USA, the purchaser has two years from the discovery of the violation or three years from the purchase date, whichever comes first, to take action.

CHAPTER 15

Pretest

STATE SECURITIES ADMINISTRATOR: THE UNIFORM SECURITIES ACT

1. An administrator may require all of the following except:
   a. Securities to be sold under a specific subscription form
   b. An agent to take an oral exam
   c. An issuer to file monthly financial reports
   d. A specimen of the security

2. A recent college graduate has just passed their Series 65 exam. The state securities administrator may deny them registration solely based on:
   I. Lack of experience
   II. Public interest
   III. Lack of training
   IV. A felony conviction two years ago prior to the application for registration
   a. I and III
   b. III and IV
   c. I, II, and III
   d. II, III, and IV

3. A New York agent calls a customer who is a New Jersey resident vacationing in Florida at his hotel. The representative recommends that the client purchase 1,000 shares of ABC. The customer informs the representative that he will call him when he returns to New Jersey the following morning. On his return, the customer calls his representative and elects to purchase the 1,000 shares of ABC. Which state administrator has jurisdiction over this transaction?
   a. New York and Florida only
   b. New Jersey and New York only
   c. New York, New Jersey, and Florida
   d. New York only

4. A state securities administrator takes action against the principal of a firm for failing to supervise the actions of one of its agents. Which of the following is true?
   I. The administrator may take action against the firm's registration.
   II. The administrator may not take action against the firm's registration.
   III. The agent's registration may be subject to action by the administrator.
   IV. Because the administrator has taken action against the supervisor, they may not take action against the agent.
   a. I and II
   b. I and III
   c. II and III
   d. II and IV

5. A state securities administrator has sent a notice of its intention to revoke a firm's registration. The firm requests a hearing in writing. The hearing will be held within:
   a. 30 days
   b. 15 days
   c. 45 days
   d. 60 days

6. Which of the following is true regarding actions taken by the administrator?
   I. An administrator may issue subpoenas.
   II. An administrator may suspend a pending registration.
   III. An administrator issues a stop order without a hearing.
   IV. An individual who displays contempt for the administrator's order may be found in contempt of court.

   a. I and II
   b. II and IV
   c. II, III, and IV
   d. I, II, III, and IV

7. An administrator may do all of the following except:
   a. Require the production of documents
   b. Administer oaths
   c. Compel testimony
   d. Order injunctions

8. The Uniform Securities Act was designed to be enforced by the:
   a. SEC
   b. FINRA
   c. State
   d. Federal government

9. Which of the following are true with regard to an investor's right of rescission?
   I. They have 30 days to accept the offer.
   II. It may be offered verbally.
   III. It must include an offer to pay interest.
   IV. They may receive punitive damages.

   a. I and II
   b. I and III
   c. I, II, and IV
   d. I, II, III, and IV

10. An agent who willfully violates the antifraud provision of the Uniform Securities Act may be subject to:

    I. Three years in prison

    II. A $5,000 fine

    III. Five years in prison

    IV. A $10,000 fine

    a. I and II
    b. II only
    c. III and IV
    d. IV only

11. A client who determines that their firm has violated the USA by selling certain securities to them has how long to take action against the firm under the USA?

    a. Six years
    b. Two years from the discovery or three years from the triggering event, whichever occurs first
    c. Five years
    d. There is no statute of limitations for violations of the USA.

12. All of the following are violations of the USA except:

    a. Buying warrants and selling the issuer's common stock short
    b. Making market predictions
    c. Telling a customer that they cannot lose money by purchasing Treasury bonds because their principal is guaranteed by the U.S. government
    d. Printing FINRA in large letters on the firm's business card

13. Which of the following is a violation of the USA?

    a. Cold calling a neighboring state
    b. Explaining to a customer that securities listed on the NYSE are safer than nonlisted securities
    c. Mailing 150 form letters to potential customers
    d. Failing to withhold capital gains taxes on the sale of a security

14. An agent may be denied a registration for all of the following reasons except:
    a. The agent is being taken to arbitration by a number of clients for allegedly mishandling their accounts.
    b. The agent has a securities-related misdemeanor.
    c. The agent was convicted of fraud eight years ago.
    d. Its solely deemed to be in the public's best interest.

15. A client who takes action against an investment adviser is entitled to all of the following under the Uniform Securities Act except:
    a. Reimbursement of fees
    b. Attorney's fees
    c. Treble damages
    d. Interest on money

16. An agent has displayed a pattern of abusive activity. The administrator may take action against which of the following?
    I. The agent
    II. The principal of the firm
    III. The firm
    IV. Industry regulators for failing to supervise the firm
    a. I only
    b. I and III
    c. I, II, and III
    d. I, II, III, and IV

17. A customer who has rejected a broker dealer's offer of rescission may do which of the following under the Uniform Securities Act?
    a. Reserve the right to accept the offer at a later date.
    b. Sue the firm in court.
    c. Take the firm to arbitration.
    d. The customer has given up their rights of recovery.

18. A state securities administrator may take action against an issuer for all of the following reasons except:
    a. The promoter's fees are excessive.
    b. The registration statement is incomplete.
    c. The prospects for the issuer's industry are not strong.
    d. The issuer has relied on an exemption from registration based on a misleading application.

19. A broker dealer has withdrawn their state registration. Their request to withdraw their registration will become effective in:
    a. 45 days
    b. 30 days
    c. 60 days
    d. 90 days

20. An offer of securities is subject to the jurisdiction of all of the following state securities administrators except the state where the:
    a. Offer originated
    b. Issuer is headquartered
    c. Offer was directed
    d. Offer was accepted

Answer Keys

CHAPTER 1: EQUITY SECURITIES

1. (D) As a common stock holder, you will have the right to receive your percentage of any residual assets.
2. (D) All listed are ways that a company can pay a dividend.
3. (C) The yield on the stock will have gone up as the price has fallen because the dividend has remained constant.
4. (D) All dividends are taxed at a rate of 15% for the year in which they were received.
5. (B) A stockholder does not get to vote directly for executive compensation.
6. (B) Each ADR represents between one to 10 shares, and ADR holders have the right to vote and receive dividends. Foreign governments put restrictions on the foreign ownership of stock from time to time.
7. (B) The current yield is found by using the following formula: Annual income/current market price of $10/$110 = 9.1%.
8. (C) First you must determine the number of shares. Par/conversion price = 100/20 = 5 multiplied by the number of preferred shares: 5 × 100 = 500.
9. (B) An ADR may represent more than one share of the company's common stock and may be exchanged for the ordinary common shares. The dividend, however, is paid in the foreign currency and is received by the investor in U.S. dollars; as a result, the investor is subject to currency risk.
10. (D) The investor will receive $8 per share × 100 shares: $800 plus $1 per share because it is participating, so $800 + $100 = $900.
11. (C) The investor who buys a 7% preferred stock is entitled to $7 per year or $3.50 every six months.

12. (C) A holder of a cumulative preferred has all of the rights listed, except the right to convert the preferred into common stock.
13. (B) Authorized stock is all of the answers listed, except the number of authorized shares may be changed by a vote of the shareholders.
14. (D) Common stockholders do not have voting power in the matter of bankruptcy.
15. (D) Dividend yield (or current yield) is found by dividing the annual income by the current market price.
16. (C) 800 shares × 5% = 40 shares.
17. (A) In addition to maintaining control, a company may want to increase its earnings per share, fund employee stock option plans, or use shares to pay for a merger or acquisition.

CHAPTER 2: CORPORATE AND MUNICIPAL DEBT SECURITIES

1. (A) One bond point is worth $10.00; 1.25 points, therefore, is worth: $12.50 × 10 bonds = $125.
2. (D) Bonds registered as to principal only will still require the investor to clip coupons.
3. (A) The real interest rate will determine the return after inflation.
4. (D) Bearer bonds are issued without a name on them, meaning that whoever has possession of the bond may clip the coupons and claim the interest.
5. (C) All of the choices listed are reasons a corporation would attach warrants to their bonds, except to increase the number of shares outstanding.
6. (B) A mortgage bond is secured by real estate.
7. (D) Collateral trust certificates have pledged securities, which they own, issued by another company as collateral for the issue.
8. (C) An investor who has purchased an 8% corporate bond will receive the principal payment plus the last semiannual interest payment at maturity for a total of $1,040.
9. (B) The parity price of the stock is found by using the following formulas: No. of shares = PAR/CVP, 1,000/20 = 50, parity price = CMV of bond/No. of shares = 1,100/50 = 22.

10. (A) The YTM for a bond purchased at a premium is found using the following formula: (Annual income – annual premium)/(price paid + par)/2 60/1,100 = 5.45%.
11. (C) The parity price is found by determining the number of shares that can be received upon conversion par/conversion price = 1,000/25 = 40 shares, then the parity price equals the current market value of the convertible/ No. of shares, 1,200/40 = $30.
12. (C) Of all the choices listed, only an industrial revenue bond pays interest; all of the other choices are issued at a discount.
13. (A) An investor would expect to realize the largest gain by purchasing bonds when rates are high. The bond with the longest time left to maturity will become worth the most as interest rates fall.

CHAPTER 3: GOVERNMENT AND GOVERNMENT AGENCY ISSUES

1. (A) The minimum dollar amount to purchase a GNMA pass-through certificate is $1,000.
2. (C) T-bonds are quoted as a percentage of par to 32nds of 1%. A quote of 103.16 = 103
16/32% × 1,000 = $1,035.
3. (A) The EE savings bonds are sold at a discount and at maturity are redeemed at face value, which includes the interest income.
4. (B) Interest earned by investors on FNMA securities is taxable at all levels: federal, state, and local.
5. (C) The investor purchased the Treasury bond at 95.03 or 95 3/32% of $1,000 = $950.9375.

CHAPTER 4: INVESTMENT COMPANIES

1. (C) An investor in a mutual fund portfolio has an undivided interest in that portfolio and is not an investor or stockholder in the fund company itself.
2. (C) A breakpoint sale is a violation committed by a representative who is trying to earn a larger commission by not informing the investor that a breakpoint sales charge reduction is available at a slightly higher dollar level.

3. (A) The investor will redeem the shares of the growth portfolio at the NAV and will purchase the shares of the biotech portfolio at the NAV because XYZ offers conversion privileges; (500 × 22.30)/17.10.
4. (C) A mutual fund's custodian maintains books and records for accumulation plans.
5. (A) A 12B-1 fee may be up to ¼ of 1% of the NAV.
6. (D) The ex date is set by the NYSE/FINRA for a closed-end fund just like for a stock.
7. (C) A mutual fund calling itself a diversified fund is limited to owning no more than 10% of any one company.
8. (C) New shares will be created for the investor as soon as the mutual fund company receives the money. The investor becomes an owner of record on that day.
9. (D) Employees with access to cash and securities must be bonded.
10. (A) A fund with a portfolio turnover ratio of 25% replaces its portfolio every four years.

CHAPTER 5: VARIABLE ANNUITIES AND RETIREMENT PLANS

1. (D) An investor may always make a contribution to their IRA as long as they have earned income.
2. (D) The individual would expect the death benefit to go down and the cash value to go up. The AIR is only concerned with the death benefit, not the cash value. As long as the performance of the separate account is positive, the cash goes up.
3. (C) This is a nonqualified plan, meaning the money is deposited after taxes so the retiree will only pay taxes on the growth.
4. (D) The maximum amount that a couple may contribute to their IRAs at any one time is $20,000. Between January 1 and April 15, a contribution may be made for the prior year, the current year, or both; $5,000 × 2 × 2 = $20,000.
5. (C) The retirement account is qualified, which means the investors have deposited the money pretax, therefore, all of the money is taxed when it is withdrawn.
6. (A) A 529 plan would allow the investor to make a lump sum deposit.

7. (A) The money has been deposited in a Roth IRA after taxes. It is allowed to grow tax deferred. If you are over 59.5 and the money has been in the IRA for at least five years, then it may all be withdrawn without paying taxes on the growth.
8. (B) A fixed annuity does not provide protection from inflation. If inflation rises, the holder of a fixed annuity may end up worse off due to the loss of value of the dollar.
9. (D) The maximum contribution for a SEP IRA is the lesser of 25% of the postcontribution income or $49,000.

CHAPTER 6: FUNDAMENTAL AND TECHNICAL ANALYSIS

1. (A) The company's EPS is determined by dividing the earnings available to commons holders by the number of outstanding shares or $2,000,000/2,000,000 = $1.
2. (D) Everything that a company owns (assets) minus everything that a company owes (liabilities) results in the corporation's net worth and the stockholders' equity.
3. (B) The current yield is found by multiplying the quarterly dividend by 4: $.70 × 4 = $2.80; then divide it by the market price: $2.80/20 = 14%.
4. (D) Capitalization refers to the overall picture of a company's financial situation, including its assets, liabilities, company's net worth, and the stockholders' equity as shown on its balance sheet.
5. (C) A high beta security is the most volatile and therefore the most risky.
6. (A) A high short interest is considered bullish.
7. (D) Systematic risk is inherent in any investment in the market. An investment may decline in value simply because prices in the overall market are falling.

CHAPTER 7: ECONOMIC FUNDAMENTALS

1. (C) During an inflationary period, the price of a treasury bond will fall the most. The fixed income security with the longest maturity will change the most in price as interest rates change.
2. (D) Rising interest rates are bearish for the stock market.

3. (B) The main theory of economics is one of supply and demand; if the supply outpaces the demand, the price of the goods will fall.
4. (D) The discount rate is the rate that is actually controlled by the Federal Reserve Board. All of the other rates are adjusted in the market place by the lenders as a result of a change in the discount rate.
5. (C) Falling inventories are a sign of a pick up in the economy.
6. (A) A bank may borrow money from another bank to meet their reserve requirement and it will pay the other bank the federal funds rate.
7. (A) The two tools of the government are monetary policy which is controlled by the Federal Reserve Board and controls the money supply, and fiscal policy which is determined by the president and Congress and controls government spending and taxation.
8. (D) Fiscal policy is controlled by the president and Congress.
9. (C) The Federal Reserve sets all of those except government spending.
10. (A) A decline in the gross domestic product must last at least two quarters or six months to be considered a recession.

CHAPTER 8: RECOMMENDATIONS, PROFESSIONAL CONDUCT, AND TAXATION

1. (B) This is known as painting the tape, matched purchases, or matched sales.
2. (D) An industrial revenue bond may subject some wealthy investors to the alternative minimum tax.
3. (B) Of all the investments listed, only the Ginnie Mae pass-through certificate will provide income. Ginnie Maes pay monthly interest and principal payments.
4. (D) This client is concerned about legislative risk: The risk that the government will do something that adversely affects your investment.
5. (A) The investor has a large position in a thinly traded stock; as a result, the investor is subject to a large amount of liquidity risk.
6. (B) An investor who is concerned with the changes in interest rates would be least likely to purchase long-term bonds. As interest rates change, the price of the long-term bonds will fluctuate the most.
7. (B) Bankers' acceptances are money market instruments and short term; Series HH government bonds can only be exchanged for mature

Series EE; and convertible-preferred stock is a security with risk. A 90-day T-bill is considered a risk-free investment.

8. (D) Using the pending dividend to create an urgency on the part of the investor to purchase this stock is a perfect example of this violation, and the results are listed in answers A, B, and C.
9. (D) An investor in a low tax bracket seeking current income would be best suited for a corporate bond fund.
10. (B) This is a violation known as trading ahead.
11. (D) An investor seeking protection from interest rate risk will most likely be best suited for a portfolio of Treasury bills. As the bills mature, the investor can roll over their position into the newly issued bills with new interest rates.
12. (B) Of all the choices listed, only the Treasury bond pays interest. Commercial paper and bankers' acceptance are issued at a discount. An income bond will only pay interest if the company has enough income to do so.
13. (D) The greatest risk when purchasing a CMO is the risk of early refinancing or prepayment risk.
14. (C) Treasury STRIPS are government-issued zero-coupon bonds. They are issued at a discount and mature at par or $1,000. For the exam, they are the best answer for college expense planning if the question is asking for an investment recommendation, not the type of account that it is deposited into.
15. (D) Showing a client the past performance for a mutual fund that has only been around for three years is in line with the regulations. All of the other choices are violations.
16. (A) If an investor may lose part or all of his capital, it is called capital risk.
17. (C) A money market fund is the best recommendation for investors who will need access to their funds in the next few years.

CHAPTER 9: SECURITIES INDUSTRY RULES AND REGULATIONS

1. (D) The Securities Exchange Act of 1934 regulates the secondary market.
2. (C) The SEC is the ultimate industry authority in regulating conduct.
3. (A) All of the choices listed must be included, except for the name of the principal who approved the ad for use.

4. (D) The Maloney Act of 1938 was an amendment to the Securities Exchange Act of 1934 and established the NASD as the self-regulator organization for the over-the-counter market. The NASD is now part of FINRA.
5. (D) All of the items listed are considered to be retail communication if even a single individual investor can see any part of the choices listed.
6. (D) A principal is designated to supervise all of the actions of a firm and its employees; a principal must prevent any violation of industry, state, or federal laws or regulations but need not approve all transactions prior to their execution.
7. (B) Brokerage firms must maintain their advertising for at least three years.
8. (D) Generic advertising may not contain information about past recommendations.
9. (D) All of the parties listed may be held liable to the purchasers of the new issue.
10. (D) All of the items listed must appear in the tombstone ad.

CHAPTER 10: TRADING SECURITIES

1. (A) When acting as a market maker, the firm is trading for its own account and is acting as a dealer.
2. (D) In order to establish a short position would enter a sell stop order for the security. Buy orders would not be used to sell short and AON is not a sell order. AON stands for "all or none" and sets a volume limit for the order. An AON modifier may be attached to either buy or sell orders.
3. (D) An allied member may not trade on the floor. They are only allowed to call themselves a member and have electronic access to the exchange.
4. (C) Firms that act as market makers in Nasdaq securities are trying to make the spread that is the difference between the bid and the ask.
5. (D) Mini/maxi and best efforts are types of underwriting commitments, not types of orders.
6. (C) A technical analyst would want to buy the stock when it breaks through resistance.
7. (A) Selling stock short will expose an investor to unlimited risk because there is no limit to how high as stock price can go.

8. (A) The inside market is the highest bid and the lowest offer.
9. (B) An investor who purchases a straddle is neither bullish nor bearish.
10. (B) The order has been elected since the stock has traded though the stop price. The order has now become a limit order to sell the stock at 160.

CHAPTER 11: OPTIONS

1. (B) Your maximum gain when you sell an option with no other positions in the account is always the premium received; 5.70 × 1,000 = $5,700.
2. (C) With the opening sale of a naked option, the maximum gain is always the premium received.
3. (B) To gain some protection and take in premium income, you would sell 100 XYZ Oct 45 calls.
4. (D) I is incorrect in that an option is a contract between two parties, which determines the time and price at which a security may be bought or sold.
5. (C) Call sellers and put buyers are both bearish. They want the value of the stock to fall.
6. (B) Option trades settle the next day.
7. (B) The OCC or Options Clearing Corporation issues all standardized options.
8. (D) The investor made $3,900. The options are worth $7,000 at expiration; they paid $3,100; the profit, therefore, is $3,900.
9. (A) The Options Clearing Corporation issues all option contracts and guarantees their performance.

CHAPTER 12: DEFINITION OF TERMS

1. (C) A minor is not considered a person because they may not enter into a legally binding contract.
2. (C) The pledge of securities as collateral for a margin loan is not considered a sale. All of the other choices constitute a sale including a bonus security attached to another security, such as a warrant.
3. (D) A qualified purchaser must have at least $5,000,000 in assets. A family-owned business with $5,000,000 in investments is also a qualified purchaser.

4. (C) All of the choices listed are institutional investors except an employee benefit plan with $800,000 in assets. In order for the plan to be an institutional investor, it must have more than $1,000,000 in assets.
5. (B) A trust indenture is the contract between a corporate issuer of debt securities and a trustee and is not a security.
6. (D) A gift of assessable stock is considered to be a sale. Assessable stock can require the owner to make additional payments.
7. (A) The publisher of a market report that is based on market events is an investment adviser.
8. (D) A family-owned business with at least $5,000,000 is a qualified purchaser.
9. (B) XYZ is a federally covered security and is given an exemption from state registration because it trades on a U.S. exchange.
10. (D) An interest in any of the items listed is a security.
11. (B) Only the company and the publisher of the market letter are investment advisors. Individuals are investment adviser representatives.
12. (D) The promise of a profit is not one of the requirements of the Howey test.
13. (D) A broker is a "person" who executes an order for their own account or for the account of others.
14. (D) An offer of securities is made through a prospectus.
15. (C) A corporation that issues securities or simply proposes to issue securities is considered an issuer.
16. (D) An individual representing an out-of-state broker dealer is required to register as an agent.
17. (A) A broker dealer with no office in the state who only conducts business with customers who do not reside in that state or who are in that state for less than 30 days and an out-of-state broker dealer that only conducts business with other broker dealers are not considered broker dealers in that state.
18. (D) A stock that is traded on the OTCBB is not a federally covered security. Only Nasdaq global and capital market securities are federally covered.
19. (C) A guarantee of interest or principal may be issued by all of those listed except an investment adviser.
20. (C) An offer has been made when a representative has made a recommendation.

CHAPTER 13: REGISTRATION OF BROKER DEALERS, INVESTMENT ADVISERS, AND AGENTS

1. (D) A broker dealer may not employ anyone as an agent unless they are duly registered.
2. (C) A broker dealer that meets the SEC's net capital requirement is exempt from the requirement.
3. (C) An investment adviser is limited to giving advice to five clients or less during a 12-month period under the de minimus exemption.
4. (D) All of the partners must register because all of them act in a sales capacity by managing portfolios at the time the firm initially registered. Partners who do not act in a sales capacity are not required to register.
5. (C) Commissions paid by the adviser would be considered an expense of the adviser, not soft-dollar compensation.
6. (C) An investment adviser with between \$100,000,000 and \$110,000,000 may select either federal or state registration, depending on the prospects for receiving additional funds.
7. (D) At the time a client enters into a new advisory relationship, all of the choices must be disclosed except the representative's compensation.
8. (C) An agent is exempt from registration if they represent an exempt issuer. A Canadian corporation is not an exempt issuer.
9. (D) A person who gives advice as to the value of securities would be considered to be an investment adviser.
10. (D) When an agent changes employment, the old employer, the new employer, and the agent all must notify the administrator.
11. (C) A broker dealer may also be registered as an investment adviser and may be a corporation or an individual.
12. (C) An investment adviser must keep books and records at the principal office for two years and readily accessible for five years.
13. (C) A Canadian broker dealer in good standing with a Canadian securities regulator can register through a simplified registration process.
14. (C) An investment adviser may receive all of the choices listed except a percentage of the customer's profits as long as it is all disclosed to the customer.
15. (D) If a firm becomes insolvent, all agents' registrations are canceled.
16. (C) An investment adviser who does not have custody of client funds is not subject to the \$35,000 requirement.

17. (C) The investment adviser must register in this case. An exemption is given to advisors who have given advice to five or less individuals in 12 months.
18. (A) Investors who open wrap accounts will be charged one fee for advice and execution. The investor must receive Schedule H at the time the account is opened.
19. (A) All registrations expire on December 31.

CHAPTER 14: SECURITIES REGISTRATION, EXEMPT SECURITIES, AND EXEMPT TRANSACTIONS

1. (C) This is an example of an exempt transaction. All transactions with financial institutions are exempt, regardless of the security involved.
2. (B) This is known as a manual exemption.
3. (B) A registered representative may sell an unregistered nonexempt security though a private placement.
4. (C) All unsolicited orders are exempt transactions. An unsolicited order is placed by the customer without any advice from the representative.
5. (B) Commercial paper must be issued in denominations exceeding $50,000 with a maturity of less than 270 days.
6. (C) These are examples of isolated nonissuer transactions.
7. (C) Securities given a federally covered exemption are exempt from state registration.
8. (A) Transactions with owners of a security are not exempt transactions.
9. (D) A security listed on a foreign exchange is not an exempt security.
10. (D) A state registration becomes effective after 10 days provided no stop order has been issued. A securities state registration may not become effective before its federal registration.
11. (B) A private placement may be sold to no more than 10 nonaccredited investors in a 12-month period under the Uniform Securities Act.
12. (B) State registration through coordination becomes effective at the same time as the federal registration.
13. (C) A recommendation to an investor involving a NYSE-listed security is not an exempt transaction.
14. (A) A security is not registered by application.
15. (C) A federally covered security is not required to register at the state level.

CHAPTER 15: STATE SECURITIES ADMINISTRATOR: THE UNIFORM SECURITIES ACT

1. (C) A state securities administrator may not require an issuer to file reports more than quarterly.
2. (B) An agent may be denied a registration based on lack of training or a criminal record. An agent may not be denied a registration solely based on the public interest or lack of experience.
3. (C) All three administrators would have jurisdiction over this transaction: New York because that is where the offer originated, Florida because that is where the offer was directed, and New Jersey because that is where the client accepted the offer.
4. (B) The administrator may take action against both the firm and the agent.
5. (B) The administrator must hold a hearing within 15 days of receiving a written request.
6. (D) An administrator may do all of the choices listed and an individual may be found in contempt of court for displaying contumacy.
7. (D) An administrator may not order an injunction. Only a court may order an injunction. The administrator may ask a court for an injunction, but the court must order it.
8. (C) The Uniform Securities Act was designed to be enforced and administered by the state.
9. (B) If an investor has been offered rescission, they must accept it within 30 days and the offer must pay the investor interest for the time that the money was invested.
10. (A) An individual who willfully violates the Uniform Securities Act may be fined $5,000, up to three years in prison, or both.
11. (B) An investor who discovers a violation has two years from the discovery or three years from the triggering event, whichever occurs first, to take action.
12. (A) All of the choices listed are violations except buying warrants and selling the issuer's common stock short. This is an example of an arbitrage transaction.
13. (B) Implying that one security is safer than another due to its exchange listing is a violation.
14. (D) An agent may not be denied a registration solely on the basis of the public interest.

15. (C) A client is not entitled to treble damages.
16. (C) It is highly unlikely that an administrator would try to take action against another regulator.
17. (D) A customer who has rejected an offer of rescission has forfeited his rights of recovery.
18. (C) An administrator may not take action against an issuer's registration because they do not think that the industry has good prospects for the issuer.
19. (B) The withdrawal of a registration will become effective after 30 days, as long as no action is being taken against the broker dealer.
20. (B) An offer of securities is not subject to the jurisdiction of the administrator in the state where the issuer is headquartered.

Glossary of Exam Terms

A

AAA/Aaa The highest investment-grade rating for bond issuers awarded by Standard & Poor's and Moody's ratings agencies.

acceptance waiver and consent A process used when a respondent does not contest an allegation made by FINRA. The respondent accepts the findings without admitting any wrongdoing and agrees to accept any penalty for the violation.

account executive (AE) An individual who is duly licensed to represent a broker dealer in securities transactions or investment banking business. Also known as a registered representative.

accredited investor Any individual or institution that meets one or more of the following: (1) a net worth exceeding $1,000,000, excluding the primary residence, or (2) is single and has an annual income of $200,000 or more or $300,000 jointly with a spouse.

accretion An accounting method used to step up an investor's cost base for a bond purchased at a discount.

accrued interest The portion of a debt securities future interest payment that has been earned by the seller of the security. The purchaser must pay this amount of accrued interest to the seller at the time of the transaction's settlement. Interest accrues from the date of the last interest payment date up to, but not including, the transaction's settlement date.

accumulation stage The period during which an annuitant is making contributions to an annuity contract.

accumulation unit A measure used to determine the annuitant's proportional ownership interest in the insurance company's separate account during the accumulation stage. During the accumulation stage, the number of accumulation units owned by the annuitant changes and their value varies.

acid-test ratio A measure of corporate liquidity found by subtracting inventory from current assets and dividing the result by the current liabilities.

ACT *See* Automated Transaction Comparison (ACT) service.

ad valorem tax A tax based on the value of the subject property.

adjusted basis The value assigned to an asset after all deductions or additions for improvements have been taken into consideration.

adjusted gross income (AGI) An accounting measure employed by the IRS to help determine tax liability. AGI = earned income + investment income (portfolio income) + capital gains + net passive income.

administrator (1) An individual authorized to oversee the liquidation of an intestate decedent's estate. (2) An individual or agency that administers securities' laws within a state.

ADR/ADS *See* American depositary receipt (ADR).

advance/decline line Measures the health of the overall market by calculating advancing issues and subtracting the number of declining issues.

advance refunding The early refinancing of municipal securities. A new issue of bonds is sold to retire the old issue at its first available call date or maturity.

advertisement Any material that is distributed by a broker dealer or issuer for the purpose of increasing business or public awareness for the firm or issuer. The broker dealer or issuer must distribute advertisements to an audience that is not controlled. Advertisements are distributed through any of the following: newspapers/magazines, radio, TV, billboards, telephone.

affiliate An individual who owns 10% or more of the company's voting stock. In the case of a direct participation program (DPP), this is anyone who controls the partnership or is controlled by the partnership.

agency issue A debt security issued by any authorized entity of the U.S. government. The debt security is an obligation of the issuing entity, not an obligation of the U.S. government (with the exception of Ginnie Mae and the Federal Import Export Bank issues).

agency transaction A transaction made by a firm for the benefit of a customer. The firm merely executes a customer's order and charges a fee for the service, which is known as a commission.

agent A firm or an individual who executes securities transactions for customers and charges a service fee known as a commission. Also known as a broker.

aggregate indebtedness The total amount of the firm's customer-related debts.

allied member An owner-director or 5% owner of an NYSE member firm. Allied members may not trade on the floor.

all-or-none (AON) order A non-time-sensitive order that stipulates that the customer wants to buy or sell all of the securities in the order.

all-or-none underwriting A type of underwriting that states that the issuer wants to sell all of the securities being offered or none of the securities being offered. The proceeds from the issue will be held in escrow until all securities are sold.

alpha A measure of the projected change in the security's price as a result of fundamental factors relating only to that company.

alternative minimum tax (AMT) A method used to calculate the tax liability for some high-income earners that adds back the deductions taken for certain tax preference items.

AMBAC Indemnity Corporation Insures the interest and principal payments for municipal bonds.

American depositary receipt (ADR)/American depositary security (ADS) A receipt representing the beneficial ownership of foreign securities being held in trust overseas by a foreign branch of a U.S. bank. ADRs/ADSs facilitate the trading and ownership of foreign securities and trade in the United States on an exchange or in the over-the-counter markets.

American Stock Exchange (Amex) An exchange located in New York using the dual-auction method and specialist system to facilitate trading in stocks, options, exchange traded funds, and portfolios. Amex was acquired by the NYSE Euronext and is now part of NYSE Alternext.

amortization An accounting method that reduces the value of an asset over its project useful life. Also the way that loan principal is systematically paid off over the life of a loan.

annual compliance review All firms must hold at least one compliance meeting per year with all of its agents.

annuitant An individual who receives scheduled payments from an annuity contract.

annuitize A process by which an individual converts from the accumulation stage to the payout stage of an annuity contract. This is accomplished by exchanging accumulation units for annuity units. Once a payout option is selected it cannot be changed.

annuity A contract between an individual and an insurance company that is designed to provide the annuitant with lifetime income in exchange for either a lump sum or period deposits into the contract.

annuity unit An accounting measure used to determine an individual's proportionate ownership of the separate account during the payout stage of the contract. The number of annuity units owned by an individual remains constant, and their value, which may vary, is used to determine the amount of the individual's annuity payment.

appreciation An asset's increase in value over time.

arbitrage An investment strategy used to profit from market inefficiencies.

arbitration A forum provided by both the NYSE and FINRA to resolve disputes between two parties. Only a public customer may not be forced to settle a dispute through arbitration. The public customer must agree to arbitration in writing. All industry participants must settle disputes through arbitration.

ask *See* offer.

assessed value A base value assigned to property for the purpose of determining tax liability.

assessment An additional amount of taxes due as a result of a municipal project that the homeowner benefits from. Also an additional call for capital by a direct participation program.

asset Anything of value owned by an individual or a corporation.

asset allocation fund A mutual fund that spreads its investments among different asset classes (i.e., stocks, bonds, and other investments) based on a predetermined formula.

assignee A person to whom the ownership of an asset is being transferred.

assignment (1) The transfer of ownership or rights through a signature. (2) The notification given to investors who are short an option that the option holder has exercised its right and they must now meet their obligations as detailed in the option contract.

associated person Any individual under the control of a broker dealer, issuer, or bank, including employees, officers, and directors, as well as those individuals who control or have common control of a broker dealer, issuer, or bank.

assumed interest rate (AIR) (1) A benchmark used to determine the minimum rate of return that must be realized by a variable annuity's separate account during the payout phase in order to keep the annuitant's payments consistent. (2) In the case of a variable life insurance policy, the minimum rate of return that must be achieved in order to maintain the policy's variable death benefit.

at-the-close order An order that stipulates that the security is to be bought or sold only at the close of the market, or as close to the close as is reasonable, or not at all.

at-the-opening order An order that stipulates that the security is to be bought or sold only at the opening of the market, or as close to the opening as is reasonable, or not at all.

at the money A term used to describe an option when the underlying security price is equal to the exercise price of the option.

auction market The method of trading employed by stock exchanges that allows buyers and sellers to compete with one another in a centralized location.

authorized stock The maximum number of shares that a corporation can sell in an effort to raise capital. The number of authorized shares may only be changed by a vote of the shareholders.

Automated Transaction Comparison (ACT) service ACT is the service clears and locks Nasdaq trades.

average cost A method used to determine the cost of an investment for an investor who has made multiple purchases of the same security at different times and prices. An investor's average cost may be used to determine a cost base for tax purposes or to evaluate the profitability of an investment program, such as dollar-cost averaging. Average cost is determined by dividing the total dollars invested by the number of shares purchased.

average price A method used to determine the average price paid by an investor for a security that has been purchased at different times and prices, such as through dollar-cost averaging. An investor's average price is determined by dividing the total of the purchase prices by the number of purchases.

B

BBB/Baa The lowest ratings assigned by Standard & Poor's and Moody's for debt in the investment-grade category.

backing away The failure of an over-the-counter market maker to honor firm quotes. It is a violation of FINRA rules.

back-end load A mutual fund sales charge that is assessed upon the redemption of the shares. The amount of the sales charge to be assessed upon redemption decreases the longer the shares are held. Also know as a contingent deferred sales charge.

balanced fund A mutual fund whose investment policy requires that the portfolio's holdings are diversified among asset classes and invested in common and preferred stock, bonds, and other debt instruments. The exact asset distribution among the asset classes will be predetermined by a set formula that is designed to balance out the investment return of the fund.

balance of payments The net balance of all international transactions for a country in a given time.

balance of trade The net flow of goods into or out of a country for a given period. Net exports result in a surplus or credit; net exports result in a deficit or net debit.

balance sheet A corporate report that shows a company's financial condition at the time the balance sheet was created.

balance sheet equation assets = liabilities + shareholders equity.

balloon maturity A bond maturity schedule that requires the largest portion of the principal to be repaid on the last maturity date.

bankers' acceptance (BA) A letter of credit that facilitates foreign trade. BAs are traded in the money market and have a maximum maturity of 270 days.

basis The cost that is assigned to an asset.

basis book A table used to calculate bond prices for bonds quoted on a yield basis and to calculate yields for bonds quoted on a price basis.

basis point Measures a bond's yield; 1 basis point is equal to 1/100 of 1%.

basis quote A bond quote based on the bond's yield.

bearish An investor's belief that prices will decline.

bearer bond A bond that is issued without the owner's name being registered on the bond certificate or the books of the issuer. Whoever has possession (bears) the certificate is deemed to be the rightful owner.

bear market A market condition that is characterized by continuing falling prices and a series of lower lows in overall prices.

best efforts underwriting A type of underwriting that does not guarantee the issuer that any of its securities will be sold.

beta A measure of a security's or portfolio's volatility relative to the market as a whole. A security or portfolio whose beta is greater than one will experience a greater change in price than overall market prices. A security or portfolio with a beta of less than one will experience a price change that is less than the price changes realized by the market as a whole.

bid A price that an investor or broker dealer is willing to pay for a security. It is also a price at which an investor may sell a security immediately and the price at which a market maker will buy a security.

blind pool A type of direct participation program where less than 75% of the assets to be acquired have been identified.

blue chip stock Stock of a company whose earnings and dividends are stable regardless of the economy.

block trade A trade involving 10,000 shares or market value of over $200,000.

blotter A daily record of broker dealer transactions.

Blue List A daily publication of municipal bond offerings and secondary market interest.

blue sky A term used to describe the state registration process for a security offering.

blue-sky laws Term used to describe the state-based laws enacted under the Uniform Securities Act.

board broker *See* order book official.

board of directors A group of directors elected by the stockholders of a corporation to appoint and oversee corporate management.

Board of Governors The governing body of FINRA. The board is made up of 27 members elected by FINRA's membership and the board itself.

bona fide quote *See* firm quote.

bond The legal obligation of a corporation or government to repay the principal amount of debt along with interest at a predetermined schedule.

bond anticipation note Short-term municipal financing sold in anticipation of long-term financing.

bond buyer indexes A group of yield-based municipal bond indexes published daily in the *Daily Bond Buyer.*

bond counsel An attorney for the issuer of municipal securities who renders the legal opinion.

bond fund A fund whose portfolio is made up of debt instruments issued by corporations, governments, and/or their agencies. The fund's investment objective is usually current income.

bond interest coverage ratio A measure of the issuer's liquidity. It demonstrates how many times the issuer's earnings will cover its bond interest expense.

bond quotes Corporate and government bond quotes are based on a percentage of par. Municipal bonds are usually quoted on a yield-to-maturity basis.

bond rating A rating that assesses the financial soundness of issuers and their ability to make interest and principal payments in a timely manner. Standard & Poor's and Moody's are the two largest ratings agencies. Issuers must request and pay for the service to rate their bonds.

bond ratio A measure used to determine how much of the corporation's capitalization was obtained through the issuance of bonds.

bond swap The sale and purchase of two different bonds to allow the investor to claim a loss on the bond being sold without violating wash sale rules.

book entry Securities that are issued in book entry form do not offer any physical certificates as evidence of ownership. The owner's name is registered on the books of the issuer, and the only evidence of ownership is the trade confirmation.

book value A corporation's book value is the theoretical liquidation value of the company. Book value is in theory what someone would be willing to pay for the entire company.

book value per bond A measure used to determine the amount of the corporation's tangible value for each bond issued.

book value per share Used to determine the tangible value of each common share. It is found by subtracting intangible assets and the par value of preferred stock from the corporation's total net worth and dividing that number by the amount of common shares outstanding.

branch office A branch office of a member firm is required to display the name of the member firm and is any office in which the member conducts securities business outside of its main office.

breadth A measure of the health of the broad market's health. It measures how many stocks are increasing and how many are declining.

breakdown A technical term used to describe the price action of a security when it falls below support to a lower level and into a new trading range.

breakeven point The point at which the value of a security or portfolio is exactly equal to the investor's cost for that security or portfolio.

breakout A technical term used to describe the price action of a security when it increases past resistance to a higher level and into a new trading range.

breakpoint sale The practice of selling mutual fund shares in dollar amounts that are just below the point where an investor would be entitled to a sales charge reduction. A breakpoint sale is designed for the purpose of trying to earn a larger commission. This is a violation of the Rules of Fair Practice and should never be done.

breakpoint schedule A breakpoint schedule offers mutual fund investors reduced sales charges for larger dollar investments.

broad-based index An index that represents a large cross-section of the market as a whole. The price movement of the index reflects the price movement of a large portion of the market, such as the S&P 500 or the Wilshire 5000.

broker *See* agent.

broker's broker (1) A municipal bond dealer who specializes in executing orders for other dealers who are not active in the municipal bond market. (2) A specialist on the exchange executing orders for other members or an OTC market.

broker dealer A person or firm who buys and sells securities for its own account and for the accounts of others. When acting as a broker or agent for a customer, the broker dealer is merely executing the customer's orders and charging the customer a fee known as a commission. When acting as a dealer or principal, the broker dealer is trading for its own account and participating in the customer's transaction by taking the other side of the trade and charging the customer a markup or markdown. A firm also is acting as a principal or dealer when it is trading for its own account and making markets in OTC securities.

bullish An investor who believes that the price of a security or prices as a whole will rise is said to be bullish.

bull market A market condition that is characterized by rising prices and a series of higher highs.

business cycle The normal economic pattern that is characterized by four stages: expansion, peak, contraction, and trough. The business cycle constantly repeats itself and the economy is always in flux.

business day The business day in the securities industry is defined as the time when the financial markets are open for trading.

buyer's option A settlement option that allows the buyer to determine when the transaction will settle.

buy in An order executed in the event of a customer's or firm's failure to deliver the securities it sold. The buyer repurchases the securities in the open market and charges the seller for any loss.

buying power The amount of money available to buy securities.

buy stop order A buy stop order is used to protect against a loss or to protect a profit on a short sale of stock.

C

call (1) A type of option that gives the holder the right to purchase a specified amount of the underlying security at a stated price for a specified period of time. (2) The act of exercising a call option.

callable bond A bond that may be called in or retired by the issuer prior to its maturity date.

callable preferred A preferred share issued with a feature allowing the issuing corporation to retire it under certain conditions.

call date A specific date after which the securities in question become callable by the issuer.

call feature A condition attached to some bonds and preferred stocks that allow the issuer to call in or redeem the securities prior to their maturity date and according to certain conditions.

call price The price that will be paid by the issuer to retire the callable securities in question. The call price is usually set at a price above the par value of the bond or preferred stock, which is the subject of the call.

call protection A period of time, usually right after the securities' issuance, when the securities may not be called by the issuer. Call protection usually ranges from 5 to 10 years.

call provision *See* call feature.

call risk The risk borne by the owner of callable securities that may require that the investor accept a lower rate of return once the securities have been called. Callable bonds and preferred stock are more likely to be called when interest rates are low or are falling.

call spread An option position consisting of one long and one short call on the same underlying security with different strike prices, expirations, or both.

call writer An investor who has sold a call.

capital Money and assets available to use in an attempt to earn more money or to accumulate more assets.

capital appreciation An increase in an asset's value over time.

capital assets Tangible assets, including securities, real estate, equipment and other assets, owned for the long term.

capital gain A profit realized on the sale of an asset at a price that exceeds its cost.

capitalization The composition of a company's financial structure. It is the sum of paid-in capital + paid-in surplus + long-term debt + retained earnings.

capital loss A loss realized on the sale of an asset at a price that is lower than its cost.

capital market The securities markets that deal in equity and debt securities with more than one year to maturity.

capital risk The risk that the value of an asset will decline and cause an investor to lose all or part of the invested capital.

capital stock The sum of the par value of all of a corporation's outstanding common and preferred stock.

capital structure *See* capitalization.

capital surplus The amount of money received by an issuer in excess of the par value of the stock at the time of its initial sale to the public.

capped index option An index option that trades like a spread and is automatically exercised if it goes 30 points in the money.

capping A manipulative practice of selling stock to depress the price.

carried interest	A sharing arrangement for an oil and gas direct participation program where the general partner shares in the tangible drilling costs with the limited partners.
cash account	An account in which the investor must deposit the full purchase price of the securities by the fifth business day after the trade date. The investor is not required by industry regulations to sign anything to open a cash account.
cash assets ratio	The most liquid measure of a company's solvency. The cash asset ratio is found by dividing cash and equivalents by current liabilities.
cash dividend	The distribution of corporate profits to shareholders of record. Cash dividends must be declared by the company's board of directors.
cash equivalent	Short-term liquid securities that can quickly be converted into cash. Money market instruments and funds are the most common examples.
cash flow	A company's cash flow equals net income plus depreciation.
cashiering department	The department in a brokerage firm that is responsible for the receipt and delivery of cash and securities.
cash management bill	Short-term federal financing issued in minimum denominations of $10,000,000.
cash settlement	A transaction that settles for cash requires the delivery of the securities from the seller as well as the delivery of cash from the buyer on the same day of the trade. A trade done for cash settles the same day.
catastrophe call	The redemption of a bond by an issuer due to the destruction of the facility that was financed by the issue. Issuers will carry insurance to cover such events and to pay off the bondholders.
certificates of accrual on Treasury securities	Zero-coupon bonds issued by brokerage firms and collateralized by Treasury securities.
certificate of deposit (CD)	An unsecured promissory note issued as evidence of ownership of a time deposit that has been guaranteed by the issuing bank.
change	The difference between the current price and the previous day's closing price.
Chicago Board of Trade (CBOT)	A commodity exchange that provides a marketplace for agricultural and financial futures.
Chicago Board Options Exchange (CBOE)	The premier option exchange in the United States for listed options.
Chinese wall	The physical separation that is required between investment banking and trading and retail divisions of a brokerage firm. Now known as firewall.

churning	Executing transactions that are excessive in their frequency or size in light of the resources of the account for the purpose of generating commissions. Churning is a violation of the Rules of Fair Practice.
class A share	A mutual fund share that charges a front-end load.
class B share	A mutual fund share that charges a back-end load.
class C share	A mutual fund share that charges a level load.
class D share	A mutual fund share that charges a level load and a back-end load.
classical economics	A theory stating that the economy will do the best when the government does not interfere.
clearing firm	A firm that carries its customer's cash and securities and/or provides the service to customers of other firms.
clearinghouse	An agency that guarantees and settles futures and option transactions.
close	The last price at which a security traded for the day.
closed-end indenture	A bond indenture that will not allow additional bonds to be issued with the same claim on the issuer's assets.
closed-end investment company	A management company that issues a fixed number of shares to investors in a managed portfolio and whose shares are traded in the secondary market.
closing date	The date when sales of interest in a direct participation plan will cease.
closing purchase	An order executed to close out a short option position.
Code of Arbitration Procedure	The FINRA bylaw that provides for a forum for dispute resolution relating to industry matters. All industry participants must arbitrate in public and customer must agree to arbitration in writing.
Code of Procedure	The FINRA bylaw that sets guidelines for the investigation of trade practice complaints and alleged rule violations.
coincident indicator	An economic indicator that moves simultaneously with the movement of the underlying economy.
collateral	Assets pledged to a lender. If the borrower defaults, the lender will take possession of the collateral.
collateral trust certificate	A bond backed by the pledge of securities the issuer owns in another entity.
collateralized mortgage obligation (CMO)	A corporate debt security that is secured by an underlying pool of mortgages.
collection ratio	A measure of a municipality's ability to collect the taxes it has assessed.
collect on delivery (COD)	A method of trade settlement that requires the physical delivery of the securities to receive payment.

combination An option position with a call and put on the same underlying security with different strike prices and expiration months on both.

combination fund A mutual fund that tries to achieve growth and current income by combining portfolios of common stock with portfolios of high-yielding equities.

combination preferred stock A preferred share with multiple features, such as cumulative and participating.

combination privileges A feature offered by a mutual fund family that allows an investor to combine two simultaneous purchases of different portfolios in order to receive a reduced sales charge on the total amount invested.

combined account A margin account that contains both long and short positions.

commercial paper Short-term unsecured promissory notes issued by large financially stable corporations to obtain short-term financing. Commercial paper does not pay interest and is issued at a discount from its face value. All commercial paper matures in 270 days or less and matures at its face value.

commingling A FINRA violation resulting from the mixing of customer and firm assets in the same account.

commission A fee charged by a broker or agent for executing a securities transaction.

commission house broker A floor broker who executes orders for the firm's account and for the accounts of the firm's customers on an exchange.

common stock A security that represents the ownership of a corporation. Common stockholders vote to elect the board of directors and to institute major corporate policies.

common stock ratio A measure of how much of a company's capitalization was obtained through the sale of common stock. The ratio is found by summing the par value of the common stock, excess paid in capital, and retained earnings and then dividing that number by the total capitalization.

competitive bid underwriting A method of underwriter selection that solicits bids from multiple underwriters. The underwriter submitting the best terms will be awarded the issue.

compliance department The department of a broker dealer that ensures that the firm adheres to industry rules and regulations.

concession The amount of an underwriting discount that is allocated to a syndicate member or a selling group member for selling new securities.

conduct rules The Rules of Fair Practice.

conduit theory The IRS classification that allows a regulated investment company to avoid paying taxes on investment income it distributes to its shareholders.

confirmation The receipt for a securities transaction that must be sent to all customers either on or before the completion of a transaction. The confirmation must show the trade date, settlement date and total amount due to or from the customer. A transaction is considered to be complete on settlement date.

consolidated tape The consolidated tape A displays transactions for NYSE securities that take place on the NYSE, all regional exchanges, and the third markets. The consolidated tape B reports transactions for Amex stocks that take place on the American Stock Exchange, all regional exchanges, and in the third market.

consolidation A chart pattern that results from a narrowing of a security's trading range.

constant dollar plan An investment plan designed to keep a specific amount of money invested in the market regardless of the market's condition. An investor will sell when the value of their account rises and buy when the value of the account falls.

constant ratio plan An investment plan designed to keep the investor's portfolio invested at a constant ratio of equity and debt securities.

construction loan note A short-term municipal note designed to provide financing for construction projects.

consumption A term used to describe the purchase of newly produced household goods.

constructive receipt The time when the IRS determines that the taxpayer has effectively received payment.

consumer price index (CPI) A price-based index made up of a basket of goods and services that are used by consumers in their daily lives. An increase in the CPI indicates a rise in overall prices, while a decline in the index represents a fall in overall prices.

contemporaneous trader A trader who enters an order on the other side of the market at the same time as a trader with inside information enters an order. Contemporaneous traders can sue traders who act on inside information to recover losses.

contingent deferred sales charge *See* back-end load.

contraction A period of declining economic output. Also known as a recession.

contractual plan A mutual fund accumulation plan under which the investor agrees to contribute a fixed sum of money over time. If the investor does not complete or terminates the contract early, the investor may be subject to penalties.

control The ability to influence the actions of an organization or individual.

control person A director or officer of an issuer or broker dealer or a 10% stockholder of a corporation.

control stock Stock that is acquired or owned by an officer, director, or person owning 10% or more of the outstanding stock of a company

conversion price The set price at which a convertible security may be exchanged for another security.

conversion privilege The right offered to a mutual fund investor that allows the investor to move money between different portfolios offered by the same mutual fund family without paying another sales charge.

conversion ratio The number of shares that can be received by the holder of a convertible security if it were converted into the underlying common stock.

convertible bond A bond that may be converted or exchanged for common shares of the corporation at a predetermined price.

convertible preferred stock A preferred stock that may be converted or exchanged for common shares of the corporation at a predetermined price.

cooling-off period The period of time between the filing of a registration statement and its effective date. During this time, the SEC is reviewing the registration statement and no sales may take place. The cooling-off period is at least 20 days.

coordination A method of securities registration during which a new issue is registered simultaneously at both the federal and state levels.

corporate account An investment account for the benefit of a company that requires a corporate resolution listing the names of individuals who may transact business in the company's name.

corporate bond A legally binding obligation of a corporation to repay a principal amount of debt along with interest at a predetermined rate and schedule.

corporation A perpetual entity that survives after the death of its officers, directors, and stockholders. It is the most common form of business entity.

correspondent broker dealer A broker dealer who introduces customer accounts to a clearing broker dealer.

cost basis The cost of an asset, including any acquisition costs. It is used to determine capital gains and losses.

cost depletion A method used to determine the tax deductions for investors in oil and gas programs.

cost of carry All costs incurred by an investor for maintaining a position in a security, including margin interest and opportunity costs.

coterminous Municipalities that share the same borders and have overlapping debt.

coupon bond *See* bearer bond.

coupon yield *See* nominal yield.

covenant A promise made by an issuer of debt that describes the issuer's obligations and the bondholders' rights.

covered call The sale of a call against a long position in the underlying security.

covered put The sale of a put against a short position in the underlying security or against cash that will allow the person to purchase the security if the put is exercised.

CPI *See* consumer price index (CPI).

credit agreement The portion of the margin agreement that describes the terms and conditions under which credit will be extended to the customer.

credit balance The cash balance in a customer's account.

credit department *See* margin department.

credit risk The risk that the issuer of debt securities will default on its obligation to pay interest or principal on a timely basis.

credit spread An option position that results in a net premium or credit received by the investor from the simultaneous purchase and sale of two calls or two puts on the same security.

crossed market A market condition that results when a broker enters a bid for a stock that exceeds the offering price for that stock. Also a condition that may result when a broker enters an offer that is lower than the bid price for that stock.

crossing stock The pairing off of two offsetting customer orders by the same floor broker. The floor broker executing the cross must first show the order to the crowd for possible price improvement before crossing the orders.

crossover point The point at which all tax credits have been used up by a limited partnership; results in a tax liability for the partners.

cum rights A stock that is the subject of a rights offering and is trading with the rights attached to the common stock.

cumulative preferred stock A preferred stock that entitles the holder to receive unpaid dividends prior to the payment of any dividends to common stockholders. Dividends that accumulate in arrears on cumulative issues are always the first dividends to be paid by a corporation.

cumulative voting A method of voting that allows stockholders to cast all of their votes for one director or to distribute them among the candidates they wish to vote for. Cumulative voting favors smaller investors by allowing them to have a larger say in the election of the board of directors.

current assets Cash, securities, accounts receivable, and other assets that can be converted into cash within 12 months.

current liabilities Corporate obligations, including accounts payable, that must be paid within 12 months.

current market value (CMV)/current market price (CMP) The present value of a marketable security or of a portfolio of marketable securities.

current ratio A measure of a corporation's short-term liquidity found by dividing its current assets by its current liabilities.

current yield A relationship between a securities annual income relative to its current market price. Determined by dividing annual income by the current market price.

CUSIP (Committee on Uniform Securities Identification Procedures) A committee that assigns identification numbers to securities to help identify them.

custodial account An account operated by a custodian for the benefit of a minor.

custodian A party responsible for managing an account for another party. In acting as a custodian, the individual or corporation must adhere to the prudent man rule and only take such actions as a prudent person would do for him- or herself.

customer Any individual or entity that maintains an account with a broker dealer.

customer agreement An agreement signed by a customer at the time the account is opened, detailing the conditions of the customer's relationship with the firm. The customer agreement usually contains a predispute arbitration clause.

customer ledger A ledger that lists all customer cash and margin accounts.

customer protection rule Rule 15C3-3 requires that customer assets be kept segregated from the firm assets.

cyclical industry An industry whose prospects fluctuate with the business cycle.

D

Daily Bond Buyer A daily publication for the municipal securities industry that publishes information relating the municipal bond market and official notices of sales.

dated date The day when interest starts to accrue for bonds.

dealer (1) A person or firm who transacts securities business for its own account. (2) A brokerage firm acting as a principal when executing a customer's transaction or making markets over the counter.

dealer paper Commercial paper sold to the public by a dealer, rather than placed with investors directly by the issuer.

debenture An unsecured promissory note issued by a corporation backed only by the issuer's credit and promise to pay.

debit balance The amount of money a customer owes a broker dealer.

debit spread An option position that results in a net premium paid by the investor from the simultaneous purchase and sale of two calls or two puts on the same security.

debt securities A security that represents a loan to the issuer. The owner of a debt security is a creditor of the issuing entity, be it a corporation or a government.

debt service The scheduled interest payments and repayment of principal for debt securities.

debt service account An account set up by a municipal issuer to pay the debt service of municipal revenue bonds.

debt service ratio Indicates the issuer's ability to pay its interest and principal payments.

debt-to-equity ratio A ratio that shows how highly leveraged the company is. It is found by dividing total long-term debt by total shareholder equity.

declaration date The day chosen by the board of directors of a corporation to pay a dividend to shareholders.

deduction An adjustment taken from gross income to reduce tax liability.

defeasance Results in the elimination of the issuer's debt obligations by issuing new debt instrument to pay off the outstanding issue. The old issue is removed from the issuer's balance sheet and the proceeds of the new issue are placed in an escrow account to pay off the now-defeased issue.

default The failure of an issuer of debt securities to make interest and principal payments when they are due.

default risk *See* credit risk.

defensive industry A term used to describe a business whose economic prospects are independent from the business cycle. Pharmaceutical companies, utilities, and food producers are examples of defensive industries.

deferred annuity A contract between an individual and an insurance company that delays payments to the annuitant until some future date.

deferred compensation plan A contractual agreement between an employer and an employee under which the employee elects to defer receiving money owed until after retirement. Deferred compensation plans are typically unfunded, and the employee could lose all the money due under the agreement if the company goes out of business.

deficiency letter A letter sent to a corporate issuer by the SEC, requesting additional information regarding the issuer's registration statement.

defined benefit plan A qualified retirement plan established to provide a specific amount of retirement income for the plan participants. Unlike a defined contribution plan, the individual's retirement benefits are known prior to reaching retirement.

defined contribution plan A qualified retirement plan that details the amount of money that the employer will contribute to the plan for the benefit of the employee. This amount is usually expressed as a percentage of the employee's gross annual income. The actual retirement benefits are not known until the employee reaches retirement, and the amount of the retirement benefit is a result of the contributions to the plan, along with the investment experience of the plan.

deflation The economic condition that is characterized by a persistent decline in overall prices.

delivery As used in the settlement process, results in the change of ownership of cash or securities.

delivery vs. payment A type of settlement option that requires that the securities be physically received at the time payment is made.

delta A measure of an option's price change in relation to a price change in the underlying security.

demand deposit A deposit that a customer has with a bank or other financial institution that will allow the customer to withdraw the money at any time or on demand.

Department of Enforcement The FINRA committee that has original jurisdiction over complaints and violations.

depletion A tax deduction taken for the reduction in amount of natural resources (e.g., gas, gold, oil) available to a business or partnership.

depreciation A tax deduction taken for the reduction of value in a capital asset.

depreciation expense A noncash expense that results in a reduction in taxable income.

depression An economic condition that is characterized by a protracted decline in economic output and a rising level of unemployment.

derivative A security that derives its value in whole or in part based on the price of another security. Options and futures are examples of derivative securities.

designated order An order entered by an institution for a new issue of municipal bonds that states what firm and what agent is going to get the sales credit for the order.

devaluation A significant fall in the value of a country's currency relative to other currencies. Devaluation could be the result of poor economic prospects in the home country. In extreme circumstances, it can be the result of government intervention.

developmental drilling program An oil or gas program that drills for wells in areas of proven reserves.

developmental fee A fee paid to organizers of a direct participation plan for the development of plans, obtaining financing, or zoning authorizations and other services.

diagonal spread A spread that is created through the simultaneous purchase and sale of two calls or two puts on the same underlying security that differ in both strike price and expiration months.

dilution A reduction in a stockholder's proportional ownership of a corporation as a result of the issuance of more shares. Earnings per share may also be diluted as a result of the issuance of additional shares.

direct debt The total amount of a municipality's debt that has been issued by the municipality for its own benefit and for which the municipality is responsible to repay.

direct paper Commercial paper sold to investors directly from the issuer without the use of a dealer.

direct participation program (DPP) An entity that allows all taxable events to be passed through to investors, including limited partnerships and subchapter S corporations.

discount The amount by which the price of a security is lower than its par value.

discount bond A bond that is selling for a price that is lower than its par value.

discount rate The rate that is charged to Federal Reserve member banks on loans directly from the Federal Reserve. This rate is largely symbolic, and member banks only borrow directly from the Federal Reserve as a last resort.

discretion Authorization given to a firm or a representative to determine which securities are to be purchased and sold for the benefit of the customer without the customer's prior knowledge or approval.

discretionary account An account where the owner has given the firm or the representative authority to transact business without the customer's prior knowledge or approval. All discretionary accounts must be approved and monitored closely by a principal of the firm.

disintermediation The flow of money from traditional bank accounts to alternative higher yielding investments. This is more likely to occur as the Federal Reserve tightens monetary policy and interest rates rise.

disposable income The sum of money an individual has left after paying taxes and required expenditures.

disproportional allocation A method used by FINRA to determine if a free-riding violation has occurred with respect to a hot issuer. A firm is only allowed to sell up to 10% of a new issue to conditionally approved purchasers.

disproportionate sharing An oil and gas sharing arrangement where the general partner pays a portion of the cost but receives a larger portion of the program's revenues.

distribution Cash or property sent to shareholders or partners.

distribution stage The period of time during which an annuitant is receiving payments from an annuity contract.

diversification The distribution of investment capital among different investment choices. By purchasing several different investments, investors may be able to reduce their overall risk by minimizing the impact of any one security's adverse performance.

diversified fund/diversified management company A mutual fund that distributes its investment capital among a wide variety of investments. In order for a mutual fund to market itself as a diversified mutual fund it must meet the 75-5-10 rule: 75% of the fund's assets must be invested in securities issued by other entities, no more than 5% of the fund's assets may be invested in any one issuer, and the fund may own no more than 10% of any one company's outstanding securities.

dividend A distribution of corporate assets to shareholders. A dividend may be paid in cash, stock, or property or product.

dividend department The department in a brokerage firm that is responsible for the collecting of dividends and crediting them to customer accounts.

dividend disbursement agent An agent of the issuer who pays out the dividends to shareholders of record.

dividend payout ratio The amount of a company's earnings that were paid out to shareholders relative to the total earnings that were available to be paid out to shareholders. It can be calculated by dividing dividends per share by earnings per share.

dividend yield Also known as a stock's current yield. It is a relationship between the annual dividends paid to shareholders relative to the stock's current market price. To determine a stock's dividend yield, divide annual dividends by the current market price.

DJIA *See* Dow Jones Industrial Average.

doctrine of mutual reciprocity An agreement that the federal government would not tax interest income received by investors in municipal bonds and that reciprocally the states would not tax interest income received by investors in federal debt obligations.

dollar bonds A term issue of municipal bonds that are quoted as a percentage of par rather than on a yield basis.

dollar-cost averaging A strategy of investing a fixed sum of money on a regular basis into a fluctuating market price. Over time an investor should be able to achieve an average cost per share that is below the average price per share. Dollar-cost averaging is a popular investment strategy with mutual fund investors.

donor A person who gives a gift of cash or securities to another person. Once the gift has been made, the donor no longer has any rights or claim to the security. All gifts to a minor are irrevocable.

do not reduce (DNR) An order qualifier for an order placed under the market that stipulates that the price of the order is not to be reduced for the distribution of ordinary dividends.

don't know (DK) A term used to describe a dealer's response to a confirmation for a trade they "don't know" doing.

Dow Jones Composite Average An index composed of 65 stocks that is used as an indicator of market performance.

Dow Jones Industrial Average (DJIA) An index composed of 30 industrial companies. The Dow Jones is the most widely quoted market index.

Dow Jones Transportation Average An index composed of 20 transportation stocks.

Dow Jones Utility Average An index composed of 15 utility stocks.

Dow theory A theory that believes that the health both of the market and of the economy may be predicted by the performance of the Dow Jones Industrial Average.

dry hole A term used to describe a nonproducing well.

dual-purpose fund A mutual fund that offers two classes of shares to investors. One class is sold to investors seeking income and the other class is sold to investors seeking capital appreciation.

E

early withdrawal penalty A penalty tax charged to an investor for withdrawing money from a qualified retirement plan prior to age 59 1/2, usually 10% on top of ordinary income taxes.

earned income Money received by an individual in return for performing services.

earnings per share The net amount of a corporation's earnings available to common shareholders divided by the number of common shares outstanding.

earnings per share fully diluted The net amount of a corporation's earnings available to common shareholders after taking into consideration the potential conversion of all convertible securities.

eastern account A type of syndicate account that requires all members to be responsible for their own allocation as well as for their proportional share of any member's unsold securities.

economic risk The risk of loss of principal associated with the purchase of securities.

EE savings bonds Nonmarketable U.S. government zero-coupon bonds that must be purchased from the government and redeemed to the government.

effective date The day when a new issue's registration with the SEC becomes effective. Once the issue's registration statement has become effective, the securities may then be sold to investors.

efficient market theory A theory that states that the market operates and processes information efficiently and prices in all information as soon as it becomes known.

Employee Retirement Income Security Act of 1974 (ERISA) The legislation that governs the operation of private-sector pension plans. Corporate pension plans organized under ERISA guidelines qualify for beneficial tax treatment by the IRS.

endorsement The signature on the back of a security that allows its ownership to be transferred.

EPS *See* earnings per share.

equipment leasing limited partnership A limited partnership that is organized to purchase equipment and lease it to corporations to earn lease income and to shelter passive income for investors.

equipment trust certificate A bond backed by a pledge of large equipment, such as airplanes, railroad cars, and ships.

equity A security that represents the ownership in a corporation. Both preferred and common equity holders have an ownership interest in the corporation.

equity financing The sale of common or preferred equity by a corporation in an effort to raise capital.

equity option An option to purchase or sell common stock.

ERISA *See* Employee Retirement Income Security Act of 1974.

erroneous report A report of an execution given in error to a client. The report is not binding on the firm or on the agent.

escrow agreement Evidence of ownership of a security provided to a broker dealer as proof of ownership of the underlying security for covered call writers.

eurobond A bond issued in domestic currency of the issuer but sold outside of the issuer's country.

eurodollar A deposit held outside of the United States denominated in U.S. dollars.

eurodollar bonds A bond issued by foreign issuer denominated in U.S. dollars.

euroyen bonds Bonds issued outside of Japan but denominated in yen.

excess equity (EE) The value of an account's equity in excess of Regulation T.

exchange A market, whether physical or electronic, that provides a forum for trading securities through a dual-auction process.

exchange distribution A distribution of a large block of stock on the floor of the exchange that is crossed with offsetting orders.

exchange privilege The right offered by many mutual funds that allows an investor to transfer or move money between different portfolios offered through the same fund company. An investor may redeem shares of the fund, which is being sold at the NAV, and purchase shares of the new portfolio at the NAV without paying another sales charge.

ex date/ex dividend date The first day when purchasers of a security will no longer be entitled to receive a previously declared dividend.

executor/executrix An individual with the authority to manage the affairs of a decedent's estate.

exempt security A security that is exempt from the registration requirements of the Securities Act of 1933.

exempt transaction A transaction that is not subject to state registration.

exercise An investor's election to take advantage of the rights offered through the terms of an option, a right, or a warrant.

exercise price The price at which an option investor may purchase or sell a security. Also the price at which an investor may purchase a security through a warrant or right.

existing property program A type of real estate direct participation program that purchases existing property for the established rental income.

expansion A period marked by a general increase in business activity and an increase in gross domestic product.

expansionary policy A monetary policy enacted through the Federal Reserve Board that increases money supply and reduces interest rates in an effort to stimulate the economy.

expense ratio The amount of a mutual fund's expenses relative to its assets. The higher the expense ratio, the lower the investor's return. A mutual fund's expense ratio tells an investor how efficiently a mutual fund operates, not how profitable the mutual fund is.

expiration cycle A four-month cycle for option expiration: January, April, July, and October; February, May, August, and November; or March, June, September, and December.

expiration date The date on which an option ceases to exist.

exploratory drilling program A direct participation program that engages in the drilling for oil or gas in new areas seeking to find new wells.

exploratory well Also known as wildcatting. The drilling for oil or gas in new areas in an effort to find new wells.

ex rights The common stock subject to a rights offering trade without the rights attached.

ex rights date The first day when the common stock is subject to a rights offering trade without the rights attached.

ex warrants Common trading without the warrants attached.

F

face-amount certificate company (FAC) A type of investment company that requires an investor to make fixed payments over time or to deposit a lump sum, and that will return to the investor a stated sum known as the face amount on a specific date.

face amount/face value *See* par.

fail to deliver An event where the broker on the sell side of the transaction fails to deliver the security.

fail to receive An event where the broker on the buy side of the transaction fails to receive the security from the broker on the sell side.

Fannie Mae *See* Federal National Mortgage Association.

Farm Credit Administrator The agency that oversees all of the activities of the banks in the Federal Farm Credit System.

Federal Deposit Insurance Corporation (FDIC) The government insurance agency that provides insurance for bank depositors in case of bank failure.

Federal Farm Credit System An organization of banks that is designed to provide financing to farmers for mortgages, feed and grain, and equipment.

federal funds rate The rate banks charge each other on overnight loans.

Federal Home Loan Mortgage Corporation (FHLMC; Freddie Mac) A publicly traded for-profit corporation that provides liquidity to the secondary mortgage market by purchasing pools of mortgages from lenders and, in turn, issues mortgage-backed securities.

Federal Intermediate Credit Bank Provides short-term financing to farmers for equipment.

Federal National Mortgage Association (FNMA; Fannie Mae) A publicly traded for-profit corporation that provides liquidity to the secondary mortgage market by purchasing pools of mortgages and issuing mortgage-backed securities.

Federal Open Market Committee (FOMC) The committee of the Federal Reserve Board that makes policy decisions relating to the nation's money supply.

Federal Reserve Board A seven-member board that directs the policies of the Federal Reserve System. The members are appointed by the President and approved by Congress.

Federal Reserve System The nation's central banking system, the purpose of which is to regulate money supply and the extension of credit. The Federal Reserve System is composed of 12 central banks and 24 regional banks, along with hundreds of national and state chartered banks.

fictitious quote A quote that is not representative of an actual bid or offer for a security.

fidelity bond A bond that must be posted by all broker dealers to ensure the public against employee dishonesty.

fill or kill (FK) A type of order that requires that all of the securities in the order be purchased or sold immediately or not at all.

final prospectus The official offering document for a security that contains the security's final offering price along with all information required by law for an investor to make an informed decision.

firm commitment underwriting Guarantees the issuer all of the money right away. The underwriters purchase all of the securities from the issuer regardless of whether they can sell the securities to their customers.

firm quote A quote displayed at which the dealer is obligated to buy or sell at least one round lot at the quoted price.

fiscal policy Government policy designed to influence the economy through government tax and spending programs. The President and Congress control fiscal policy.

5% markup policy FINRA's guideline that requires all prices paid by customers to be reasonably related to a security's market price. The 5% policy is a guideline, not a rule, and it does not apply to securities sold through a prospectus.

fixed annuity An insurance contract where the insurance company guarantees fixed payments to the annuitant, usually until the annuitant's death.

fixed assets Assets used by a corporation to conduct its business, such as plant and equipment.

flat A term used to describe a bond that trades without accrued interest, such as a zero-coupon bond or a bond that is in default.

floor broker An individual member of an exchange who may execute orders on the floor.

floor trader Members of the exchange who trade for their own accounts. Members of the NYSE may not trade from the floor for their own accounts.

flow of funds A schedule of expenses and interested parties that prioritizes how payments will be made from the revenue generated by a facility financed by a municipal revenue bond.

forced conversion The calling in of convertible bonds at a price that is less than the market value of the underlying common stock into which the bonds may be converted.

foreign currency Currency of another country.

foreign currency option An option to purchase or sell a specified amount of another country's currency.

Form 10-K An annual report filed by a corporation detailing its financial performance for the year.

Form 10-Q A quarterly report filed by a corporation detailing its financial performance for the quarter.

form letter A letter sent out by a brokerage firm or a registered representative to more than 25 people in a 90-day period. Form letters are subject to approval and recordkeeping requirements.

forward pricing The way in which open-end mutual funds are valued for investors who wish to purchase or redeem shares of the fund. Mutual funds usually price their shares at the end of the business day. The price to be paid or received by the investor will be the price that is next calculated after the fund receives the order.

401k A qualified retirement plan offered by an employer.

403b A qualified retirement plan offered to teachers and employees of nonprofit organizations.

fourth market A transaction between two large institutions without the use of a broker dealer.

fractional share A portion of a whole share that represents ownership of an open-end mutual fund.

fraud Any attempt to gain an unfair advantage over another party through the use of deception, concealment, or misrepresentation.

free credit balance Cash reserves in a customer's account that have not been invested. Customers must be notified of their free credit balances at least quarterly.

free look A privilege offered to purchasers of contractual plans and insurance policies that will allow the individual to cancel the contract within the free-look period, usually 45 days.

freeriding The purchase and sale of a security without depositing the money required to cover the purchase price as required by Regulation T.

freeriding and withholding The withholding of new issue securities offered by a broker dealer for the benefit of the brokerage firm or an employee.

front-end load (1) A sales charge paid by investors in open-end mutual funds that is paid at the time of purchase. (2) A contractual plan that seeks to assess sales charges in the first years of the plan and may charge up to 50% of the first year's payments as sales charges.

frozen account An account where the owner is required to deposit cash or securities up front, prior to any purchase or sale taking place. An account is usually frozen as a result of a customer's failure to pay or deliver securities.

full power of attorney A type of discretionary authority that allows a third party to purchase and sell securities as well as to withdraw cash and securities without the owner's prior consent or knowledge. This type of authority is usually reserved to trustees and attorneys.

fully registered bonds A type of bond issuance where the issuer has a complete record of the owners of the bonds and who is entitled to receive interest and principal payments. The owners of fully registered bonds are not required to clip coupons.

functional allocation An arrangement for oil and gas programs where the general partner pays the tangible drilling costs and the limited partner absorbs the intangible drilling costs.

fundamental analyst A method of valuing the company that takes into consideration the financial performance of the corporation, the value of its assets, and the quality of its management.

funded debt Long-term debt obligations of corporations or municipalities.

fungible Easily exchangeable items with the same conditions.

G

general account An insurance company's account that holds the money and investments for fixed contracts and traditional life insurance policies.

general obligation bond A municipal bond that is backed by the taxing power of the state or municipality.

general partner The partner in a general partnership who manages the business and is responsible for any debt of the program.

general securities principal An individual who has passed the Series 24 exam and may supervise the activities of the firm and its agents.

generic advertising Advertising designed to promote name recognition for a firm and securities as investments, but does not recommend specific securities.

good til cancel (GTC) An order that remains on the books until it is executed or canceled.

goodwill An intangible asset of a corporation, such as its name recognition and reputation, that adds to its value.

Government National Mortgage Association (GNMA; Ginnie Mae) A government corporation that provides liquidity to the mortgage markets by purchasing pools of mortgages that have been insured by the Federal Housing Administration and the Veterans Administration. Ginnie Mae issues pass-through certificates to investors backed by the pools of mortgages.

government security A security that is an obligation of the U.S. government and that is backed by the full faith and credit of the U.S. government, such as Treasury bills, notes, and bonds.

grant anticipation note (GAN) Short-term municipal financing issued in anticipation of receiving a grant from the federal government or one of its agencies.

greenshoe option An option given to an underwriter of common stock that will allow it to purchase up to an additional 15% of the offering from the issuer at the original offering price to cover over allotments for securities that are in high demand.

gross domestic product (GDP) The value of all goods and services produced by a country within a period of time. GDP includes government purchases, investments, and exports minus imports.

gross income All income received by a taxpayer before deductions for taxes.

gross revenue pledge A flow-of-funds pledge for a municipal revenue bond that states that debt service will be paid first.

growth fund A fund whose objective is capital appreciation. Growth funds invest in common stocks to achieve their objective.

growth stock The stock of a company whose earnings grow at a rate that is faster than the growth rate of the economy as a whole. Growth stocks are characterized by increased opportunities for appreciation and little or no dividends.

guardian An individual who has a fiduciary responsibility for another, usually a minor.

H

HH bond A nonmarketable government security that pays semiannual interest. Series HH bonds are issued with a $500 minimum value and may only be purchased by trading matured series EE bonds; they may not be purchased with cash.

halt A temporary stop in the trading of a security. If a common stock is halted, all derivatives and convertibles will be halted as well.

head and shoulders A chart pattern that indicates a reversal of a trend. A head-and-shoulders top indicates a reversal of an uptrend and is considered bearish. A head-and-shoulders bottom is the reversal of a downtrend and is considered bullish.

hedge A position taken in a security to offset or reduce the risk associated with the risk of another security.

high The highest price paid for a security during a trading session or during a 52-week period.

holder An individual or corporation that owns a security. The holder of a security is also known as being long the security.

holding period The length of time during which an investor owned a security. The holding period is important for calculating tax liability.

hold in street name The registration of customer securities in the name of the broker dealer. Most customers register securities in the name of the broker dealer to make the transfer of ownership easier.

horizontal spread Also known as a calendar spread. The simultaneous purchase and sale of two calls or two puts on the same underlying security with the same exercise price but with different expiration months.

hot issue A new issue of securities that trades at an immediate premium to its offering price in the secondary market.

HR 10 plan *See* Keogh plan.

hypothecation The customer's pledge of securities as collateral for a margin loan.

I

immediate annuity An annuity contract purchased with a single payment that entitles the holder to receive immediate payments from the contract. The annuitant purchases annuity units and usually begins receiving payments within 60 days.

immediate family An individual's immediate family includes parents, parents-in-law, children, spouse, and any relative financially dependent upon the individual.

immediate or cancel (IOC) An order that is to be executed as fully as possible immediately and whatever is not executed will be cancelled.

income bond A highly speculative bond that is issued at a discount from par and only pays interest if the issuer has enough income to do so. The issuer of the income bond only promises to pay principal at maturity. Income bonds trade flat without accrued interest.

income fund A mutual fund whose investment objective is to achieve current income for its shareholders by investing in bonds and preferred stocks.

income program A type of oil and gas program that purchases producing wells to receive the income received from the sale of the proven reserves.

income statement A financial statement that shows a corporation's revenue and expenses for the time period in question.

indefeasible title A record of ownership that cannot be challenged.

index A representation of the price action of a given group of securities. Indexes are used to measure the condition of the market as a whole, such as with the S&P 500, or can be used to measure the condition of an industry group, such as with the Biotech index.

index option An option on an underlying financial index. Index options settle in cash.

indication of interest An investor's expression of a willingness to purchase a new issue of securities after receiving a preliminary prospectus. The investor's indication of interest is not binding on either the investor or the firm.

Individual Retirement Account (IRA) A self-directed retirement account that allows individuals with earned income to contribute the lesser of 100% of earned income or the annual maximum per year. The contributions may be made with pre- or after-tax dollars, depending on the individual's level of income and whether he or she is eligible to participate in an employer's sponsored plan.

industrial development bond A private-purpose municipal bond whose proceeds are used to build a facility that is leased to a corporation. The debt service on the bonds is supported by the lease payments.

inflation The persistent upward pressure on the price of goods and services over time.

initial margin requirement The initial amount of equity that a customer must deposit to establish a position. The initial margin requirement is set by the Federal Reserve Board under Regulation T.

initial public offering (IPO) The first offering of common stock to the general investing public.

in part call A partial call of a bond issue for redemption.

inside information Information that is not known to people outside of the corporation. Information becomes public only after it is released by the corporation through a recognized media source. Inside information may be both material and immaterial. It is only illegal to trade on inside material information.

inside market The highest bid and the lowest offer for a security.

insider A company's officers, directors, large stockholders of 10% or more of the company, and anyone who is in possession of nonpublic material information, along with the immediate family members of the same.

Insider Trading and Securities Fraud Enforcement Act of 1988 Federal legislation that made the penalties for people trading on material nonpublic information more severe. Penalties for insider traders are up to the greater of 300% of the amount of money made or the loss avoided or $1,000,000 and up to 5 years in prison. People who disseminate inside information may be imprisoned and fined up to $1,000,000.

INSTINET A computer network that facilitates trading of large blocks of stocks between institutions without the use of a broker dealer.

institutional account An account in the name of an institution but operated for the benefit of others (i.e., banks and mutual funds). There is no minimum size for an institutional account.

institutional communication Any communication that is distributed exclusively to institutional investors. Institutional communications does not require the pre-approval of a principal but must be maintained for 3 years by the firm.

institutional investor An investor who trades for its own account or for the accounts of others in large quantities and is covered by fewer protective laws.

insurance covenant The promise of an issuer of revenue bonds to maintain insurance on the financed project.

intangible asset Nonphysical property of a corporation, such as trademarks and copyrights.

intangible drilling cost (IDC) Costs for an oil and gas program that are expensed in the year in which they are incurred for such things as wages, surveys, and well casings.

interbank market An international currency market.

interest The cost for borrowing money, usually charged at an annual percentage rate.

interest rate option An option based on U.S. government securities. The options are either rate-based or priced-based options.

interest rate risk The risk borne by investors in interest-bearing securities, which subjects the holder to a loss of principal should interest rates rise.

interlocking directorate Corporate boards that share one or more directors.

Intermarket Trading System/Computer-Assisted Execution System (ITS/CAES) A computer system that links the third market for securities with the exchanges.

Internal Revenue Code (IRC) The codes that define tax liabilities for U.S. taxpayers.

interpositioning The placing of another broker dealer in between the customer and the best market. Interpositioning is prohibited unless it can be demonstrated that the customer received a better price because of it.

interstate offering A multistate offering of securities that requires that the issuer register with the SEC as well as with the states in which the securities will be sold.

in the money A relationship between the strike price of an option and the underlying security's price. A call is in the money when the strike price is lower than the security's price. A put is in the money when the strike price is higher than the security's price.

intrastate offering *See* Rule 147.

intrinsic value The amount by which an option is in the money.

introducing broker *See* correspondent broker dealer.

inverted yield curve A yield curve where the cost of short-term financing exceeds the cost for long-term financing.

investment adviser Anyone who charges a fee for investment advice or who holds themselves out to the public as being in the business of giving investment advice for a fee.

Investment Advisers Act of 1940 The federal legislation that sets forth guidelines for business requirements and activities of investment advisers.

investment banker A financial institution that is in the business of raising capital for companies and municipalities by underwriting securities.

investment company A company that sells undivided interests in a pool of securities and manages the portfolio for the benefit of the investors. Investment companies include management companies, unit investment trusts, and face-amount companies.

Investment Company Act of 1940 Federal legislation that regulates the operation and registration of investment companies.

investment-grade security A security that has been assigned a rating in the highest rating tier by a recognized ratings agency.

investment objective An investor's set of goals as to how he or she is seeking to make money, such as capital appreciation or current income.

investor The purchaser of a security who seeks to realize a profit.

IRA rollover The temporary distribution of assets from an IRA and the subsequent reinvestment of the assets into another IRA within 60 days. An IRA may be rolled over only once per year and is subject to a 10% penalty and ordinary income taxes if the investor is under 59 1/2 and if the assets are not deposited in another qualified account within 60 days.

IRA transfer The movement of assets from one qualified account to another without the account holder taking possession of the assets. Investors may transfer an IRA as often as they like.

issued stock Stock that has actually been sold to the investing public.

issuer Any entity that issues or proposes to issue securities.

J

joint account An account that is owned by two or more parties. Joint accounts allow either party to enter transactions for the account. Both parties must sign a joint account agreement. All joint accounts must be designated as joint tenants in common or with rights of survivorship.

joint tenants in common (JTIC) A joint account where the assets of a party who has died transfer to the decedent's estate, not the other tenant.

joint tenants with rights of survivorship (JTWROS) A joint account where the assets of a party who has died transfer to the surviving party, not the decedent's estate.

joint venture An interest in an operation shared by two or more parties. The parties have no other relationship beyond the joint venture.

junk bond A bond with a high degree of default risk that has been assigned a speculative rating by the ratings agencies.

junk bond fund A speculative bond fund that invests in high-yield bonds in order to achieve a high degree of current income.

K

Keogh plan A qualified retirement account for self-employed individuals. Contributions are limited to the lesser of 20% of their gross income or $51,000.

Keynesian economics An economic theory that states that government intervention in the marketplace helps sustain economic growth.

know-your-customer rule Industry regulation that requires a registered representative to be familiar with the customer's financial objectives and needs prior to making a recommendation; also known as Rule 405.

L

lagging indicator A measurement of economic activity that changes after a change has taken place in economic activity. Lagging indicators are useful confirmation tools when determining the strength of an economic trend. Lagging indicators include corporate profits, average duration of unemployment, and labor costs.

last in, first out (LIFO) An accounting method used that states that the last item that was produced is the first item sold.

leading indicator A measurement of economic activity that changes prior to a change in economic activity. Leading economic indicators are useful in predicting a coming trend in economic activity. Leading economic indicators include housing permits, new orders for durable goods, and the S&P 500.

LEAPS (long-term equity anticipation securities) A long-term option on a security that has an expiration of up to 39 months.

lease rental bonds A municipal bond that is issued to finance the building of a facility that will be rented out. The lease payments on the facility will support the bond's debt service.

legal list A list of securities that have been approved by certain state securities regulators for purchase by fiduciaries.

legal opinion An opinion issued by a bond attorney stating that the issue is a legally binding obligation of the state or municipality. The legal opinion also contains a statement regarding the tax status of the interest payments received by investors.

legislative risk The risk that the government may do something that adversely affects an investment.

letter of intent (LOI) A letter signed by the purchaser of mutual fund shares that states the investor's intention to invest a certain amount of money over a 13-month period. By agreeing to invest this sum, the investor is entitled to receive a lower sales charge on all purchases covered by the letter of intent. The letter of intent may be backdated up to 90 days from an initial purchase. Should the investor fail to invest the stated sum, a sales charge adjustment will be charged.

level load A mutual fund share that charges a flat annual fee, such as a 12B-1 fee.

level one A Nasdaq workstation service that allows the agent to see the inside market only.

level two A Nasdaq workstation service that allows the order-entry firm to see the inside market, to view the quotes entered by all market makers, and to execute orders.

level three A Nasdaq workstation service that allows market-making firms to see the inside market, to view the quotes entered by all market makers, to execute orders, and to enter their own quotes for the security. This is the highest level of Nasdaq service.

leverage The use of borrowed funds to try to obtain a rate of return that exceeds the cost of the funds.

liability A legal obligation to pay a debt either incurred through borrowing or through the normal course of business.

life annuity/straight life An annuity payout option that provides payments over the life of the annuitant.

life annuity with period certain An annuity payout option that provides payments to the annuitant for life or to the annuitant's estate for the period certain, whichever is longer.

life contingency An annuity payout option that provides a death benefit in case the annuitant dies during the accumulation stage.

limit order An order that sets a maximum price that the investor will pay in the case of a buy order or the minimum price the investor will accept in the case of a sell order.

limited liability A protection afforded to investors in securities that limits their liability to the amount of money invested in the securities.

limited partner A passive investor in a direct participation program who has no role in the project's management.

limited partnership (LP) An association of two or more partners with at least one partner being the general partner who is responsible for the management of the partnership.

limited partnership agreement The foundation of all limited partnerships. The agreement is the contract between all partners, and it spells out the authority of the general partner and the rights of all limited partners.

limited power of attorney/limited trading authorization Legal authorization for a representative or a firm to effect purchases and sales for a customer's account without the customer's prior knowledge. The authorization is limited to buying and selling securities and may not be given to another party.

limited principal An individual who has passed the Series 26 exam and may supervise Series 6 limited representatives.

limited representative An individual who has passed the Series 6 exam and may represent a broker dealer in the sale of mutual fund shares and variable contracts.

limited tax bond A type of general obligation bond that is issued by a municipality that may not increase its tax rate to pay the debt service of the issue.

liquidity The ability of an investment to be readily converted into cash.

liquidity risk The risk that an investor may not be able to sell a security when needed or that selling a security when needed will adversely affect the price.

listed option A standardized option contract that is traded on an exchange.

listed security A security that trades on one of the exchanges. Only securities that trade on an exchange are known as listed securities.

loan consent agreement A portion of the margin agreement that allows the broker dealer to loan out the customer's securities to another customer who wishes to borrow them to sell the security short.

locked market A market condition that results when the bid and the offer for a security are equal.

LOI *See* letter of intent.

London Interbank Offered Rate (LIBOR) The interbank rates for dollar-denominated deposits in England.

long A term used to describe an investor who owns a security.

long market value The total long market value of a customer's account.

long-term gain A profit realized through the sale of a security at a price that is higher than its purchase price after a being held for more than 12 months.

long-term loss A loss realized through the sale of a security at a price that is lower than its purchase price after being held for more than 12 months.

loss carry forward A capital loss realized on the sale of an asset in one year that is carried forward in whole or part to subsequent tax years.

low The lowest price at which a security has traded in any given period, usually measured during a trading day or for 52 weeks.

M

M1 The most liquid measure of the money supply. It includes all currency and demand and NOW deposits (checking accounts).

M2 A measure of that money supply includes M1 plus all time deposits, savings accounts, and noninstitutional money market accounts.

M3 A measure of money supply that includes M2 and large time deposits, institutional money market funds, short-term repurchase agreements, and other large liquid assets.

maintenance call A demand for additional cash or collateral made by a broker dealer when a margin customer's account equity has fallen below the minimum requirement of the NYSE or that is set by the broker dealer.

maintenance covenant A promise made by an issuer of a municipal revenue bond to maintain the facility in good repair.

Major Market Index (XMI) An index created by the Amex to track 15 of the 30 largest stocks in the Dow Jones Industrial Average.

Maloney Act of 1938 An amendment to the Securities Exchange Act of 1934 that gave the NASD (now part of FINRA) the authority to regulate the over-the-counter market.

managed underwriting An underwriting conducted by a syndicate led by the managing underwriter.

management company A type of investment company that actively manages a portfolio of securities in order to meet a stated investment objective. Management companies are also known as mutual funds.

management fee (1) The fee received by the lead or managing underwriter of a syndicate. (2) The fee received by a sponsor of a direct participation program.

managing partner The general partner in a direct participation program.

managing underwriter The lead underwriter in a syndicate who is responsible for negotiating with the issuer, forming the syndicate, and settling the syndicate account.

margin The amount of customer equity that is required to hold a position in a security.

margin account An account that allows the customer to borrow money from the brokerage firm to buy securities.

margin call A demand for cash or collateral mandated by the Federal Reserve Board under Regulation T.

margin department The department in a broker dealer that calculates money owed by the customer or money due the customer.

margin maintenance call *See* maintenance call.

mark to the market The monitoring of a the current value of a position relative to the price at which the trade was executed for securities purchased on margin or on a when-issued basis.

marketability The ability of an investment to be exchanged between two investors. A security with an active secondary market has a higher level of marketability than one whose market is not as active.

market arbitrage A type of arbitrage that consists of purchasing a security in one marketplace and selling it in another to take advantage of price inefficiencies.

market letter A regular publication, usually issued by an investment adviser, that offers information and/or advice regarding a security, market conditions, or the economy as a whole.

market maker A Nasdaq firm that is required to quote a continuous two-sided market for the securities in which it trades.

market not held A type of order that gives the floor broker discretion over the time and price of execution.

market on close An order that will be executed at whatever price the market is at, either on the closing print or just prior to the closing print.

market on open An order that will be executed at whatever price the market is at, either on the opening print or just after the opening print.

market order A type of order that will be executed immediately at the best available price once it is presented to the market.

market-out clause A clause in an underwriting agreement that gives the syndicate the ability to cancel the underwriting if it finds a material problem with the information or condition of the issuer.

market risk/ systematic risk The risk inherent in any investment in the market that states an investor may lose money simply because the market is going down.

market value The value of a security that is determined in the marketplace by the investors who enter bids and offers for a security.

markdown The profit earned by a dealer on a transaction when purchasing securities for its own account from a customer.

markup The compensation paid to a securities dealer for selling a security to a customer from its inventory.

markup policy FINRA's guideline that states that the price that is paid or received by an investor must be reasonably related to the market price for that security. FINRA offers 5% as a guideline for what is reasonable to charge investors when they purchase or sell securities.

material information Information that would affect a company's current or future prospects or an investor's decision to invest in the company.

maturity date The date on which a bond's principal amount becomes payable to its holders.

member A member of FINRA or one of the 1,366 members of the NYSE.

member firm A firm that is a member of the NYSE, FINRA, or another self-regulatory organization.

member order A retail order entered by a member of a municipal bond syndicate for which the member will receive all of the sales credit.

mini maxi underwriting A type of best efforts underwriting that states that the offering will not become effective until a minimum amount is sold and sets a maximum amount that may be sold.

minimum death benefit The minimum guaranteed death benefit that will be paid to the beneficiaries if the holder of a variable life insurance policy dies.

minus tick A trade in an exchange-listed security that is at a price that is lower than the previous trade.

modern portfolio theory An investing approach that looks at the overall return and risk of a portfolio as a whole, not as a collection of single investments.

modified accelerated cost recovery system (MACRS) An accounting method that allows the owner to recover a larger portion of the asset's value in the early years of its life.

monetary policy Economic policy that is controlled by the Federal Reserve Board and controls the amount of money in circulation and the level of interest rates.

monetarist theory A theory that states that the money supply is the driving force in the economy and that a well-managed money supply will benefit the economy.

money market The secondary market where short-term highly liquid securities are traded. Securities traded in the money market include T-bills, negotiable CDs, bankers' acceptances, commercial paper, and other short-term securities with less than 12 months to maturity.

money market mutual fund A mutual fund that invests in money market instruments to generate monthly interest for its shareholders. Money market mutual funds have a stable NAV that is equal to $1, but it is not guaranteed.

money supply The total amount of currency, loans, and credit in the economy. The money supply is measured by M1, M2, M3, and L.

moral obligation bond A type of municipal revenue bond that will allow the state or municipality to vote to cover a short fall in the debt service.

multiplier effect The ability of the money supply to grow simply through the normal course of banking. When banks and other financial institutions accept deposits and subsequently loan out those deposits to earn interest, the amount of money in the system grows.

municipal bond A bond issued by a state or political subdivision of a state in an effort to finance its operations. Interest earned by investors in municipal bonds is almost always free from federal income taxes.

municipal bond fund A mutual fund that invests in a portfolio of municipal debt in an effort to produce income that is free from federal income taxes for its investors.

Municipal Bond Investors Assurance Corp. (MBIA) An independent insurance company that will, for a fee received from the issuer, insure the interest and principal payments on a municipal bond.

municipal note A short-term municipal issue sold to manage the issuer's cash flow, usually in anticipation of the offering of long-term financing.

Munifacts A service that provides real-time secondary market quotes. Munifacts is now known as Thomson Muni Market Monitor.

Municipal Securities Rulemaking Board (MSRB) The self-regulatory organization that oversees the issuance and trading of municipal bonds. The MSRB's rules are enforced by other industry SROs.

mutual fund An investment company that invests in and manages a portfolio of securities for its shareholders. Open-end mutual funds sell their shares to investors on a continuous basis and must stand ready to redeem their shares upon the shareholder's request.

mutual fund custodian A qualified financial institution that maintains physical custody of a mutual fund's cash and securities. Custodians are usually banks, trust companies, or exchange member firms.

N

naked The sale of a call option without owning the underlying security or the sale of a put option without being short the stock or having cash on deposit that is sufficient to purchase the underlying security.

narrow-based index An index that is based on a market sector or a limited number of securities.

NASD (National Association of Securities Dealers) The industry self-regulatory agency that was authorized by the Maloney Act of 1938 and empowered to regulate the over-the-counter market. The NASD is now part of FINRA.

NASD bylaws The rules that define the operation of the NASD and how it regulates the over the counter market. The four major bylaws are the Rules of Fair Practice, the Uniform Practice Code, the Code of Procedure, and the Code of Arbitration. Now known as FINRA bylaws.

NASD Manual An NASD publication that outlines the rules and regulations of NASD membership. Now known as the FINRA Manual.

National Securities Clearing Corporation (NSCC) The clearing intermediary through which clearing member firms reconcile their securities accounts.

NAV (net asset value) The net value of a mutual fund after deducting all its liabilities. A mutual fund must calculate its NAV at least once per business day. To determine NAV per share, simply divide the mutual fund's NAV by the total number of shares outstanding.

negotiability The ability of an investment to be freely exchanged between noninterested parties.

negotiable certificate of deposit A certificate issued by a bank for a time deposit in excess of $100,000 that can be exchanged between parties prior to its maturity date. FDIC insurance only covers the first $250,000 of the principal amount should the bank fail.

NOW (negotiable order of withdrawal) Account A type of demand deposit that allows the holder to write checks against an interest-bearing account.

net change The difference between the previous day's closing price and the price of the most recently reported trade for a security.

net current assets per share A calculation of the value per share that excludes fixed assets and intangibles.

net debt per capita A measure of a municipal issuer's ability to meet its obligations. It measures the debt level of the issuer in relation to the population.

net debt to assessed valuation A measure of the issuer's ability to meet its obligations and to raise additional revenue through property taxes.

net direct debt The total amount of general obligation debt, including notes and short-term financing, issued by a municipality or state.

net interest cost (NIC) A calculation that measures the interest cost of a municipal issue over the life of all bonds. Most competitive underwritings for municipal securities are awarded to the syndicate that submits the bid with the lowest NIC.

net investment income The total sum of investment income derived from dividend and interest income after subtracting expenses.

net revenue pledge A pledge from a revenue bond that pays maintenance and operation expenses first, then debt service.

net total debt The total of a municipality's direct debt plus its overlapping debt.

net worth The value of a corporation after subtracting all of its liabilities. A corporation's net worth is also equal to shareholder's equity.

new account form Paperwork that must be filled out and signed by the representative and a principal of the firm prior to the opening of any account being opened for a customer.

new construction program A real estate program that seeks to achieve capital appreciation by building new properties.

new housing authority (NHA) A municipal bond issued to build low-income housing. NHA bonds are guaranteed by the U.S. government and are considered the safest type of municipal bonds. NHA bonds are not considered to be double-barreled bonds.

new issue *See* initial public offering (IPO).

New York Stock Exchange (NYSE) A membership organization that provides a marketplace for securities to be exchanged in one centralized location through a dual-auction process.

no-load fund A fund that does not charge the investor a sales charge to invest in the fund. Shares of no-load mutual funds are sold directly from the fund company to the investor.

nominal owner An individual or entity registered as the owner of record of securities for the benefit of another party.

nominal quote A quote given for informational purposes only. A trader who identifies a quote as being nominal cannot be held to trading at the prices that were clearly identified as being nominal.

nominal yield The yield that is stated or named on the security. The nominal yield, once it has been set, never changes, regardless of the market price of the security.

noncompetitive bid A bid submitted for Treasury bills where the purchaser agrees to accept the average of all yields accepted at the auction. Noncompetitive tenders are always the first orders filled at the auction.

noncumulative preferred A type of preferred stock whose dividends do not accumulate in arrears if the issuer misses the payment.

nondiscrimination A clause that states that all eligible individuals must be allowed to participate in a qualified retirement plan.

nondiversification An investment strategy that concentrates its investments among a small group of securities or issuers.

nondiversified management company An investment company that concentrates its investments among a few issuers or securities and does not meet the diversification requirements of the Investment Company Act of 1940.

nonfixed UIT A type of UIT that allows changes in the portfolio and traditionally invests in mutual fund shares.

nonqualified retirement plan A retirement plan that does not allow contributions to be made with pre-tax dollars; that is, the retirement plan does not qualify for beneficial tax treatment from the IRS for its contributions.

nonsystematic risk A risk that is specific to an issuer or an industry.

not-held (NH) order An order that gives the floor broker discretion as to the time and price of execution.

note An intermediate-term interest-bearing security that represents an obligation of its issuer.

numbered account An account that has been designated a number for identification purposes in order to maintain anonymity for its owner. The owner must sign a statement acknowledging ownership.

O

odd lot A transaction that is for less than 100 shares of stock or for less than 5 bonds.

odd lot differential An additional fee that may be charged to an investor for the handling of odd lot transactions (usually waived).

odd lot theory A contrarian theory that states that small investors will invariably buy and sell at the wrong time.

offer A price published at which an investor or broker dealer is willing to sell a security.

offering circular The offering document that is prepared by a corporation selling securities under a Regulation A offering.

office of supervisory jurisdiction (OSJ) An office identified by the broker dealer as having supervisory responsibilities for agents. It has final approval of new accounts, makes markets, or structures offerings.

Office of the Comptroller of the Currency An office of the U.S. Treasury that is responsible for regulating the practices of national banks.

official notice of sale The notice of sale published in the *Daily Bond Buyer* by a municipal issuer that is used to obtain an underwriter for municipal bonds.

official statement The offering document for a municipal issuer that must be provided to every purchaser if the issuer prepares one.

oil and gas direct participation program A type of direct participation program designed to invest in oil and gas production or exploration.

oil depletion allowance An accounting method used to reduce the amount of reserves available from a producing well.

omnibus account An account used by an introducing member to execute and clear all of its customer's trades.

open-end investment company *See* mutual fund.

open-end covenant A type of bond indenture that allows for the issuance of additional bonds with the same claim on the collateral as the original issue.

option A contract between two investors to purchase or sell as security at a given price for a certain period of time.

option agreement A form that must be signed and returned by an option investor within 15 days of the account's approval to trade options.

Options Clearing Corporation (OCC) The organization that issues and guarantees the performance of standardized options.

option disclosure document A document that must be furnished to all option investors at the time the account is approved for options trading. It is published by the Options Clearing Corporation (OCC), and it details the risks and features of standardized options.

order book official (OBO) Employees of the CBOE who are responsible for maintaining a fair and orderly market in the options assigned to them and for executing orders that have been left with them.

order department The department of a broker dealer that is responsible for routing orders to the markets for execution.

order memorandum/ order ticket The written document filled out by a registered representative that identifies, among other things, the security, the amount, the customer, and the account number for which the order is being entered.

original issue discount (OID) A bond that has been issued to the public at a discount to its par value. The OID on a corporate bond is taxed as if it was earned annually. The OID on a municipal bond is exempt from taxation.

OTC market *See* over-the-counter (OTC) market.

out of the money The relationship of an option's strike price to the underlying security's price when exercising the option would not make economic sense. A call is out of the money when the security's price is below the option's strike price. A put is out of the money when the security's price is above the option's strike price.

outstanding stock The total amount of a security that has been sold to the investing public and that remains in the hands of the investing public.

overlapping debt The portion of another taxing authority's debt that a municipality is responsible for.

overriding royalty interest A type of sharing arrangement that offers an individual with no risk a portion of the revenue in exchange for something of value, such as the right to drill on the owner's land.

over-the-counter (OTC) market	An interdealer market that consists of a computer and phone network through which broker dealers trade securities.

P

par	The stated principal amount of a security. Par value is of great importance for fixed-income securities such as bonds or preferred stock. Par value for bonds is traditionally $1,000, whereas par for a preferred stock is normally $100. Par value is of little importance when looking at common stock.
participation	The code set forth in the Employee Retirement Income Security Act of 1974 that states who is eligible to participate in an employer sponsored retirement plan.
parity	A condition that results when the value of an underlying common stock to be received upon conversion equals the value of the convertible security.
partial call	A call of a portion of an issuer's callable securities.
pass-through certificate	A security that passes through income and principal payments made to an underlying portfolio of mortgages. Ginnie Mae is one of the biggest issuers of this type of security.
passive income	Income received by an individual for which no work was performed, such as rental income received from a rental property.
passive loss	A loss realized on an investment in a limited partnership or rental property that can be used to offset passive income.
pass-through certificate	Securities issued by Ginnie Mae to investors that pay monthly interest and principal.
payment date	The day when a dividend will actually be sent to investors. The payment date is set by the corporation's board of directors at the time when they initially declare the dividend.
payout stage	The period during which an annuitant receives payments from an annuity contract.
payroll deduction plan	A nonqualified retirement plan where employees authorize the employer to take regular deductions from their paychecks to invest in a retirement account.
pension plan	A contractual retirement plan between an employee and an employer that is designed to provide regular income for the employee after retirement.
percentage depletion	An accounting method that allows for a tax deduction for the reduction of reserves.

periodic payment plan A contract to purchase mutual fund shares over an extended period of time, usually in exchange for the fund company waiving its minimum investment requirement.

person Any individual or entity that can enter into a legally binding contract for the purchase and sale of securities.

personal income Income earned by an individual from providing services and through investments.

phantom income (1) A term used to describe the taxable appreciation on a zero-coupon bond. (2) The term used to describe taxable income generated by a limited partnership that is not producing positive cash flow.

Philadelphia Automated Communication Execution System (PACE) The computerized order-routing system for the Philadelphia Stock Exchange.

pink sheets An electronic quote service containing quotes for unlisted securities that is published by the National Quotation Bureau; operated as the PINK over-the-counter market.

placement ratio A ratio that details the percentage of municipal bonds sold, relative to the number of bonds offered in the last week, published by the *Daily Bond Buyer*.

plus tick A transaction in an exchange-listed security that is higher than the previous transaction.

point An increment of change in the price of a security: 1 bond point equals 1% of par or 1% of $1,000, or $10.

POP *See* public offering price (POP).

portfolio income Interest and dividends earned through investing in securities.

portfolio manager An entity that is hired to manage the investment portfolios of a mutual fund. The portfolio manager is paid a fee that is based on the net assets of the fund.

position The amount of a security in which an investor has an interest by either being long (owning) or short (owing) the security.

power of substitution *See* stock power.

preemptive right The right of a common stockholder to maintain proportional ownership interest in a security. A corporation may not issue additional shares of common stock without first offering those shares to existing stockholders.

preferred stock An equity security issued with a stated dividend rate. Preferred stockholders have a higher claim on a corporation's dividends and assets than common holders.

preferred stock ratio A ratio detailing the amount of an issuer's total capitalization that is made up of preferred stock. The ratio is found by dividing the total par value of preferred stock by the issuer's total capitalization.

preliminary prospectus/red herring A document used to solicit indications of interest during the cooling-off period for a new issue of securities. All of the information in the preliminary prospectus is subject to revision and change. The cover of a preliminary prospectus must have a statement saying that the securities have not yet become registered and that they may not be sold until the registration becomes effective. This statement is written in red ink, and this is where the term *red herring* comes from.

price-earnings ratio (PE) A measure of value used by analysts. It is calculated by dividing the issuer's stock price by its earnings per share.

price spread A term used to describe an option spread where the long and short options differ only in their exercise prices.

primary earnings per share The amount of earnings available per common share prior to the conversion of any outstanding convertible securities.

prime rate The interest rate that banks charge their best corporate customers on loans.

principal (1) The face amount of a bond. (2) A broker dealer trading for its own account. (3) An individual who has successfully completed a principal exam and may supervise representatives.

principal transaction A transaction where a broker dealer participates in a trade by buying or selling securities for its own account.

priority The acceptance of bids and offers for exchange-listed securities on a first-come, first-serve (FCFS) basis.

private placement The private sale of securities to a limited number of investors. Also known as a Regulation D offering.

profit sharing plan A plan that allows the employer to distribute a percentage of its profits to its employees at a predetermined rate. The money may be paid directly to the employee or deposited into a retirement account.

progressive tax A tax structure where the tax rate increases as the income level of the individual or entity increases.

project note A municipal bond issued as interim financing in anticipation of the issuance of new housing authority bonds.

prospectus *See* final prospectus.

proxy A limited authority given by stockholders to another party to vote their shares in a corporate election. The stockholder may specify how the votes are cast or may give the party discretion.

proxy department The department in a brokerage firm that is responsible for forwarding proxies and financial information to investors whose stock is held in street name.

prudent man rule A rule that governs investments made by fiduciaries for the benefit of a third party. The rule states that the investments must be similar to those that a prudent person would make for on him- or herself.

public offering The sale of securities by an issuer to public investors.

public offering price (POP) The price paid by an investor to purchase open-end mutual fund shares. Also the price set for a security the first time it is sold to the investing public.

put An option contract that allows the buyer to sell a security at a set price for a specific period of time. The seller of a put is obligated to purchase the security at a set price for a specific period of time, should the buyer exercise the option.

put buyer A bearish investor who pays a premium for the right to sell a security at a set price for a certain period of time.

put spread An option position created by the simultaneous purchase and sale of two put options on the same underlying security that differ in strike prices, expiration months, or both.

put writer A bullish investor who sells a put option in order to receive the option premium. The writer is obligated to purchase the security if the buyer exercises the option.

Q

qualified legal opinion A legal opinion containing conditions or reservations relating to the issue. A legal opinion is issued by a bond counsel for a municipal issuer.

quick assets A measure of liquidity that subtracts the value of a corporation's unsold inventory from its current assets.

quick ratio *See* acid-test ratio.

qualified retirement plan A retirement plan that qualifies for favorable tax treatment by the IRS for contributions made into the plan.

quote A bid and offer broadcast from the exchange or through the Nasdaq system that displays the prices at which a security may be purchased and sold and in what quantities.

R

range The price difference between the high and low for a security.

rate covenant A promise in the trust indenture of a municipal revenue bond to keep the user fees high enough to support the debt service.

rating A judgment of an issuer's ability to meet its credit obligations. The higher the credit quality of the issuer is, the higher the credit rating. The lower the credit quality is, the lower the credit rating, and the higher the risk associated with the securities.

rating service Major financial organizations that evaluate the credit quality of issuers. Issuers have to request and pay for the service. Standard and Poor's, Moody's, and Fitch are the most widely followed rating services.

raw land program A type of real estate limited partnership that invests in land for capital appreciation.

real estate investment trust (REIT) An entity that is organized to invest in or manage real estate. REITs offer investors certain tax advantages that are beyond the scope of the exam.

real estate limited partnership A type of direct participation program that invests in real estate projects to produce income or capital appreciation.

real estate mortgage investment conduit (REMIC) An organization that pools investor's capital to purchase portfolios of mortgages.

realized gain A profit earned on the sale of a security at a price that exceeds its purchase price.

realized loss A loss recognized by an investor by selling a security at a price that is less than its purchase price.

reallowance A sales concession available to dealers who sell securities subject to an offering who are not syndicate or selling group members.

recapture An event that causes a tax liability on a previously taken deduction, such as selling an asset above its depreciated cost base.

reclamation The right of a seller to demand or claim any loss from the buying party due to the buyer's failure to settle the transaction.

recourse loan A loan taken out by a limited partnership that allows the lender to seek payment from the limited partners in the case of the partnership's failure to pay.

recession A decline in GDP that lasts for at least 6 months but not longer than 18 months.

record date A date set by a corporation's board of directors that determines which shareholders will be entitled to receive a declared dividend. Shareholders must be owners of record on this date in order to collect the dividend.

redeemable security A security that can be redeemed by the issuer at the investor's request. Open-end mutual funds are an example of redeemable securities.

redemption The return of an investor's capital by an issuer. Open-end mutual funds must redeem their securities within seven days of an investor's request.

red herring *See* preliminary prospectus.

registered A term that describes the level of owner information that is recorded by the security's issuer.

registered as to principal only A type of bond registration that requires the investor to clip coupons to receive the bond's interest payments. The issuer will automatically send the investor the bonds principal amount at maturity.

registered options principal (ROP) An individual who has passed the Series 4 exam.

registered principal A supervisor of a member firm who has passed the principal examination.

registered representative An individual who has successfully completed a qualified examination to represent a broker dealer or issuer in securities transactions.

registrar An independent organization that accounts for all outstanding stock and bonds of an issuer.

registration statement The full disclosure statement that nonexempt issuers must file with the SEC prior to offering securities for sale to the public. The Securities Act of 1933 requires that a registration statement be filed.

regressive tax A tax that is levied on all parties at the same rate, regardless of their income. An example of a regressive tax is a sales tax. A larger percentage of a low-income earner's income is taken away by the tax.

regular-way settlement The standard number of business days in which a securities transaction is completed and paid for. Corporate securities and municipal bonds settle regular way on the third business day after the trade date with payment due on the fifth. Government securities settle the next business day.

regulated investment company An investment company that qualifies as a conduit for net investment income under Internal Revenue Code subchapter M, so long as it distributes at least 90% of its net investment income to shareholders.

Regulation A A small company offering that allows company to raise up to $5,000,000 in any 12-month period, without filing a full registration.

Regulation D A private placement or sale of securities that allows for an exemption from registration under the Securities Act of 1933. A private placement may be sold to an unlimited number of accredited investors but may only be sold to 35 nonaccredited investors in any 12-month period.

Regulation G Regulates the extension of credit for securities purchases by other commercial lenders.

Regulation T Regulates the extension of credit by broker dealers for securities purchases.

Regulation U Regulates the extension of credit by banks for securities purchases.

Regulation X Regulates the extension of credit by overseas lenders for securities purchases.

Rehypothecation The act of a broker dealer repledging a customer's securities as collateral at a bank to obtain a loan for the customer.

REIT *See* real estate investment trust (REIT).

rejection The act of a buyer of a security refusing delivery.

reorganization department The department in a brokerage firm that handles changes in securities that result from a merger or acquisition or calls.

repurchase agreement (REPO) A fully collateralized loan that results in a sale of securities to the lender, with the borrower agreeing to repurchase them at a higher price in the future. The higher price represents the lender's interest.

reserve maintenance fund An account set up to provide additional funds to maintain a revenue-producing facility financed by a revenue bond.

retail communication Any communication that may be seen in whole or in part by an individual investor. Retail communication must be approved by a principal prior to first use and maintained by the firm for 3 years.

reserve requirement A deposit required to be placed on account with the Federal Reserve Board by banks. The requirement is a percentage of the bank's customer's deposits.

resistance A price level to which a security appreciates and attracts sellers. The new sellers keep the security's price from rising any higher.

restricted account (1) A long margin account that has less than 50% equity but more than 25%. (2) A customer account that has been subject to a sellout.

restricted stock A nonexempt unregistered security that has been obtained by means other than a public offering.

retained earnings The amount of a corporation's net income that has not been paid out to shareholders as dividends.

retention The amount of a new issue that an underwriter allocates to its own clients.

retention requirement The amount of equity that must be left in a restricted margin account when withdrawing securities.

return on equity A measure of performance found by dividing after-tax income by common stockholders' equity.

return on investment (ROI) The profit or loss realized by an investor from holding a security expressed as a percentage of the invested capital.

revenue anticipation note A short-term municipal issue that is sold to manage an issuer's cash flow in anticipation of other revenue in the future.

reverse repurchase agreement A fully collateralized loan that results in the purchase of securities with the intention of reselling them to the borrower at a higher price. The higher price represents the buyer's/lender's interest.

reverse split A stock split that results in fewer shares outstanding, with each share being worth proportionally more.

reversionary working interest A revenue-sharing arrangement where the general partner shares none of the cost and receives none of the revenue until the limited partners have received their payments back, plus any predetermined amount of return.

right A short-term security issued in conjunction with a shareholders preemptive right. The maximum length of a right is 45 days, and it is issued with a subscription price, which allows the holder to purchase the underlying security at a discount from its market price.

rights of accumulation A right offered to mutual fund investors that allows them to calculate all past contributions and growth to reach a breakpoint to receive a sales charge discount on future purchases.

rights agent An independent entity responsible for maintaining the records for rights holders.

rights offering The offering of new shares by a corporation that is preceded by the offering of the new shares to existing shareholders.

riskless simultaneous transaction The purchase of a security on a principal basis by a brokerage firm for the sole purpose of filling a customer's order that the firm has already received. The mark up on riskless principal transactions has to be based on the firm's actual cost for the security.

rollover The distribution of assets from a qualified account to an investor for the purpose of depositing the assets in another qualified account within 60 days. An investor may only roll over an IRA once every 12 months.

round lot A standard trading unit for securities. For common and preferred stock, a round lot is 100 shares. For bonds, it is 5 bonds.

Rule 144 SEC rule that regulates the sale of restricted and control securities requiring the seller to file Form 144 at the time the order is entered to sell. Rule 144 also regulates the amount of the securities that may be sold.

Rule 145 SEC Rule that requires a corporation to provide stockholders with full disclosure relating to reorganizations and to solicit proxies.

Rule 147 An intrastate offering that provides an exemption from SEC registration.

Rule 405 The NYSE rule that requires that all customer recommendations must be suitable and that the representative must "know" the customer.

S

Sale *See* sell.

sales charge *See* commission.

sales literature Written material distributed by a firm to a controlled audience for the purpose of increasing business. Sales literature includes market letters, research reports, and form letters sent to more than 25 customers.

sales load The amount of commission charged to investors in open-end mutual funds. The amount of the sales load is added to the net asset value of the fund to determine the public offering price of the fund.

satellite office An office not identified to the public as an office of the member, such as an agent's home office.

savings bond A nonnegotiable U.S. government bond that must be purchased from the government and redeemed to the government. These bonds are generally known as series EE and HH bonds.

scale A list of maturities and yields for a new serial bond issue.

Schedule 13D A form that must be filed with the SEC by any individual or group of individuals acquiring 5% or more of a corporation's nonexempt equity securities. Form 13D must be filed within 10 days of the acquisition.

scheduled premium policy A variable life insurance policy with fixed premium payments.

SEC *See* Securities and Exchange Commission (SEC).

secondary distribution A distribution of a large amount of securities by a large shareholder or group of large shareholders. The distribution may or may not be done under a prospectus.

secondary offering An underwriting of a large block of stock being sold by large shareholders. The proceeds of the issue are received by the selling shareholders, not the corporation.

secondary market A marketplace where securities are exchanged between investors. All transactions that take place on an exchange or on the Nasdaq are secondary market transactions.

sector fund A mutual fund that invests in companies within a specific business area in an effort to maximize gains. Sector funds have larger risk-reward ratios because of the concentration of investments.

Securities Act of 1933 The first major piece of securities industry legislation. It regulates the primary market and requires that nonexempt issuers file a registration statement with the SEC. The act also requires that investors in new issues be given a prospectus.

Securities Act Amendments of 1975 Created the Municipal Securities Rulemaking Board (MSRB).

Securities Exchange Act of 1934 Regulates the secondary market and all broker dealers and industry participants. It created the Securities and Exchange Commission, the industry's ultimate authority. The act gave the authority to the Federal Reserve Board to regulate the extension of credit for securities purchases through Regulation T.

Securities and Exchange Commission The ultimate securities industry authority. The SEC is a direct government body, not a self-regulatory organization. The commissioners are appointed by the U.S. President and must be approved by Congress.

Securities Investor Protection Corporation (SIPC) The industry's nonprofit insurance company that provides protection for investors in case of broker dealer failure. All member firms must pay dues to SIPC based upon their revenue. SIPC provides coverage for each separate customer for up to $500,000, of which a maximum of $250,000 may be cash. The Securities Investor Protection Act of 1970 created SIPC.

security Any investment that can be exchanged for value between two parties that contains risk. Securities include stocks, bonds, mutual funds, notes, rights, warrants, and options, among others.

segregation The physical separation of customer and firm assets.

self-regulatory organization (SRO) An industry authority that regulates its own members. FINRA, the NYSE, and the CBOE are all self-regulatory organizations that regulate their own members.

sell The act of conveying the ownership of a security for value to another party. A sale includes any security that is attached to another security, as well as any security which the security may be converted or exchanged into.

sell out A transaction executed by a broker dealer when a customer fails to pay for the securities.

sell-stop order An order placed beneath the current market for a security to protect a profit, to guard against a loss, or to establish a short position.

seller's option A type of settlement option that allows the seller to determine when delivery of the securities and final settlement of the trade will occur.

selling away Any recommendation to a customer that involves an investment product that is not offered through the employing firm without the firm's knowledge and consent. This is a violation of industry regulations and may result in action being taken against the representative.

selling concession *See* concession.

selling dividends The act of using a pending dividend to create urgency for the customer to purchase a security. This is a violation and could result in action being taken against the representative.

selling group A group of broker dealers who may sell a new issue of securities but who are not members of the syndicate and who have no liability to the issuer.

separate account The account established by an insurance company to invest the pooled funds of variable contract holders in the securities markets. The separate account must register as either an open-end investment company or as a unit investment trust.

separate trading of registered interest and principal securities (STRIPS) A zero-coupon bond issued by the U.S. government. The principal payment due in the future is sold to investors at a discount and appreciates to par at maturity. The interest payment component is sold to other investors who want some current income.

serial bonds A bond issue that has an increasing amount of principal maturing in successive years.

series EE bond A nonmarketable U.S. government zero-coupon bond that is issued at a discount and matures at its face value. Investors must purchase the bonds from the U.S. government and redeem them to the government at maturity.

series HH bond A nonmarketable U.S. government interest-bearing bond that can only be purchased by trading in matured series EE bonds. Series HH bonds may not be purchased with cash and are issued with a $500 minimum denomination.

settlement The completion of a securities transaction. A transaction settles and is completed when the security is delivered to the buyer and the cash is delivered to the seller.

settlement date The date when a securities ownership changes. Settlement dates are set by FINRA's Uniform Practice Code.

75-5-10 diversification The diversification test that must be met by mutual funds under the Investment Company Act of 1940 in order to market themselves as a diversified mutual fund: 75% of the fund's assets must be invested in other issuer's securities, no more than 5% of the fund's assets may be invested in any one company, and the fund may own no more than 10% of an issuer's outstanding securities.

shareholders equity *See* net worth.

share identification The process of identifying which shares are being sold at the time the sale order is entered in order to minimize an investor's tax liability.

shelf offering A type of securities registration that allows the issuer to sell the securities over a two-year period.

short A position established by a bearish investor that is created by borrowing the security and selling in the hopes that the price of the security will fall. The investor hopes to be able to repurchase the securities at a lower price, thus replacing them cheaply. If the security's price rises, the investor will suffer a loss.

short against the box A short position established against an equal long position in the security to roll tax liabilities forward. Most of the benefits of establishing a short against the box position have been eliminated.

short straddle The simultaneous sale of a call and a put on the same underlying security with the same strike price and expiration. A short straddle would be established by an investor who believes that the security price will move sideways.

simplified arbitration A method of resolving disputes over $50,000 or less. There is no hearing; one arbitrator reads the submissions and renders a final decision.

Simplified Employee Pension (SEP) A qualified retirement plan created for small employers with 25 or fewer employees that allows the employees' money to grow tax-deferred until retirement.

single account An account operated for one individual. The individual has control of the account, and the assets go to the individual's estate in the case of his or her death.

sinking fund An account established by an issuer of debt to place money for the exclusive purpose of paying bond principal.

special assessment bond A municipal bond backed by assessments from the property that benefits from the improvements.

specialist Members of an exchange responsible for maintaining a fair and orderly market in the securities that they specialize in and for executing orders left with them.

specialist book A book of limit orders left with the specialist for execution.

special situation fund A fund that seeks to take advantage of unusual corporate developments, such as take mergers and restructuring.

special tax bond A type of municipal revenue bond that is supported only by revenue from certain taxes.

speculation An investment objective where the investor is willing to accept a high degree of risk in exchange for the opportunity to realize a high return.

split offering An offering where a portion of the proceeds from the underwriting goes to the issuer and a portion goes to the selling shareholders.

spousal account An IRA opened for a nonworking spouse that allows a full contribution to be made for the nonworking spouse.

spread (1) The difference between the bid and ask for a security. (2) The simultaneous purchase and sale of two calls or two puts on the same underlying security.

spread load plan A contractual plan that seeks to spread the sales charge over a longer period of time, as detailed in the Spread Load Plan Act of 1970. The maximum sales charge over the life of the plan is 9%, while the maximum sales charge in any one year is 20%.

standby underwriting An underwriting used in connection with a preemptive rights offering. The standby underwriter must purchase any shares not subscribed to by existing shareholders.

stabilizing The only form of price manipulation allowed by the SEC. The managing underwriter enters a bid at or below the offering price to ensure even distribution of shares.

statutory disqualification An individual who has been barred or suspended or convicted of a securities-related crime.

statutory voting A method of voting that requires investors to cast their votes evenly for the directors they wish to elect.

stock ahead A condition that causes an investor's order not to be executed, even though the stock is trading at a price that would satisfy the customer's limit order, because other limit orders have been entered prior to the customer's order.

stock certificate Evidence of equity ownership.

stock or bond power A form, that when signed by the owner and attached to a security, makes it negotiable.

stock split A change in the number of outstanding shares, the par value, and the number of authorized shares that has been approved through a vote of the shareholders. Forward-stock splits increase the number of shares outstanding and reduce the stock price in order to make the security more attractive to individual investors.

stop limit order An order that becomes a limit order to buy or sell the stock when the stock trades at or through the stop price.

stop order An order that becomes a market order to buy or sell the stock when the stock trades at or through the stop price.

stopping stock A courtesy offered by a specialist to public customers, whereby the specialist guarantees a price but tries to obtain a better price for the customer.

straddle The simultaneous purchase or sale of a call and a put on the same security with the same strike price and expiration.

straight line depreciation An accounting method that allows an owner to take equal tax deductions over the useful life of the asset.

strangle The purchase or sale of a call and a put on either side of the current market price. The options have the same expiration months but different strike prices.

stripped bond A bond that has had its coupons removed by a broker dealer and that is selling at a deep discount to its principal payment in the future.

stripper well An oil well that is in operation just to recover a very limited amount of reserves.

subchapter S corporation A business organization that allows the tax consequences of the organization to flow through to the owners.

subscription agreement An application signed by the purchaser of an interest in a direct participation plan. An investor in a limited partnership does not become an investor until the general partner signs the subscription agreement.

subscription right *See* right.

suitability A determination that the characteristics of a security are in line with an investor's objectives, financial profile, and attitudes.

Super Display Book System (SDBK) The electronic order-routing system used by the NYSE to route orders directly to the trading post.

supervise The actions of a principal that ensure that the actions of a firm and its representatives are in compliance with industry regulations.

support The price to which a security will fall and attract new buyers. As the new buyers enter the market, it keeps the price from falling any lower.

surplus fund An account set up for funds generated by a project financed by a municipal revenue bond to pay a variety of expenses.

syndicate A group of underwriters responsible for underwriting a new issue.

systematic risk A risk inherent in any investment in the market. An investor may lose money simply because the market is going down.

T

takedown The price at which a syndicate purchases a new issue of securities from the issuer.

tax anticipation note (TAN) A short-term note sold by a municipal issuer as interim financing in anticipation of tax revenue.

tax and revenue anticipation note A short-term note sold by a municipal issuer as interim financing in anticipation of tax and other revenue.

tax-deferred annuity A nonqualified retirement account that allows an investor's money to grow tax deferred. A tax-deferred annuity is a contract between an insurance company and an investor.

tax equivalent yield The interest rate that must be offered by a taxable bond of similar quality in order to be equal to the rate that is offered by a municipal bond.

tax-exempt bond fund A bond fund that seeks to produce investment income that is free from federal tax by investing in a portfolio of municipal bonds.

tax liability The amount of money that is owed by an investor after realizing a gain on the sale of an investment or after receiving investment income.

tax preference item An item that receives preferential tax treatment and must be added back into income when calculating an investor's alternative minimum tax.

tax-sheltered annuity (TSA) A qualified retirement plan offered to employees of governments, school systems, or nonprofit organizations. Contributions to TSAs are made with pre-tax dollars.

technical analysis A method of security analysis that uses past price performance to predict the future performance of a security.

Telephone Consumer Protection Act of 1991 Legislation that regulates how potential customers are contacted by phone at home.

tenants in common *See* joint tenants in common.

tender offer An offer to buy all or part of a company's outstanding securities for cash or cash and securities.

term bond A bond issue that has its entire principal due on one date.

term maturity A type of bond maturity that has all principal due on one date.

testimonial The use of a recognized expert or leader to endorse the services of a firm.

third market A transaction in an exchange-listed security executed over the Nasdaq workstation.

third-party account An account that is managed for the benefit of a customer by another party, such as an investment adviser, a trustee, or an attorney.

30-day visible supply The total par value of all new issue municipal bonds coming to market in the next 30 days.

time deposit An account that is established by a bank customer where the customer agrees to leave the funds on deposit for an agreed upon amount of time.

time value The value of an option that exceeds its intrinsic value or its in the money amount.

tombstone ad An announcement published in financial papers advertising the offering of securities by a group of underwriters. Only basic information may be contained in the tombstone ad, and all offers must be made through the prospectus only.

top heavy rule The rule that states the maximum salary for which a Keogh contribution may be based. This is in effect to limit the disparity between high- and low-salary employees.

trade confirmation The printed notification of a securities transaction. A confirmation must be sent to a customer on or before the completion of a transaction. The completion of a transaction is considered to be the settlement date.

trade date The day when an investor's order is executed.

tranche A class of collateralized mortgage obligation (CMO) that has a predicted maturity and interest rate.

transfer agent An independent entity that handles name changes and records the names of security holders of record and ensures that all certificates are properly endorsed.

transfer and hold in safekeeping A request by customers for the brokerage firm to transfer their securities into the firm's name and to hold them in safekeeping at the firm. A brokerage may charge a fee for holding a customer's securities that have been registered in its name.

transfer and ship A request by customers for the brokerage firm to transfer their securities into their name and to ship them to their address of record.

Treasury bill A U.S. government security that is issued at a discount and matures at par in 4, 13, 26, and 52 weeks.

Treasury bond A long-term U.S. government security that pays semiannual interest and matures in 10 to 30 years.

Treasury note An intermediate-term U.S. government security that pays semiannual interest and matures in 1 to 10 years.

Treasury receipt A zero-coupon bond created by a brokerage firm that is backed by U.S. government securities. It issued at discount and matures at par.

treasury stock Stock that has been issued by a corporation and that has subsequently been repurchased by the corporation. Treasury stock does not vote or receive dividends. It is not used in the calculation of earnings per share.

trendline A line used to predict the future price movement for a security. Drawing a line under the successive lows or successive highs creates a trendline.

trough The bottoming out of the business cycle just prior to an new upward movement in activity.

true interest cost (TIC) A calculation for the cost of a municipal issuer's interest expense that includes the time value of money.

Trust Indenture Act of 1940 Regulates the issuance of corporate debt in excess of $5,000,000 and with a term exceeding one year. It requires an indenture between the issuer and the trustee.

trustee A person who legally acts for the benefit of another party.

12B-1 fee An asset-based distribution fee that is assessed annually and paid out quarterly to cover advertising and distribution costs. All 12B-1 fees must be reasonable.

two-dollar broker An independent exchange member who executes orders for commission house brokers and other customers for a fee.

type A classification method for an option as either a call or a put.

U

uncovered *See* naked.

underlying security A security for which an investor has an option to buy or sell.

underwriting The process of marketing a new issue of securities to the investing public. A broker dealer forwards the proceeds of the sale to the issuer minus its fee for selling the securities.

unearned income Any income received by an individual from an investment, such as dividends and interest income.

uniform delivery ticket A document that must be attached to every security delivered by the seller, making the security "good delivery."

Uniform Gifts to Minors Act (UGMA) Sets forth guidelines for the gifting of cash and securities to minors and for the operation of accounts managed for the benefit of minors. Once a gift is given to a minor, it is irrevocable.

Uniform Practice Code The FINRA bylaw that sets guidelines for how industry members transact business with other members. The Uniform Practice Code establishes such things as settlement dates, rules of good delivery, and ex dividend dates.

Uniform Securities Act (USA) The framework for state-based securities legislation. The act is a model that can be adapted to each state's particular needs.

Uniform Transfer to Minors Act (UTMA) Legislation that has been adopted in certain states, in lieu of the Uniform Gifts to Minors Act. UTMA allows the custodian to determine the age at which the assets become the property of the minor. The maximum age for transfer of ownership is 25.

unit investment trust (UIT) A type of investment company organized as a trust to invest in a portfolio of securities. The UIT sells redeemable securities to investors in the form of shares or units of beneficial interest.

unit of beneficial interest The redeemable share issued to investors in a unit investment trust.

unit refund annuity An annuity payout option that will make payments to the annuitant for life. If the annuitant dies prior to receiving an amount that is equal to their account value, the balance of the account will be paid to the annuitant's beneficiaries.

unqualified legal opinion A legal opinion issued by a bond attorney for the issue where there are no reservations relating to the issue.

unrealized A paper profit or loss on a security that is still owned.

V

variable annuity A contract issued by an insurance company that is both a security and an insurance product. The annuitant's contributions are invested through the separate account into a portfolio of securities. The annuitant's payments depend largely on the investment results of the separate account.

variable death benefit The amount of a death benefit paid to a beneficiary that is based on the investment results of the insurance company's separate account. This amount is over the contract's minimum guaranteed death benefit.

variable life insurance A life insurance policy that provides for a minimum guaranteed death benefit, as well as an additional death benefit, based on the investment results of the separate account.

variable rate municipal security Interim municipal financing issued with a variable rate.

vertical spread The simultaneous purchase and sale of two calls or two puts on the same underlying security that differ only in strike price.

vesting The process by which an employer's contributions to an employee's retirement account become the property of the employee.

visible supply *See* 30-day visible supply.

voluntary accumulation plan A method, such as dollar-cost averaging, by which an investor regularly makes contributions to acquire mutual fund shares.

voting right The right of a corporation's stockholders to cast their vote for the election of the corporation's board of directors as well as for certain major corporate issues.

W

warrant A long-term security that gives the holder the right to purchase the common shares of a corporation for up to 10 years. The warrant's subscription price is always higher than the price of the underlying common shares when the warrant is initially issued.

wash sale The sale of a security at a loss and the subsequent repurchase of that security or of a security that is substantially the same within 30 days of the sale. The repurchase disallows the claim of the loss for tax purposes.

western account A type of municipal security syndicate account where only the member with unsold bonds is responsible for the unsold bonds.

when-issued security A security that has been sold prior to the certificates being available for delivery.

wildcatting An exploratory oil- and gas-drilling program.

wire room *See* order department.

withdrawal plan The systematic removal of funds from a mutual fund account over time. Withdrawal plans vary in type and availability among fund companies.

workable indication An indication of the prices and yields that a municipal securities dealer may be willing to buy or sell bonds.

working capital A measure of a corporation's liquidity that is found by subtracting current liabilities from current assets.

working interest An interest that requires the holder to bear the proportional expenses and allows the holder to share in the revenue produced by an oil or gas project in relation to the interest.

workout quote A nonfirm quote that requires handling and settlement conditions to be worked out between the parties prior to the trade.

writer An investor who sells an option to receive the premium income.

writing the scale The procedure of assigning prospective yields to a new issuer of serial municipal bonds.

Y

Yellow Sheets A daily publication published by the national quotation bureau providing quotes for corporate bonds.

yield The annual amount of income generated by a security relative to its price; expressed as a percentage.

yield-based option An interest rate option that allows the holder to receive the in the money amount in cash upon exercise or expiration.

yield curve The rate at which interest rates vary among investments of similar quality with different maturities. Longer-term securities generally offer higher yields.

yield to call An investor's overall return for owning a bond should it be called in prior to maturity by the issuer.

yield to maturity An investor's overall return for owning a bond if the bond is held until maturity.

Z

zero-coupon bond A bond that is issued at a discount from its par value and makes no regular interest payments. An investor's interest is reflected by the security's appreciation towards par at maturity. The appreciation is taxable each year even though it is not actually received by the investor (phantom income).

zero-minus tick A trade in an exchange-listed security that occurs at the same price as the previous transaction, but at a price that is less than the last transaction that was different.

zero-plus tick A trade in an exchange-listed security that occurs at the same price as the previous transaction, but at a price that is higher than the last transaction that was different.

Index

H

I

J

N

O

P